AMONG CONGO PIGMIES

AMS PRESS

NEW YORK

THE LAND OF THE PIGMIES IN THE DEPTHS OF THE
PRIMEVAL FOREST

AMONG
CONGO PIGMIES

by

Paul Schebesta

Translated from the German by
GERALD GRIFFIN

WITH 89 PHOTOGRAPHS AND THREE MAPS

London
HUTCHINSON & CO. (Publishers) LTD.

Library of Congress Cataloging in Publication Data

Schebesta, Paul, 1887-1967.
  Among Congo pigmies.

    Translation of Bambuti, die zwerge vom Kongo.
    Reprint of the 1933 ed. published by Hutchinson,
London.
    Includes index.
    1. Bambute. 2. Ethnology—Zaire. I. Title.
DT650.B36S3413   1977   967.5'15'02   74-15085
ISBN 0-404-12135-7

Reprinted from an original copy in the collections
of the University of Connecticut Library

From the edition of 1933, London
First AMS edition published in 1977
Manufactured in the United States of America

AMS PRESS INC.
NEW YORK, N. Y.

PREFACE

THE struggle for existence of a little nomad race which is perhaps the immediate successor in the progress of civilisation to the "dawn man," is vividly set before us in the following narrative of Dr. Paul Schebesta's adventures during his stay of eighteen months among the Congo pigmies.

But Dr. Schebesta deprecates the suggestion that he aims just at providing the reader with thrills. The thrills are merely incidental to his work, whose purpose is strictly anthropological. His expedition to the Congo was undertaken with a view to following up the research work on the origin of man which he had previously carried out among other aboriginal stocks.

All previous explorers had only obtained very impressionist glimpses of pigmy culture, and were unanimous in maintaining, *inter alia*, that they had discovered a race that had no religion and no conception of the soul as a separate entity from the body. Biologists, with an ultra-materialistic kink, fastened on this pseudo-discovery as bearing out their contention that primitive man had no religion.

Dr. Schebesta completely explodes this fallacy. He shows how these little African gipsies, who dwell in temporary huts made of leaves and twigs, and are the nearest approach in primitiveness to the wild animals on which they prey, have a definite religious cult and ethical and social codes of their own.

GERALD GRIFFIN

CONTENTS

LIST OF ILLUSTRATIONS

9

INTRODUCTION

THE Congo-Nile watershed which runs from north to south, west of the great African lakes, is a tableland rising in places to more than 7600 feet above sea-level. From it spring three mighty tributaries of the brackish Congo River—the Nepolo, Lindi and Ituri, whose basins drain the great stretches of the Ituri Forest, where rank luxuriance riots in the tropical heat.

Many decades back the German pioneers, Emin Pascha and Stuhlmann, penetrated the western hinterlands of this region, and just fifty-five years ago, Stanley succeeded in crossing the forest from end to end. He was the first white man to accomplish this feat. To-day, scarcely a generation later, civilization is struggling to stretch its tentacles into the primeval forest, and the first motor track, thousands of miles in length, has been cut right through its heart. Europe is shaking the giant, striving to rouse him from the slumber of centuries, but as yet the result is almost negligible. Heedless of the itching and tickling in its entrails, the Ituri Forest still sleeps its age-long sleep. It is too vast, too mighty, too primeval, to be scared from its repose by the clattering and clanking of Europe's civilization.

Countless streams, now babbling and murmuring, now thundering and roaring, flow through the maze of trees, luxuriating in evergreen freshness as their vigour is constantly renewed by the persistent rain ; for except during the months of January and February, it rains almost daily in the Ituri Forest, and the streams, tinged with greyish loam, are ever in full spate, overflowing their banks and even carrying away trees in their course.

The Equator cuts diagonally through the tropical zone of this virgin forest ; yet, however fiercely the African sun may beat down and shroud the forest in steam and mist, in the undergrowth it is always cool, though sluggish and moist.   Here the fierce rays of the sun never penetrate.   The Ituri shelters two mysteries in its depths, the tiny pigmies and the timid okapi.   The latter, a species of wood giraffe, still roams in fairly large herds over remote reaches, as yet hardly known to the white hunter.   Almost as timid as the okapi is his hunter, the pigmy, the aboriginal inhabitant of the region.   While he does not shun the negro villager, the pigmy avoids the inquisitive white man, who attempts to track him down and intrude on his privacy.   A white man may often travel through the forest for many miles without catching sight of one of these tiny people, for their huts lie off the beaten track, buried away where the shadows of the trees and the undergrowth are most dense.   It is not alone the abodes of the white man that are shunned ;   even the very paths he treads are avoided.   Should you happen to blunder upon a bunch of pigmies you may be sure that they will vanish into the forest's gloom like a flash.   Were it not for the tiny footprints that you see here and there, you would think it uninhabited ;   and, indeed, for the most part, it is.   It was only in the course of centuries that isolated groups of negroes penetrated its pathless jungle, and laid down for themselves slender lines of communication.   In doing so they blundered upon the aborigines.   Gradually the latter overcame their timidity, and formed alliances with the invaders against whom at first they fought, and eventually the negroes became the masters of the pigmies.

This diminutive African race is not the only one of its kind.   Similar dwarfs are to be found in other parts of the world.   The Semangs in Malacca and the Minokopies of the Andaman Islands resemble them closely in their primitive forest community life ;   but their nearest cousins dwell in the woods of Gabun and in the Cameroons on the West Coast of Africa.   The bushmen of the Kalahari Desert, who are frequently mistaken for pigmies, seem in fact to be very far removed cousins of theirs.

This book will be devoted to the Iturian pigmies, and will tell all that is known of them and their habits.   The reader will not experience the disillusionment that I so often felt when I picked up a book which pretentiously promised to describe the Congo pigmies, but in fact dismissed them with a few random remarks, and went on to deal with negroes. My book aims exclusively at a portrayal of these Lilliputians. I shall not touch at all upon the mongrel dwarfs and the negroes whom I encountered.

This is the first detailed account of my pioneer trip in the years 1929 and 1930 to the pigmies of the Congo, a task the difficulties of which can be appreciated fully only by a man who has himself tried to live with aboriginal nomadic folk.

In order to attain my goal two courses were open to me. Either I could attach myself to one or more groups in a limited area, spend the entire period at my disposal with them, and thus study in detail every possible angle in the various phases of their life ; or I could wander through the whole region of the forest, trail any pigmy camps I was able to, tarry here and there as long as possible, and gain a general impression of these tiny people and their civilization as a whole. I had good reason for deciding on the latter, withal, the more difficult course. If the pigmies had a uniform cultural code, it would have sufficed to study them in some definite district, where I could have obtained a faithful picture of pigmy life and activity in general. Such a presumption is, however, by no means correct, as the reader will readily see for himself. Indeed, the pigmies, racially, have undergone a transformation through inter-breeding with people of different stocks. The Batwas of Ruanda and the Batschwas of the Equator are good examples of this, for they are no longer 100 per cent pigmies. External forces have made a still greater impression upon pigmy civilization. There is no uniformity even in the civilization of the pure-bred Iturian pigmies. The influence of the negroes has actually transformed their culture into a baroque mosaic. My investigations have led me to this conclusion, although at the same time they have established the fact that the general principles of pigmy civilization obtrude themselves repeatedly in every tribe, like the leit-motif of a musical composition.

My work has paved the way for a more thorough investigation, and it now seems to be the opportune moment for this task. Moreover, there is no time to be lost. Who can say how many years will elapse before the

Congo pigmies are pounded into unrecognizable pulp in the mortar of European civilization ? Will they, in the near future, strut before us in morning-coats and wing collars like so many of the semi-civilized races, with the result that we can only surmise their aboriginality from their physical formation, for they will have become externally like all civilized " wild men " ?

The expedition with which this book deals in part is a continuation of the pioneer trip which I undertook in the years 1924 and 1925 among the aborigines of Malacca, when my aim was to throw a further searchlight on the origin of man.

My deepest gratitude is due to the Society for the Furtherance of German Science, which placed at my disposal a considerable sum for my expedition to the land of the pigmies.

PAUL SCHEBESTA.

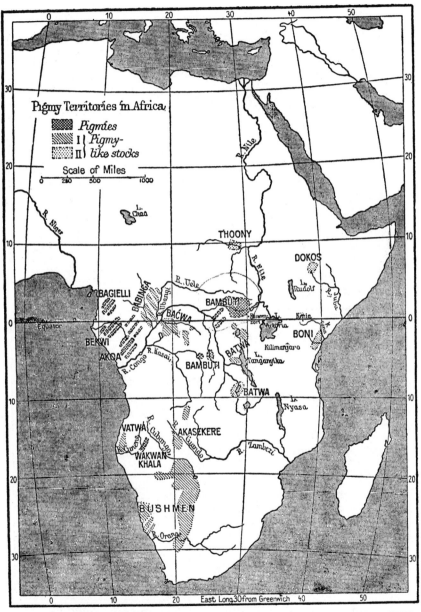

MAP OF AFRICA SHOWING EXTENT OF PIGMY TERRITORIES RELATIVE
TO THE AREA OF THE CONTINENT

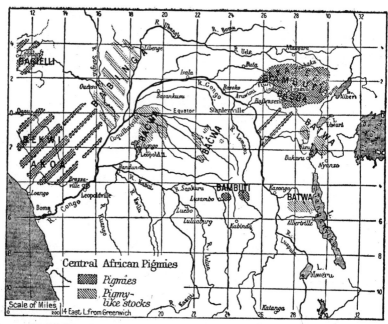

VAST TRACTS THROUGH WHICH 20,000 ITURI PIGMIES ROAM

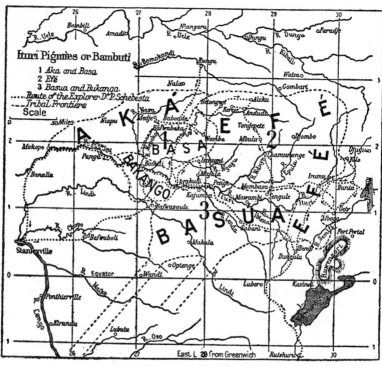

DR. PAUL SCHEBESTA'S ROUTE

AMONG CONGO PIGMIES

CHAPTER I

FIRST MEETING WITH THE BAMBUTI

BEFORE me lies a quaint document of olden days—
the text of a letter of the great Pharaoh Nefrikare,
which contains the oldest, and probably the first
information on the legendary pigmies. This letter from
the King to his Commander-in-Chief, Herihuf, runs thus :
" I have noted the contents of your letter to me, your
King. I learn from it that you have penetrated with your
troops into the land of Iman.

" In your letter you also state that you are preparing
to bring with you many choice gifts, which Hator, the
goddess of Iman, has prepared for the person of Nefrikare.

" I further learn from your letter that you are bringing
a pigmy with you, who dances the dance of the Gods in the
land of legend, a dwarf apparently like the one whom the
treasure-keeper of the Gods, Baured, brought from Punt
in the days of Aosis. You also inform my majesty that
never was anything to equal him in value, brought home
before by any servant of my majesty.

" You have the pigmy in your retinue whom you have
brought from the Land of Legend, so that he may dance
the dance of the Gods, and thereby fill the heart of King
Nefrikare with joy.

" When you bring him to the ship, choose reliable men
to keep watch on both sides of the vessel, lest perchance
he may fall into the water, and when he sleeps at night
tell off ten stout fellows to sleep alongside him.

" My majesty yearns mightily to see this pigmy.

" See that you bring the pigmy alive, hale and sound

to my palace, and then my majesty will confer on you far higher awards than those given by the treasurer of the Gods in the days of Aosis. From this gauge how great is the yearning of my majesty to see this pigmy."

Thus in the quaint phraseology of ancient Egypt did the great Pharaoh Pepi II (Nefrikare) of the sixth dynasty, give vent to his unrestrained childish joy to his commander-in-chief who reported the imminent arrival of a pigmy along with other booty from Central Africa.

And so among all the vaunted treasures, the dwarf was the most important, the most interesting, and the dearest one—the one whose arrival he awaited with impatience. How touching sound the instructions to guard the pigmy so carefully, so that no harm should come to him !

This unique document in the picturesque script of ancient Egypt is, as already stated, the first authentic information available on the existence of African dwarfish beings, who, in those remote days, fascinated people quite as much as they do to-day throughout the world.

Even the very aboriginal negroes of the Congo, neighbours of the pigmies, who only know by hearsay of the existence of the dwarfs in the woods close by, flock in curious crowds whenever real flesh-and-blood pigmies appear among them. What an outstanding event it was, only last year in Stanleyville, when on the occasion of the Belgian centenary celebrations, a Government official brought a tribe of pigmies to that town and paraded them in procession before the curious citizens ! Stanleyville, built on the verge of the primitive forest, and one of the largest and finest towns in the Congo, has no pigmies in its vicinity. Long before the Europeans had penetrated into the country, they had retired hundreds of miles into the backwoods, and the black population rarely saw a single member of their race. The news of their arrival spread like wildfire. Crowds swarmed in front of the compound where they were housed. The black mob yelled and jostled, clambered over the barriers and frightened the pigmies, huddled together in terror, with all kinds of mischievous capers. To the natives they were not human beings, but weird creatures, fairies, or maybe, beast-men. In the procession that followed, the tribe of pigmies, as may well be imagined, attracted the most attention, and were greeted with great noise and cheering, which the panic-stricken dwarfs mistook for threats. Whereupon their chief stepped boldly out of the ranks, and casting fierce glances on all sides, he bared his teeth, and swore to kill anybody who laid a hand on one of his subjects. His threat took immediate effect, and led to a proclamation by the authorities that anyone who tormented the pigmies would be sent to prison. No further demonstrations were made, and the pigmies returned unmolested to their native woods.

Negroes who live in constant touch with them, soon get accustomed to these quaint people, and yet they still regard them as being somewhat uncanny. Superstition, which is extremely rife among the negroes, is mainly responsible for this. One cannot wonder at it, when even European nations weave fairy tales and myths about this curious race, and regard them as genuine creatures of magic. The aura of mystery that shrouds this tiny people seems to increase with distance. In the litany of sagas on the race, which has extended throughout all Africa, the most fantastic have been invented in the regions most remote from the tropical forest.

It seems probable then that such legends were known in ancient Egypt, so that one can quite understand the exuberant glee, even of a great Pharaoh like Pepi II, at the prospect of getting possession of a real live pigmy from the heart of Africa.

Even Homer sings about these goblin men, and historians and philosophers of antiquity write gravely about them, and try to fathom their nature. Thus Herodotus tells us of the expedition of the Nasamones, who after wandering for a long time in the wilderness, arrived in a state of utter prostration at an oasis, and fed sumptuously on the fruits of its trees. In the middle of their feast they were surprised by a horde of little men, captured, and led to a village in the heart of the swamp. That was how the Nasamones came in contact with the dark-skinned pigmies and their camp.

I have no time just now to argue with the scholars as to whether the little men Herodotus speaks of were pigmies, and if they were, what stock or tribe. Neither have I time to examine Saint Augustine's views on the descent of the pigmies from Noah.   I merely wish to emphasize that everywhere throughout the ages tales about the pigmies always appealed to the popular imagination.

With the beginning of the Christian missions to Central Africa in the seventeenth century, more definite news about the Bambuti filtered through to Europe.   Take, for instance, Dapper's quaint statement on the Bakke-bakke or Mimos on the Loango coast :

" His black majesty of Loango," he says, " was attended by dwarf pages, and the black men said that a certain wilderness was inhabited exclusively by dwarfs like these, who were wont to kill considerable numbers of elephants."

This report is probably based on negro sources, because apparently the white men in those days never came into any kind of contact with the pigmies.   However, we know to-day that he was recording facts.   Dapper's Bakke-bakke are the modern Bekwi or Akoa of Gabun, in West Africa.

To Schweinfurth belongs the honour of having been the first to bring the civilized world into contact with the pigmies.   During his journey to the Uele (1868–1871) he met the first pigmies at Munza's court, and named them Akka, as they are still called in that region.   With regard to information about the pigmies Schweinfurth's expedition has proved more valuable than Stanley's journey three years later, when he met the Wambuti, as he called them, in the Ituri district.

Since the days of Schweinfurth and Stanley, many explorers and travellers have striven to lift the veil from the Ituri Forest, and to solve the riddle of the pigmies. But the forest refused to give up the key to the mysteries hidden in its depths.   Scrappy items of information about the pigmies leaked out, it is true ; many travellers got into touch with them in a tentative sort of way ; but broadly speaking the forest pigmy remained an enig-matical, aloof creature, utterly unfathomable and in-scrutable.   He was elusive and impalpable.   Far from the buzz of civilization, he hunts his prey through the shades of the dim forest, and avoids the path of the stranger, like the timid okapi, which, also a pigmy of its own species, flees from the trail of the hunter. The okapi and the Bambuti have continued to be the most weird and wonderful creatures of the Ituri Forest all through the ages until the present day.

. . . . . .

A lucky chance brought me to Central Africa, right to the very heart of the ancient forest, the home of the pigmies, and I endeavoured to solve the riddle of this race by following closely on their tracks. I took the greatest pains to " listen in " to them and observe their ways, and I was successful in my efforts. From January 1929 until September 1930 I followed their paths through the virgin forest, and trailed the pigmies so thoroughly that both negroes and dwarfs alike nicknamed me " Baba wa Bambuti "—" the father of the pigmies." I am rather proud, by the way, of this soubriquet. It gives a sort of cachet to my achievements, and I look upon it as the finest reward for the many great hardships I had to face during the course of my work.

Fortified though I was by my previous extensive experience in dealing with timid nomad forest-dwellers during my stay in the remote wilds of India, I felt at the beginning of my Congo trip an unaccountable anxiety lest I might not be as successful with the Bambuti as I had been with the Semangs of Malacca. Fear on this score kept nagging at me constantly as I waited in Bafwasende, on the banks of the Lindi, for a favourable opportunity to get into touch with the pigmies. At length natives in the vicinity gave me an approximate idea of the nearest pigmy camp, and as Commissioner Daout, an obliging and courteous official, cordially supported my project, and Père Cawaters, a missionary who happened to be there at the time, urged friendly negroes to assist me, things began to assume a very cheerful outlook.

Accompanied by a Babali native, I struck out in a north-westerly direction for Bombali, in Ituri. Just outside the village our caravan left the main track. Heavy with foliage, giant trees bowed their mighty heads down to the narrow but clearly defined trail, which presently led us through a wretched straggling native village. After travelling for hours through the silence of

the forest we came to the Apare River, which forms the
western boundary of the pigmies and which they rarely
cross. On the opposite bank the fierce rays of the midday
sun beat down on a few native huts, surrounded by
succulent green oil-palm trees. The negroes, crouched in
the shade of their verandas, were puffing away at their
long banana-stalk pipes. They looked up in alarm when
our vanguard hailed them ; then a giant figure rose
languidly, dodged among the huts, and after a while came
down to the bank, carrying a paddle. After a prolonged
parley the man put across in a canoe, and in two trips
took us all to the other side. A short delay in the village
was unavoidable as some of my bearers hailed from it,
and chattered and drank palm wine with their friends.
Incidentally it was very refreshing after our long tramp
in the clammy heat of the forest. My spirits rose, not only
on account of the exhilarating effect of the excellent
" Malofu," which they call their wine, but also owing to
the good news that pigmies were ahead of me in the
village of Zongere.

At last, I felt, I was nearing my goal. I determined to
finish my journey that very evening, if possible. On our
way small Babali villages appeared here and there in the
gloomy depths of the giant forest, whose silence was
broken now and again by the croaking of the horn-bills,
which birds are sacred among the aborigines. The heavy
beat of their wings above the tree-tops reminded me of
the soughing of the monsoon. The sun's rays gleaming
through the dense foliage, flickered along the trail ahead
in delicate patterns, but the greenery above protected my
head so well that I took off my sun-helmet and stepped
gaily forward.

Our caravan halted in the village of Tomos, and, as I
did not know the way, I yielded to the suggestions of my
boys that we should spend the night in the village. I had
no notion that I was going to sleep almost within view of
the longed-for pigmies, and that my guides had been
pulling my leg !

At dawn we were on the march. Soon we reached
another native village, swarming with life like an ant-hill.
Negroes and negresses darted past one another. Others
rushed to their doors to catch a glimpse of the queer

white man who had travelled across the seas just to see
the Bambuti. My fame had gone before me. By this
time youngsters from all the villages we had passed
through had swelled our retinue to enormous proportions, and our vanguard spread the report everywhere :
" Here comes the Baba wa Bambuti."

We had almost reached the foot of the slope—the
village was built on the summit of a hill—when a deafening din arose. The natives yelled as though possessed ;
even my bearers threw down their bundles, and ran in the
same direction towards a particular hut. I stood dumbfounded, staring after the vanishing heels. What was the
meaning of this skedaddle ?

Before the hut swayed a seething mass of men and
women, screaming wildly and jostling one another. At
length the mob opened up, and from the struggling crowd
of humanity there emerged a wee bearded creature, in the
grip of an immense negro who was dragging him towards
me. The first pigmy !

Haltingly, with faltering steps and with a venomous
expression on his features, the tiny thing was hauled
along. The yells and brawlings of the mob made the
little fellow even more terrified. He struggled in the
grip of the huge negro like a fish on a hook. His large
dark eyes stared with terror from under their bushy
brows, while a galvanic grin distorted a face, which, at
its best, was fearfully repulsive.

The whole thing struck me as so exceedingly funny
that, I regret to say, I burst into a hearty fit of laughter.
This completely unnerved the poor pigmy.

There he stood, the aborigine of the forest, a pigmy, a
specimen of the strangest race on earth, a genuine
Bambuti.

He looked exactly like a hobgoblin on the cover of a
book of fairy tales. However, he understood me when I
spoke to him. He even replied to some of the questions I
put to him in Kingwana, the Swahili dialect of the district.
He frequently stammered, and seemed embarrassed.
Perhaps he could not quite follow me. Maybe terror
gripped his throat. His eyes roamed uneasily in all
directions, seemingly seeking some means of escape. The
hopelessness of such an attempt soon dawned on him

when he saw the serried ranks of men surrounding him.

A fistful of salt and another of tobacco put an end to his fear, and he quickly realized that I meant him no harm. The villagers cast envious glances at the salt and tobacco, and almost certainly would have tried to take them from him if they could. For all that some of them handed him a few banana leaves, in which he wrapped his treasures. Even among pigmies the way to the heart is through the stomach ! Which fact I had many excellent opportunities of confirming during the long months I spent with them.

My new-found friend tied the two packets together with bast, and trotted alongside me towards his village close by, where the whole tribe of pigmies were awaiting me.

Agali, as the sinister-looking dwarf was called, stayed by my side when the path permitted, and when it narrowed, he ran sometimes ahead, sometimes behind me. He was a man in the prime of life, stoutly built with a massive angular head perched on his short neck. His uncanny face, enveloped in a thick beard, appeared almost bestial. His cheek-bones protruded abnormally, and his broad misshapen short nose seemed fixed in his face like a squat knob. Behind such a mask I could not imagine there would be a trace of humanity or kindness, but quickly dismissed these unpleasant thoughts when I remembered his people were to be my companions for many months to come.

And I may add that most decidedly at that moment I had no reason to feel uneasy about the wee thing who kept chattering glibly and confidingly as he trotted along.

My pigmy was quite unarmed. Around his loins flapped a dirty rag of plaited marumba bark, which hung apron-wise between his legs. A broad woven hip-belt, which Agali told me was made of " Kenge skin," kept the apron in position. The " Kenge," I learned later, is the okapi. Two little wooden ornaments, amulets of some kind, were suspended round his neck by twisted coils of cord, while one wrist was bound with a strip of spotted snake skin. Neither the skin cap nor the plaited rush cowl, the usual headgear of the Bambuti in that district, decked his curly head.

Whenever he ran ahead of me, my eyes took in the strange contours of his clayish yellow body. It is only among pigmies that one finds such a strange conglomeration of physical abnormalities. Actually, in addition to their short stature and their queer-shaped heads, their bodily proportions, or rather disproportions, form such a striking feature that you could never mistake them for specimens of any other race. The short thin legs are in direct contrast to the long, thick trunk, with its square broad shoulders. Their arms are abnormally long, but their hands and feet seem almost shapely, although the latter are frequently somewhat introverted.

Though his legs, arms and chest were covered with a fairly thick coat of hair, my companion's body was not nearly as hirsute as those of other pigmies I met later. To complete the picture, Agali was hideously ugly. I sought comfort in the hope that his fellow tribesmen might have more pleasant and attractive features. In this I was utterly mistaken. Almost all the pigmies that I met later—and they numbered thousands—were indescribably repulsive, many so hideous that they made me shudder. The children for a few years are quite attractive, but nobody can blame the pigmies if they harbour a grudge against their creator for making them so appallingly ugly; although maybe all primitive men in bygone ages looked as repellent as they.

Another striking characteristic among the majority of pigmies is their bright brown skin. There are some dark manikins, and even jet-black ones. The latter, however, are very rare, and are found exclusively on the outskirts of the forest, so that, in all probability, they are halfbreeds. The bright tint of the Bambuti skin appeals so much to the negroes that they often refer to them as their brothers. When I occasionally suggested they should deprecate the idea of a kinship that was by no means flattering, and asked for the grounds of their contention, they replied : " Well, their skin is beautiful, like yours."

With a little fortitude one becomes accustomed to anything, no matter how loathsome it may be. It is common knowledge that negroes exude a strong odour,

which at times is extremely offensive, especially inside
the walls of their huts. Even frequent washing has very
little effect, for every new bout of perspiring envelops
the negro in the all-pervading aroma. Should the white
man complain too much, a courageous native is quite
likely to retort : " You smell, too." For they find the
body odour of Europeans just as offensive as we do theirs,
and say that it reminds them of a corpse.

The emanation from the skin of pigmies is more pronounced and even more unpleasant. This may be due to
their proverbial uncleanliness. As a rule they shun the
wash-tub, and I never recollect having seen one of them
wash his face. The wee fellows may occasionally take a
dip in a river, although they are very squeamish about
doing so, and it is rather to cool themselves than with
any conscious idea of cleanliness. It is no wonder that
the forest dwarf gives out an extraordinary unescapable
blend of stenches such as impinged my nose whenever
Agali came near me. For all that, in the course of
eighteen months I grew accustomed to this nuisance and
to many other unpleasant habits among the pigmies.

I was also struck by the shortness of my companion.
Surrounded by the negroes, he definitely appeared a
dwarf. His height I gauged roughly at four feet ten
inches. I learned later that the average height of the
Bambuti male is four feet eight inches, and that of the
women four feet four.

The pigmies are rightly described as dwarfs, but to call
them negrillos, or little negroes, as do the French, is
absolutely incorrect. The pigmies racially are quite
distinct from the negroes. Naturally on a casual glance
their curly hair might suggest kinship, although even on
this point a difference can be detected on close inspection.
Actually the pigmy stock is quite as remote from that of
the negro as is our own. One can easily understand why
the French anthropologist, M. Hainy, coined the term
" Negrillos " for the Central African dwarfs, for in his day
very little was known about these wee people, and the
swarthy skin of the frontier pigmies led to their being
mistaken for little negroes.

Agali still kept up his incessant chatter as we trudged
through the forest, when suddenly I heard the strains of

music. " The Bambuti ! " cried my dusky guides, and
rushed forward. Halting for a moment, I listened
to the strange melody. On an eminence ahead of us
stood a village. Agali came close to me and looked up
wonderingly, as, lost in my dreams, I gazed ahead.
Maybe he was sizing up my appearance, as I had his only
a short while before. For was I not the first white man
that he had ever laid eyes on ?

Hardly had we topped the hill when I saw men, women
and children swaying in a measured dance. There they
were, those golden-brown Congo dwarfs with their queer
angular faces that I had so often seen in pictures. At
first sight their dancing seemed unrhythmical, even stiff
and constrained. My sudden appearance seemingly
made them self-conscious. The women danced a kind of
one-step in a wide circle around the men, and clapped
their hands, which they held to the left and level with
their faces. The men's movements were more agile, and
as they danced they played flutes. The strains of these
reed instruments sounded so impressive and haunting
that they put me under a spell. Played with taste,
feeling, and a curious sense of rhythm, they harmonized
as effectively as so many tiny organ pipes, producing a
very simple, but well-rounded orchestral effect.

Delighted though I was with this weird music, I felt
somewhat disappointed as I noticed the preoccupied,
listless movements of the dancers. I seemed to be a
source of amusement to them. They showed a furtive
curiosity, glancing in my direction as they whirled
mechanically around. Perhaps it was silly of me to be
piqued by the attitude of these guileless children of the
forest, for, after all, it was at the instigation of the
negroes that they had come into the village to welcome
me. Perhaps the wee creatures were frightened at the
sight of the big white man, and were really only anxious
to take to their heels.

I decided to break the spell that bound them, and
right away to win their confidence by telling my bearers
to give them salt and tobacco. Immediately all the
elfin creatures raised a chorus : " Get the banana leaves !
The big white man is giving us salt and tobacco ! Salt
and tobacco ! " Then followed a deafening pandemonium

in a tongue of which I could not understand a single word. The almost naked figures formed a semicircle, and there was a sudden lull as they held out their banana leaves for my gifts. Scarcely had they tied up their parcels when the dance began again, but this time with a definite zest. Even the old women, who previously had crouched apathetically in the shadows of the huts, swung into the ring with decided élan. The woods around rang to the din of the merry-making. Perspiration streamed down the bronzed bodies, and mingled with the dust whirled up by their crazy gyrations.

After a short rest we set off for the village of Zongere, where there was a rest hut. On our way we had to cross a deep gorge which lay between the two villages. During the whole time a motley throng of pigmies capered in my rear, while two sturdy lads walked either side of me.

I stayed in the rest hut for several days. My object was to strengthen the bond I had just established with the pigmies, and also to find a suitable camping ground, where I could settle down in their midst.

As usual the negroes were the ones to strut and swagger about, while the pigmies crouched shyly in the background behind some oil lamps, and stared at me wide-eyed. The former were dragging their wicker-work arm-chairs towards the veranda, so as to take stock of me and my possessions with greater comfort. I stopped them and beckoned to the pigmies. With very bad grace the natives made way for the little forest goblins and shepherded them into the hut, taunting and jostling them.

Presuming that the pigmies must have some kind of overlord, I enquired for their chief. I was presented to a hale, elderly dwarf named Alianga, who wore a rush cap decorated with a cluster of sky-blue feathers. Alianga was calm and dignified, but somewhat aloof. He had a slight stutter. Later we became fast friends.

It was extremely fortunate that I was able to converse with the pigmies from the first, without any intermediary, in Kingwana, a Swahili dialect which has spread along the Ituri and over the entire eastern Congo territory. Introduced some eighty years ago by the Zanzibar slave-traders, the development of the Kiswahili dialect

GROUP OF BAKANGO PIGMIES FROM ASUNGUDA

(Page 28)

AGALI, THE SULLEN PIGMY
(Page 24)

ALIANGA, THE CHIEF OF THE BAFWAGUDA
CAMP, WITH THE AUTHOR
(Page 28)

was as swift as the progress of their power. The enslaved negroes, as well as those who came under the influence of the Wangwana—as the successors of the slave-traders were called—quickly adopted the new language. They moulded it in certain respects to suit their own idiom, and a common *lingua franca* evolved, which is spoken and understood throughout the Congo. A considerable number of pigmies are able to understand Kingwana and even to speak it, especially those who use the Babira dialect in the camps.

As might be expected, some of the more bumptious negroes butted in while we were chatting, and frequently answered for the still timid pigmies. However, as it kept the conversation going, it was all to the good.

After our palaver I encircled Alianga's neck with a string of gaudy glass beads and a gay medal—incidentally, given to me at home by some thoughtful friends, as an attractive bauble to be used as a special gift on some epoch-making occasion ! The old man was quite bewildered when he saw that the resplendent " Sultan's chain "—the envy of so many negroes—was his very own. In the Congo it is customary for the administration to present privileged negro chiefs with necklaces and medallions attached as badges of honour.

In the presence of the negroes and the pigmies Alianga was elevated to the rank of a " medalled chief." He looked radiantly proud of his new dignity. I noticed a few days later that the gew-gaw no longer glistened on his dirty neck. Apparently his negro protector had taken it away from him.

When I asked him about his family, Alianga introduced me to a strapping lad of about seventeen, named Mangbendu. He was one of the youngsters who had trotted by my side on the way to the village. I gave him a bright string of beads, to which he attached a medallion made out of a bit of tinfoil from a cigarette packet. So he, too, was a chief—by his own act of grace ! The vain youth was vastly pleased with the necklace. Weeks later I noticed that he was still wearing it.

The sequence was rather embarrassing to me. Shortly after Mangbendu had strutted among his pals with his decoration, he came to my veranda accompanied by another youth. He took me aside confidentially and told me, without, however, venturing to look me in the face, that his father was old and weak on his legs, and was no longer any good as a Sultan (among the pigmies the chiefs are called Sultans). He added that he himself was young and strong, and had the right stuff in him for a really first-rate Sultan, and told me the lad with him was his policeman.

As I looked obtuse at his hints, and pretended not to understand what he was really driving at, he became quite blunt and asked me to appoint him as Sultan in place of his father.

I still do not know whether he realized that I was deaf to all his suggestions. I was so amused that I burst out laughing. However, fearing that he might go away for good, I gave his policeman pal some beads, and they both went off highly delighted. During my stay in the camp Mangbendu's friend was known as " Policy," and I used to employ him running errands, which, however, he had a habit of dodging, whenever he felt like it. Occasionally, too, when I was particularly pleased with him, I addressed Mangbendu as " Sultan," to his intense delight.

I could never really understand why the conceited Mangbendu, right from the start, showed his ambitious inclinations so blatantly. As will be seen later, there is really no scope for the ambitions of chieftainship in the social organization of the pigmies, and Mangbendu's mental bias must be explained in some other way. He, like all pigmies, knew that it was the white men who appointed the so-called overlords in the various negro villages. Hence, apparently, he came to the conclusion that I, the " Baba wa Bambuti," would do likewise among the pigmies ; and evidently considered that he was the most suitable, both for the rôle of chief and that of intermediary between me and his people.

I was aware that both the negroes and the pigmies who had heard that I was coming to the forest, looked on me as a kind of pigmy official. A few days before my arrival, negroes spread the rumour that a white man was on his way, whose mission was " exclusively for the Bambuti." The view is held generally that all white men who come to the forest, whether officials, merchants or missionaries, are there merely in the interests of the negroes, and the latter thought it strange that a white man should come over the seas to look after such scum as pigmies.

I saw no reason for disillusioning either the pigmies or the negroes, and decided to make capital out of this rumour. I always strove to settle disputes, brought before me by the pigmies, in accordance with their racial code. Hitherto a· pigmy had never brought a dispute with a negro before a white official, knowing full well that the latter would be sure to back the negro. During my stay among them, however, the little fellows repeatedly asked me to be their umpire when they fell foul of the negroes ; and so from the very outset, without at first realizing it, I had been playing a winning game with them. As a rule they rushed forward to greet me whenever I appeared, whereas usually they give the white man a very wide berth.

I now understand how I came by the grand title " Baba wa Bambuti," which originated among the negroes, and which obviously expressed their surmises regarding my mission to the forest. They regarded me as the advocate of the Bambuti, bent on helping them in every possible way.

As time went on my popularity among the pigmies made the negroes jealous. They frequently vented their spite by refusing to supply me with provisions and bearers. I was " the white man of the Bambuti," they said sullenly ; well, let them do my jobs for me. The result was that I frequently found myself in an awkward and unpleasant position from which I occasionally had to extricate myself with my bare fists !

The paternal solicitude of Baba wa Bambuti was destined to find an outlet very soon. On my instructions negro women fetched bananas which were divided among the pigmies. The poor little devils were desperately hungry, for they had had nothing to eat since the previous day. Very opportunely my negro huntsman had also brought in a magnificent chimpanzee, which was divided among the pigmies. Negroes abhor monkey's flesh. To them the chimpanzee is a species of man ; and yet some years ago those very negroes were cannibals. The pigmies also thought that the " Sheko," as they call the anthropoid ape, was a kind of man, but they deprecated my suggestion that by eating him they were cannibals. The Sheko did not know the use of fire and so was not a real man, was their jesuitical defence! The casuistry of this explanation left me speechless. I dropped the subject for the moment, as, at any rate, my little comrades were chewing up the chimpanzee with appreciative gusto. The women had cut up the carcase into huge chunks which they roasted. Bananas peeled and boiled in earthenware pots were also served up.

Before the chimpanzee was dismembered, I took a snapshot of him and Alianga side by side. The juxtaposition of " man-ape " and " ape-man " tickled my fancy. I fixed the dead monkey in a sitting position, when he was as tall as the pigmy, who posed crouching beside him. The resemblance between man and beast was particularly striking.

Late in the afternoon the dance was resumed. The dwarfish figures reacted rhythmically to the beating of the negro drums. Whenever I approached the dancers, Alianga darted forward, and with yells and facial contortions inspired his men to more frenzied gyrations.

The negroes, men and women, sat in groups at the doors of their huts, and enjoyed the spectacle of the Bambuti dancers. A gentle evening breeze had sprung up, and acted as a soothing anodyne on the minds of all. A spirit of festivity pervaded the village of Zongere.

Long after I had retired to my bunk, the singing and dancing went on with unabated zest. The full moon stood high in the sky, its rays lighting up the festal scene in a weirdly grotesque fashion that was suggestive of the " Walpurgis night " interlude from *Faust*. It was long after midnight when the revels ended, leaving a breathless silence brooding over the forest, holding me in a spell of awe and sadness. For hours I lay there, wide-eyed, weaving fantastic dreams before I fell asleep.

Next morning torrents of rain fell from a grey sky. What rotten luck! On the previous day I had arranged with the pigmies and negroes to take a trip into the forest to see the Bambuti camp. Nobody wanted to move on that chilly dripping day. The journey was too long, they said, and owing to the rain the pace would be too slow. They insisted, too, that there would be no chance of getting back before dark. I refused to listen to these excuses, and peremptorily ordered the young " Sultan " and his "policeman " to accompany me. The effect was magical. The two chosen ones stepped forward proudly, and when the rest saw that I was in dead earnest, more pigmies and negroes joined us.

Had I paused for a moment to recall my experiences in my travels through the Indian forests, I should not have started on this journey in such a downpour. At first our route lay through the " kongo," a desolate weed-covered plantation, overgrown with brambles and tall grass which was almost impassable owing to the rain. I was soon drenched to the skin. The dripping branches lashed my face, and all the time I kept slipping and slithering on the sticky trail that zig-zagged through a maze of hillocks and hollows. Once I bumped my head against an overhanging branch, for my eyes were constantly fixed on the ground to obviate the risk of tripping over the ropes of trailing liana and the stumps of trees. At last we reached the great forest, and the vista between the trees expanded. I gave a sigh of relief as we quickened our pace. The rain ceased, but there was a steady drip-drip from the trees.

Casting a glance behind me I suddenly became aware of the numbers of my retinue. In addition to men and women, there were also negro girls who at a bend in the road suddenly left us, apparently in order to herald our approach. A negro from a wayside village, through which we passed, announced himself as a patron of the Bambuti, and assumed the rôle of guide at the head of the procession. After an exhausting tramp of three hours we reached a little banana plantation. Scarcely had I entered a cane-brake hut, when its owner, the Mubali negro, our recent self-appointed guide, issued a series of commands. I was informed that here he was the master and patron of a group of pigmies.

A pigmy woman fearfully disfigured with sores crawled out of the hut. She was Alianga's wife, the mother of the young " Sultan." I learned later from Alianga himself that he had long ago ceased to live with the invalid woman and had married a widow, leaving his first wife

c

to be supported by the Babali. She was far better off
with the latter than in the pigmy camp, for she was quite
unfit for the constant trekking of her husband's nomad
race.

Meanwhile the friendly negro treated me to a sugar
cane which he had cut and peeled for me. My retinue,
both negroes and pigmies, scattered through the plantation, obviously in quest of edible fruit. The little negro
village comprised only a few huts. It owed its existence,
in reality, to its alliance with the pigmies. Some fifty
feet from the end of the plantation tiny huts peeped out
of the high grass. They were pigmy houses, built in the
same style as those of the negroes, but much smaller.
The entrances were so low and narrow that I was unable
to squeeze my way through them. In the nearby bush
stood the ruins of some beehive huts of a type that I
frequently saw later on.

So this was the pigmy camp ! What a disillusionment !
At most it could accommodate twenty people, and yet
fifty pigmies had gathered around me in the village of
Zongere. How had the rest encamped ? The proximity
of the negroes was, moreover, very distasteful to me.
Nothing would induce me to erect my hut in the midst of
a negro plantation. It had been my earnest wish to live
among the pigmies alone. There was still another and a
very important reason why the place dissatisfied me.
There was no stream, and consequently no water in the
vicinity.

Although we had hit upon a more comfortable trail for
our return journey, and the sun shone gaily through the
tree-tops, I felt in very bad humour. As soon as we
reached the camp I gave the people my views, quite
candidly, on the camp we had just seen. My suggestion
that all the pigmies should settle in one camp met with
no opposition. They were fully prepared to trek in
another direction right away. After a short parley with
the negroes, they agreed upon a spot which they thought
would meet with my approval ; and that was the origin
of the camp on the Asunguda River.

I myself had nothing to do with the selection of the
site, for, having decided to stay two months with my
new friends, I had to hurry back to Bafwasende to

collect my luggage. I gave the Zongere negroes the commission to build huts for me and my servants, while the pigmies were to erect their own themselves. On my return I paid my first visit to the new camp. As may be imagined, my progress along the fresh trail was excessively slow, for it had only recently been opened up, and with its tortuous twists and turns was not made for European travellers. There was a short cut across water and morass, which I tried only once. Ever afterwards, when I had to go into the negro village, I preferred the serpentine and laborious route to wading through the stinking, fetid marsh. The camp was some two hours' journey from the village of Zongere. Thus, while on the one hand the distance was great enough to prevent the too frequent visits of the negroes annoying me, on the other hand I had comparatively easy means of procuring a sufficient supply of bananas for my servants and the pigmies. From the very start it had been clear to me that the only method of keeping the Bambuti loyal was by accepting the responsibility for the greater part of their daily food. Through the medium of M. Daout, the administrator, the chiefs of the outlying villages had received instructions to sell me their bananas, instead of delivering them, as usual, to the Wegebau Station. At that time a motor road was being built through the forest, and the negro villages, even the far distant ones, had, for a truly meagre remuneration, to deliver bananas and other food supplies regularly at certain fixed points. As the negroes sometimes had to travel a distance of thirty-five miles, while fulfilling their contract, they were extremely pleased with the order to supply me with food. Even so they often delivered the bananas with a very bad grace.

When I appeared for the first time in the new camp, the pigmies were already living in their huts, but my abode was still far from being finished. Accordingly I lent a hand myself to speed up the erection of the building. The hut was thatched with phrynium leaves, which the pigmy women collected. The boys and men felled trees and made posts and rafters. Soon, however, I noticed that this sort of work was not congenial to the Bambuti. They were so listless that they constantly had to be bullied by their taskmasters, the negroes, to get them to work at all. Had it not been for the aid of the negroes the work would never have been finished.

The Bambuti had constructed the camp in the shape of a horse-shoe, with their huts facing mine. From the front of my house I had a full view of the camp. As the ground was very damp, I had my hut built on piles, so that the floor was about a yard from the earth. In this way I always managed to have dry boards under my feet. The side walls were made of phrynium leaves. A partition, also made of these leaves, divided the abode into two rooms. In front was an open veranda, where I spent most of my time. There, too, I took my meals and chatted with the pigmies for hours at a time. I developed my photographs and did all my writing there, and often spent half the night in my arm-chair, when the camp was silent, and I could do my work undisturbed. Sometimes I dreamily watched figures, silhouetted against the fitful gleam of the smoking camp fires, appearing and vanishing into the shadows. Now and again the profound silence of the gloomy forest would be broken by the faint wail of a baby and the soothing croon of its mother.

My bedroom, as I have said, was separated from the veranda by a partition of leaves. My bed, actually a bunk made of rattan by the pigmies, was overhung with a mosquito net. The provisions were also kept in the bedroom.

My black servants had built a hut of leaves for themselves, close to mine. At first the life in the forest appealed to them immensely, and they appeared to get on very well together. It was only natural that I found them always ready to score over me or over the pigmies, whom they regarded as creatures of a far lower order than themselves.

The huntsman went daily in quest of game, and regularly returned with some Kema monkeys. I adapted myself to such an extent to my environment that I even ate the monkey meat. It was very luscious and had an excellent flavour. After a few days, however, I noticed that it was too strong for my stomach, and decided to abstain from the delicacy in future.

At the end of my second week in the pigmy camp I

noted signs of unrest and boredom among my retinue. A little later they started squabbling among themselves. I had brought with me a half-breed Mombuti, named Adzapori, as a sort of interpreter and steward. He was a sturdy fellow, healthy in body and mind, and he amused me vastly with his naive primitive ways. The three others, the huntsman, cook and valet, were pure negroes, and intensely disliked the half-breed, who could only speak a pidgin Kingwana. One morning I saw that Adzapori was building a hut for himself. Reading the question registered by my astounded expression, he explained apologetically that the other hut was too small for four people, and that he was building one for himself. All four of them had lived for nearly three weeks in one hut, and it was quite big enough for them ; but now it had suddenly become too small! Nevertheless, I humoured him, as I did not want to get mixed up in their squabbles.

Adzapori was an excellent servant, and did his utmost to assist me in my exploration work, a field in which the others took no interest whatsoever. Moreover, he had a good deal of personal charm, which was a great asset to me in dealing with the Bambuti.

We were about five weeks in the camp when Adzapori surprised me with the news that he intended to marry a pigmy beauty from the camp, a young widow with one child. I stared at him astounded, and flatly refused to permit it.

"While you are in my service you must not get married," I replied. "When you leave me, you can do as you like."

Perplexed as he was, Adzapori tried to coax me to change my mind, but I was firm. Whereupon he declared that he would stay with me as long as I would permit him. When I left the camp some weeks later, he resigned his post, so apparently he preferred to marry the widow to remaining with me.

Adzapori belonged to a particular tribe, " Basua wa mungine," i.e. " village Bambuti." The genuine pigmies are called " Basua wa pori "—" forest Bambuti." It seems very probable that at one time there was some common link between them, although to-day the " Basua wa mungine " resemble the Babali negroes more than they do the Bambuti. Yet I found some of the village Bambuti who bore the racial marks of the pigmies. A typical case was Ponde, the uncle of Adzapori, to all appearances a genuine pigmy.

At the present day the " Basua wa mungine " live together in villages, just like the Babali, and they marry Babali or pigmy girls. They have, however, a language of their own. In their outlook, too, they differ, in some respects, from both stocks. As only four settlements of these village Bambuti are still in existence, they are of extreme importance to the explorer. If one credits a tradition common to them and to the Babali, they followed the Babali negroes, their masters, into the forest region of the Apare River. According to this legend they would seem to be a blend of pigmy and negro.

Adzapori, who was an offshoot of this stock, and who showed scarcely a trace of pigmy ancestry in his features, exhibited one trait, his love of hunting, which he must have acquired from this source.

I have already mentioned that the Bambuti are called Basua by the Babali negroes ; but the pigmies call themselves Bakango, at least in this territory. The names Basua, Batua, Basa and Batchwa are applied to the central African pigmies over various widely scattered areas. Every negro tribe gives a particular name to its specific group of pigmies, which sometimes has no relation to their ancestral title.

Linguistically, too, the pigmies are an exceedingly interesting people, as I noticed even in the early days of my stay in the Asunguda camp. Almost all of them spoke several languages. Invariably the majority had a certain acquaintance with the trading lingo, Kingwana, and all of them spoke the dialects of the Babali negroes fluently. They seemed familiar, too, with the speech of their half-cousins, the " Basua wa mungine " ; but it was their camp argot that especially fascinated me. This was a strange patois, with musical cadences, and I found it extremely difficult to follow. After some time, however, I could gather the gist of it, and I realized that it was a corruption of Kibira, the ancient language of the negroes. I was greatly disappointed at this discovery, as I had thought, at first, that I was hot on the trail of a genuine pigmy language. Among the philologists there is a general, but erroneous, consensus of opinion that the pigmies speak negro dialects only. As we go on, we shall go into this question more fully. The Bakango, at all events, spoke the language of the Babira, and though they have no dealings with one another at the present day, they must have lived in community at some earlier period. In my travels, later on, southward of the Asunguda River, I met the Babira, and I have no doubt at all in my own mind that they were formerly patrons of the Bakango, and that the latter were driven from their ancestral territory by the Babali. The Bambuti must have remained in the occupied territory and made terms with the new conquerors. One comes across many similar linguistic freaks in the Congo forest territories, and it seems that the dialects of the pigmies afford the best clue to the wanderings of the negro tribes.

During the first weeks of my stay in the Ituri region I was amazed to learn the extraordinary number of different negro tribes, each of whom had a language, or at any rate a dialect of its own. I have to thank the missionaries in the various areas for helping me to solve this difficult problem, for at first I was absolutely confused by the maze of tribes and tongues. As I penetrated deeper into the forest I gradually began to see a coordination between this medley of languages and dialects, and eventually had a tolerably good knowledge of the territorial distribution of all the negro stocks in the tropics, and was able to make copious notes of almost all the forest dialects.

Unfortunately I failed to find the key to the pigmy languages, mainly because those little people do not show the faintest trace of a consciousness of a clear differentiation of tribes. Accordingly I had to be satisfied either with grouping the pigmies among the negro tribes, with whom they lived in community, or with finding out the basis of the dialects spoken by the little men. I decided upon the latter course, and after arduous research, I was successful in my object.

The Iturian pigmies are unquestionably a distinct race ; moreover, they are exceedingly conscious of their racial cohesion. Not only are they regarded as foreigners by the negroes ; they even proudly assert the fact themselves. They are unanimous in the belief that they are the aborigines of the primeval forest regions, which were their domain before the incursions of the negroes. Almost all the pigmy tribes have stories of their fierce wars with the invaders. A negro would never dream of putting himself on the same social plane as pigmies, and he would never regard them as even human. He calls himself a " man," but to him the pigmies, whether they term themselves " Bambuti " or " Basua," are merely " man-apes," like the chimpanzees.

Despite the race-consciousness of all the pigmies, they lack any idea of unity or of the cohesion essential to a distinct stock. Their peculiar circumstances make this impossible for them. They have been so completely split up by the multiplicity of languages spoken among them, that at the present day an individual unit has far closer ties with its negro neighbours than with its own kith and kin living any distance away. In reality, only groups living close together have any intercourse with one another. So absolute has the cleavage between the tribes become, that their very systems of life and their customs are different. Despite this the explorer can still trace a definite fundamental similarity in the material, social and spiritual outlook of all pigmies, which enables him to visualize them as a distinct entity.

On the basis of language, I divide the pigmies of the Ituri Forest into three groups. The Aká, who were discovered by Schweinfurth, and later by other explorers, hold the north-western area between Nepoko and Bomokandi, and live in community with the Medje, Babeyru and the Majogu. In this area, too, live the pigmies of the Balika tribe and some of the Wabudu. Their patrons are, for the most part, Sudanese tribes, and they speak a Sudanese dialect.

Southward of them the Bambuti occupy a very extensive territory. To their breed belong the Bakango, already mentioned. Originally they had the Babira-Bakumu as their sole patrons ; but when the latter were driven out by tribes, who swept down probably from the north-west, the pigmies allied themselves with the new invaders, the Babali, Bandaka and the Barumba. The name Bambuti, originally applied solely to the Kabira-speaking dwarfs, gradually spread, after the Wangwana conquests, to all the pigmies.

The eastern group, extending as far as the steppes, are the Efé. These are decidedly the most numerous, and, racially, the most pure of all pigmy stocks. They would even appear to have preserved their primitive language to the present day. The influence of the invaders on them such as the Mombutu, Mamvu, Balese and Bambuba has, so far, been almost negligible. The handful of Banyari and the Balendu pigmies may be counted among the Efé.

The Efé dwell on the upper reaches of the Nepoko, on the Nduye and Epulu rivers, and stretch westwards, over a narrow strip of country, to the other side of the Ituri, nearly as far as Beni. The Bambuti (Basua), on the other hand, occupy both banks of the Ituri as far as Mombasa. Their largest numbers are between the Ituri and the middle reaches of the Lindi, and along the banks of the Lenda to the summit of the Beni, from which their camps extend again as far as Ruwenzori.

It is difficult to imagine how the pigmies lived before the negroes invaded the tropical forest, and I doubt very much whether the Bambuti of to-day could survive without the aid of the negro plantations. It is quite evident that long ago they must have managed to do so somehow, but in those days they were even more primitive than they are now. As economically the weaker stock, they gradually became entirely dependent on the negro peasants. While it is not exactly a condition of slavery that has gradually evolved, there exists a sort of community life, in which the pigmies, in the long run, get the worst of the bargain. In the forest, as everywhere else in the world, the weaker are exploited by the stronger. The pigmy is merely a hunter and a harvester. He never does any planting, and though game is at times fairly abundant, meat is by no means his chief sustenance. The produce of the forest, such as roots, leaves, nuts and various fruits, is at times very scanty, and at best a rather meagre and unsubstantial diet. The demand for nourishing food in abundance can only be satisfied by the banana plantations, oil palm trees, sugar-canes, manioc roots and other succulent dainties which are the exclusive property of the negroes. Pigmies consider bananas particularly appetizing food, and they are ready to barter, not only their game, but to a certain extent their very freedom, to satisfy their craving. The negro has exploited this very natural desire of the pigmies for nourishing diet, and has constituted himself their overlord. The position is, at the present time, that a horde of pigmies is attached to almost every negro village, in such a manner that an individual negro is patron over one or more groups of pigmies, which he has inherited from his father, and which in turn he will pass on to his son. The pigmies are entitled to receive from time to time supplies of bananas, sugar-cane and other food, in return for which they are obliged to supply him with game, the produce of the woods, and if required, their personal services. The tribute to be levied is usually decided by the patron himself. He regards the group of pigmies as his personal property, of which no other negro can deprive him with impunity. Of course the pigmies beg or buy food from other negroes, but primarily the patron is responsible for their maintenance. As the Bambuti know absolutely nothing about iron-working, they also buy their weapons, such as iron arrows and spears, from the negroes.

Owing to this community life the pigmies try to pitch their camps close to the negro villages, so as to be in closer touch with the plantations. However, as the little fellows frequently help themselves without leave to the produce of the plantations, if they think their patron miserly, the black men try to prevent the pigmies from camping too close to them and often compel them to move farther on.

It would be a mistake to infer from what I have just said that the negroes interfere in the private social life of the Bambuti. Taking everything into consideration, they permit them to continue their nomad life in accordance with their ancestral ways. The fact, however, that the negro patron appoints one of his group of pigmies as chief, and through him communicates his desires or commands to the camp, might be considered by some as an attempt to meddle in their social organization.

On the other hand the negro tries to bind his group of pigmies closer to him by introducing them into his own social schemes. Among other privileges he allows them to take part in the " clan initiation " ceremonials—a rather cunning, but withal, a gracious political gesture, which might serve as a lesson to all colonial empires ! On the other hand, as the pigmy always remains an outcast, his closer connection with the negroes is of little use to him. He is only too well aware that the big fellow is all the time out to rob him with as little fuss as possible. Many of the Bambuti complained to me on this score, and begged me to protect them against the browbeating methods of the negroes.

The pigmy is far too proud to put up with anything like a state of slavery. He is always ready to defend himself with arms if necessary. Hence there are squabbles and fights in plenty between pigmies and negroes. The Bambuti are very dexterous with the bow and arrow, which they do not hesitate to use when wantonly attacked by their bigger brothers. Given sufficient provocation they will even kill their patrons.

Some years ago, I was informed, a group of pigmies overpowered a negro, who had been bullying them unmercifully, bound him, and handed him over to the local " white administrator." This, however, must have been an isolated case. As a rule, when harshly treated, they administer the unwritten law themselves.

If the negro looks down on the pigmy as a " beast-man," he is treated with scant respect by the little fellow. One day I had an opportunity of witnessing an instance of this attitude. I was having a breezy chat with a group of pigmies when a negro joined us. I asked who he was, and a scrubby little pigmy answered in a most contemptuous tone : " Iko Muschenzi wangu ! " It is necessary to understand what the word " Muschenzi " means among negroes, to grasp the abysmal scorn implied by the term. Among the Mohammedan Wamgewana every heathen is a " Muschenzi," i.e. a " savage " ; and this was the term which my scrubby little pigmy had applied to the negro—incidentally his patron ! The latter was his " savage," whose business it was to supply him with bananas ! From this interlude, one can infer what little effect the lordly pretensions of the negroes have upon the pigmies.

In the opinion of the Bambuti the negro peasants are morally bound to place the plantations at their disposal. They maintain that they have an hereditary right to them, and, as a basis for this view, quote myths and traditions which they share alike with the negroes.

I heard one such legend time and again in various widely distant places. Told in the quaint idiom of the Bambuti, it shows that the latter regard the chimpanzee as a sort of pioneer of civilization.

" In ancient times a pigmy, while out hunting one day, came upon a chimpanzee village. He was astounded at the many strange things he saw, and at once returned home and reported his discovery. Accompanied by a negro, he set off again. The first sight that met their eyes was a magnificent plantation, abounding with green trees that were laden with bunches of golden bananas. At first neither of the two ventured to touch the beautiful ripe fruit. They had never seen anything like it before, and for all they knew it might be poisonous. Then the wary and cunning negro urged the pigmy to taste one. He pointed out to him that he was in the habit of eating many different kinds of wild products of the forest, and argued that, as none of these had ever done him any harm, it was scarcely probable that this new discovery would be injurious to him.

" The Mombuti gazed longingly at the luxurious festoons. At last he took heart, and, somewhat timidly, ate a banana. He announced that it tasted delicious. The negro watched him enviously, but was afraid as yet to touch the fruit himself.

" When evening came, they both lay down in the chimpanzee village ; but, for the negro, it was a sleep-less night. He was still unconvinced that the fruit was not poisonous, and kept fretting about the dwarf, although the latter was sleeping soundly.

" Before dawn the negro aroused the pigmy, and asked him how he felt. The little chap rubbed his eyes, replied that he had never felt better, and at once resumed his eulogy on the flavour of bananas. The negro had no further anxiety. Back they went to the plantation, and had a hearty breakfast on their new-found fruit.

"Suddenly the thought struck the negro that it would be an excellent idea to grow this delicacy in his own village. The Mombuti fell in with the suggestion, and they set to work at once. While the dwarf collected the most luxurious clusters with the intention of sowing the fruit in the earth, the negro, to the intense amusement of his small companion, broke off branches, which he took home and planted round his hut. The dwarf, on the other hand, laid row after row of bananas in the ground. The very next morning, the negro's shoots drooped and withered. The pigmy laughed heartily at the man, and, for some time, kept taunting and teasing him for his silly whim. But the negro was cunning, and let the manikin have his little joke.

"The pigmy waited in vain for his bananas to sprout. Eventually he dug up the ground, and saw that the fruit had become rotten. However, he consoled himself with the thought that the negro had had similar bad luck with his branches ; so he took his bow and arrows and resumed his quest of game.

"When months later he returned to the negro's hut, he could scarcely believe his eyes. A luxurious banana plantation had grown around the little dwelling. Now was the negro's turn to laugh, but the pigmy, concealing his annoyance, remarked diplomatically : ' I knew I had not the stuff for a farmer in me. That's more in your line, I prefer to stick to my hunting. You can go on planting bananas, and I shall eat them, for it was I who introduced them to you.' "

It is on this legend that the pigmies base their claim to the negro plantations.

I heard a variant of this theme from an old man in the Asunguda camp. He told me that the Bambuti were the first to discover bananas. It was common knowledge that they grew wild in the forest, but they had always been regarded as poisonous, until, one day, a pigmy tasted one, and found that it was delicious. He took some of the fruit back to his comrades. Whereupon great jubilation broke out in the camp, which was immediately transferred to the shade of the banana clump.

Some time later, the Bambuti, following their usual custom, moved farther on, and some negroes, finding banana peels lying around, nibbled them, and then tasted the fruit itself, which they found very palatable. So they transplanted all the trees to their village.

When the pigmies returned to the district they found no trace of their bananas. They wandered about in quest of them, and came at last to the negro village where they recognized their trees. " Why did you steal our bananas ? " they indignantly asked the negroes. Then they plucked all the fruit, and brought it back to their own camp. And they continue to do so to this very day.

There are many legends telling of other advantages that the negroes have gained through the ingenuity of the pigmies. It seems singular that the very negroes who look on the Bambuti as being far inferior to themselves, regard them, nevertheless, as their precursors, to whom they owe many of the amenities of civilization. On the other hand, I must repeat once again that there is no doubt that without the aid of the negroes the pigmies could scarcely manage to exist at the present day.

CHAPTER II

IN THE BAFWAGUDA CAMP

NO very intense research was called for on my part to learn the name that the Bambuti give to themselves. Mainly it was a matter of chance. Incidentally, my attempts at the pronunciation of it afforded the pigmies much amusement. Known to the negroes as " Basua," they call themselves, as I have said before, " Bakango." Despite all my efforts, I was unable to discover the origin of this name, although I found later that some primitive negro tribes in these districts are also named thus. Even so, I could trace no real connection between the two.

Alianga, the Bambuti chief, was the first to initiate me into the mysteries of the geography of the Congo. He enumerated all the camps in the vicinity for me, together with the rivers that formed their natural boundaries. I put question after question to him as we sat in the shade with our backs against a tree-trunk, and his replies proved a considerable help in my work later on.

Above, the rays of the sun were beating down through the forest trees, and shining with a garish gleam on the huts of the pigmies. Alianga was making a dog collar, and chatted animatedly and freely. I learned that he belonged to the tribe, or more strictly, to the clan (tribal unit) of the Bafwaguda. Every member of the camp was also Bafwaguda, a fact I had not realized before. The other camps in the vicinity belonged to different clans. He mentioned the Bepieli, Baboti, Bafwabane, and the Bafwasengwe, and the almost extinct Bataro. They were all Bakango, he said, and dwelt in the Apare River district as far as the Ituri. He said he could not state their numbers, but according to my reckoning there were about four hundred in all.

At the end of our conversation I was getting ready to return to Zongere—this was before my hut was quite finished—and suggested to the old fellow that he might accompany me. With great alacrity he stuffed the dog collar into the leafy roof of his hut, and shouted to a woman who was about to fetch some water. We stepped out, and he showed me a short cut along the river by the morass. The going was so muddy that my shoes were oozing mire, and squelching, for hours after.

I had found the roundabout way to the camp and back rather tedious. The short cut through the marsh was infinitely worse, while this third route was very little better, and I made up my mind that in future I should take the longest way round with all its drawbacks.

Alianga returned with me the same evening, so as to be ready the next morning with his people, who were to be my bearers. As the natives of Zongere had expressed their willingness to co-operate with me for a small gift of salt, everything went swimmingly. As you may well imagine, I was in really good spirits that morning. I felt that it was a most satisfactory achievement to have built my hut in the midst of those very pigmies, of whose actual whereabouts I had had only an extremely hazy idea two months before. I was fairly satisfied that my present good relations with the pigmies would continue, and was determined to do nothing that would lead to a rupture. The little folk had quickly won my sympathy, for they were an enslaved and harassed people—a type that my heart always goes out to.

I spent the whole day improving and putting the finishing touches to my forest quarters, the negroes and pigmies lending a hand. I wished to make it as comfortable as possible, as I had decided to remain for at least two months on this spot.

That night, dog-tired, I threw myself down on my bunk. I had hardly closed my weary eyes, when a maddening itching pain on my feet, hands and face abruptly woke me. I felt as though I was lying in a bed of nettles. I quickly flashed on my electric torch, swearing, I might add, volubly. I know of nothing more liable to wring a string of curses from a man than my predicament of that moment, and I feel sure that anyone who has suffered the torments of being aroused from his sleep by myriads of mosquitoes and midges will agree with me on this point. I felt in a helpless rage. My torturers on this particular night were not mosquitoes. I could see nothing, and reluctantly lay down again, pulling the sheet over my face. It was absolutely useless. In a few minutes my agony was resumed. I rubbed and scratched my hands and face, and peered round in quest of the little wretches. At length I saw countless wee midges, scarcely as big as pin-points. They were sand-midges, so tiny that they were even able to squeeze through the meshes of my mosquito net. My night's rest was over. I protected myself as best I could by pulling socks over my hands and feet and tying up my head in a cloth. Thus wrapped up, I sweated and gasped my way through the tropical night. At last towards morning, overcome by utter exhaustion, I fell asleep.

The next day everybody stared in astonishment at my prickled and swollen face. My servants advised me to cover the hut on all sides so thoroughly with leaves, that no light, and consequently no midges could enter it. I refused to entertain this suggestion for a moment, as I had no wish to be suffocated! I preferred old Alianga's idea of lighting a fire beneath the hut in the hope that the smoke would keep the midges away. I followed his suggestion the next night. The experiment was a success. True, I was nearly smoked out of my hut, but that was more endurable than the plague of midges. I thought that the breeding ground of the midges might have been the morass at the back of my log home which separated the camp from the Asunguda River. It had to be crossed by anyone going to the river for water. The Bambuti worried very little about sinking knee deep in mire, but marsh baths had no appeal for me, and hoping at the same time to decrease the numbers of midges, I set about bridging the bog with boughs and leaves, with the aid of Pembereko, a half-breed pigmy.

Every day, early in the morning and at midday, I was in the habit of bathing in the nearby river. It was an amusing spectacle for the pigmies. I was generally alone at the riverside in the mornings, but in the afternoons I always had a numerous escort accompanying me. My

D

followers were not crazy about bathing—far from it ; they were merely curious spectators. To the pigmies it was extremely funny to watch the " white man " splashing about in the water. They must have regarded it as an exceptionally good show, for a crowd of youths and boys formed my daily bodyguard. I usually asked a couple of them to accompany me. This was the signal for a general rush to carry my soap, towel and wash-basin. They all started at a run for the river bank.

After a little while my example proved infectious. Gradually, one by one, they decided to try the cooling river—at first tentatively and timidly, but very soon with confidence and courage. They enjoyed it immensely when I chased them in the water, or dived at their feet. If I cornered any of them, they would entangle themselves in the trailing liana, that hung down into the river, whereupon I would grasp the coils and swing them to and fro. They would cling on like monkeys, laughing and screaming with delight.

It would never occur to a pigmy to start the day with bathing or washing. When he awakes, he rubs his eyes— and that completes his day's toilet. Normally, shortly before dawn there are signs of life about the camp, but if the morning is rainy, or cold and dull with a steady drip from the trees, there is not a stir until fairly late. As soon as the smoke of the first fire curls up from a leaf-thatched hut, however, it is the signal for all to get up, even if the rain has not yet cleared. There is a loud hum of conversation forthwith. Soon somebody pokes his head out to see what the weather is like. Later a more daring fellow ventures fully into the open, hugging himself against the cold, but in a few seconds he dives back again under the thatch and crouches over the warm fire. On days like this the camp remains dead and silent.

When the morning is sunny and warm, the camp awakes to greet the new day with zest and clamour. Everyone moves about briskly. All are in high spirits. A snatch of song in a girlish voice rings out on the morning air. Others take up the refrain. Many a morning I have watched one lithe young maiden, Arao, stretching her arms with a languid sleepy yawn at the door of her hut, like a bird preening its feathers before leaving its nest. Then her clear, though hardly melodious voice, would ring out in song. One dance tune after another she would trill forth to the torpid tropical forest. It was the greeting of the dawn by the Bafwaguda.

Arao was an alert, vital girl, although she must have been tubercular, I think, for every now and then her song was interrupted by a convulsive cough ; but she always started afresh with renewed zest. Another young woman, Mazeru, even more enamoured of song than Arao, if that were possible, accompanied her in a cracked soprano, typical of the harsh, cacophonous singing of her race. The other women kept time to the rhythmic song of the two girls with a droning hum, bustling nimbly the while about the fires ; and all the time the men and children would keep hopping in and out of their huts. The striplings and the men always stood apart in groups in the mornings and took no notice of the women. Here and there, one of them played on a musical bow, or remained buried in an ecstasy of languorous indolence. The first sign of real activity among the jabbering men was shown when Agali began to fill his long tobacco pipe made from banana leaves. Scarcely had he exhaled the first clouds of smoke when three of his chums gathered round him to get a few puffs. A moment or so later all the others darted back into their huts, whence they presently emerged with pipes into which they crammed tobacco.

The first jarring note that marred this peaceful awakening of the forest aborigines was the hullabaloo of my servants. They placed pots in front of the huts, and in abusive language bellowed to the women to fetch water. The pigmies themselves were none too quiet as they buzzed around, but the clatter of the negroes was far worse. My servants had made a pact with the camp women, whereby the latter supplied the kitchen with water and firewood, for which they were paid in salt. The black men deemed it beneath their dignity to do these jobs themselves.

At a signal half the women in the camp, with an infernal jabbering and screaming, darted towards the river with pots on their shoulders. They were headed by the children who had previously been playing gaily before the

huts, where they tumbled and danced around in the
puddles, remnants of the recent downpour. This liking
of the little ones for puddles and ditches always remained
a puzzle to me, when I knew how water-shy were their
parents. The minute the children saw their mothers start
for the river, they stopped their splashing and ran after
them. The tiniest of them, who were barely able to
toddle, hung on to the aprons of the water-carriers, and
raised an infernal yell, until some of the women, not
already burdened with a nursling, picked up the brats,
scolding them the while. Over the fires, the earthenware
pots were simmering with vegetables for the grown-ups
and gruel for the children. Many of the women produced
a small supply of bananas remaining from the previous
evening. Adengu's wife, a heavy, selfish and phlegmatic
woman—an unusual type among pigmies—peeled banana
after banana, flinging the peels backwards over her hut
into the bush. Others, less lazy, carefully collected
the peels and put them on the refuse heap behind the
huts.

The aged, invalid Asangwa crouched before a smoking
fire, and shelled nuts, about the size of our hazel-nuts,
which he roasted, one by one, in the coals between two
stones, and popped them into his withered mouth. This
was his breakfast.

While the fires burned gaily and the pots simmered, the
girls and young women were not idle. Indolently reclining
on a broad reed chair, one of them, Majanga, stretched her
limbs while a friend dressed her hair for her. Mazeru
squatted nearby and sang, while every now and then she
dipped her finger in a vessel full of a dark fluid, prepared
from charcoal and the juice of a gum fruit, with which
she smeared her body in the most peculiar way. She
painted her hips and thighs pitch-black, which made her
look as if she were wearing bathing drawers.

With extreme care she traced geometric designs on her
calves. Then Bakbara, who had been lazily looking on,
skilfully decorated her friend's buttocks with all manner
of lines and fantastic patterns. Next she "made up"
Mazeru's face, not with rouge or lipstick, but with the
same jet-black mixture, which she applied carefully with
little sticks. The Bambuti term this art of body painting

AN ARCHERY CONTEST AMONG THE BAKANGO
(*Page* 56)

A PIGMY BEAUTY-PARLOUR IN AN ASUNGUDA CAMP
(*Page* 52)

AN ASUNGUDA GRANDMOTHER "MAKING UP"
HER GRANDCHILD'S FACE

(Page 53)

MOTHERS CARRY THEIR CHILDREN IN SASHES
OF WILD BOAR OR ANTELOPE HIDE

(Page 61)

" Ebembe." If the pigmy women want to look especially attractive, they apply the " Ebembe " in red as well as black, and sometimes even in white.

I do not think, however, that this mania for painting themselves is inspired merely by coquetry, for I have noticed scarcely any propensity for flirting among them. I am rather inclined to think that the reason lies in the mere delight in gaudy lines and fantastic designs. Even the lads and young men do not scorn to " make up " their faces. The fact that many Bambuti often look almost black is due to this Ebembe, which is frequently applied during the week, but never washed off. Consequently it is very difficult to tell what is the natural colour of a group of pigmies that you may come upon suddenly in the forest. The older men and women seem to be above this childish craze for body decoration. The fact, however, that withered old crones lovingly paint their grand-children with Ebembe shows that an appreciation of flashy ornamentation remains even with the aged. How touch-ing I thought the spectacle of a child of about six stretch-ing its little head towards its grandma, who deftly and caressingly painted the little face with slow gentle touches ! What tender solicitude was shown in this picture !

As I looked at the aged woman and the babe, I could not help wondering if I were really among " savages " ; among " beast-men," who, in our view, have almost no attributes beyond animal instincts. Here I was, living with a group of people who were absolutely primitive, relics, almost, of a prehistoric age, but who were, in fact, " savages " in name only ; men, who would never dream of snatching food from one another, but who would stand by one another ; men, whose hearts glowed with kindly feelings towards one another. I could see that among these people there were strong family ties. The affection for father and mother, brother and sister, meant to them exactly what it means to us, differing only, in that their demonstrations of love and affection were more naïve, more undemonstrative, and, possibly, therefore, more real than ours. This poor little camp had an air of con-tentment and peace about it, only because it was the sanctuary of men, not one of whom possessed more than his brother ; little men, linked together by their harsh elemental environment in a communal existence, where there was scant scope for envy or greed.

These lowly camp amenities which I saw every day, again and again, under the most touching circumstances, gave me a deep insight into the ways of life and thought, not only of this group as a whole, but of many individuals themselves. These conclusions are not based on questions ; they were not necessary, and might have been, to a certain extent, unsatisfactory. All I had to do was to keep my eyes open to see the very soul of the primitive man laid bare. On such occasions the veils that screened their minds fell apart, as the petals of a rose-bud expand in the sun. This was the more beautiful aspect of their life that I was seeing. Later on, I was to catch a glimpse of the uglier side.

The morning toilet of the young folk is always accompanied by merry laughter and joking. First of all the hairdressers line up. Mangbendu, with head bowed, squats in front of a girl who sharpens a little shearing knife on the palm of her hand. She cuts all manner of patterns in her client's hair, shaving him close to the scalp. She literally mows lanes through the tousled mop. Beside her is a pot of water, into which she dips her fingers every now and again, and moistens Mangbendu's scalp. This makes the woolly locks fall more easily before the blade. The patterns cut through the hair become more and more eccentric. Just above the forehead is a small half-moon design, shaved close to the scalp, while a larger one is cut at the back of the head. It all depends on the whim of the moment. Mangbendu's style seems to have established a special school of hairdressing, for I noticed that an ever increasing number of youths and lads adopted his fantastic coiffure. Emulating the dandy Mangbendu, they entrusted their woolly heads to the fair ones, who plied their shearing with the greatest zest. I took a snapshot of four of these weirdly tonsured Bambuti heads. I can still conjure up the picture of the fantastic grimaces that the young fellows made, through sheer exuberance of spirits, as they faced the camera.

Fantastic arabesques shaved through the mazes of woolly hair are to the Bambuti Beau Brummels what

Ebembe dressing is to the women. The older females are wont to shave their heads bare, and so too are the old men. The pigmies do not wear ornamental combs, but one very frequently sees the young men running fine-toothed wooden ones through their hair, with a view to getting rid of the vermin that plague them. They very rarely adorn their tresses with flowers, but are fond of swathing their bodies with girdles of leaves. Almost invariably you will find them covered in greenery on their homeward trips from the forest. Their dancing garb consists of the dressed skin of the wild-cat, while both sexes wear tufts of ornamental grass fixed in their girdles.

I noticed this love of decoration showed itself in many other quaint ways among the Bambuti. The short aprons of the women, made of tanned tree bark about the size of a pocket handkerchief, often look quite attractive with artistic groupings of red and black spots and stripes. In her leisure time a woman will fetch her apron, get out the Ebembe pot, and start painting one quaint pattern after another, following some sudden caprice. Should she not have sufficient time to complete the design at one sitting, she will roll up the garment very carefully, and secrete it under the roof of her hut, to resume her work at the first opportunity. As a proof of the value that the pigmy women put on these decorated aprons, I may mention that I found it exceedingly difficult to get a few of them in exchange for some large rolls of cotton.

The calmer temperament and sedateness of the older men make them much more pleasant company than the somewhat turbulent young fellows, with whom they associate very little. They prefer sitting quietly in small groups, chatting or doing some odd job.

Once while I was strolling through the camp, I came upon the sullen Agali on the point of finishing a new bow. He held it over the fire for a moment, tested it to see if it curved properly, and examined both ends to make sure that they tapered proportionately and were smoothly rounded. At last he was satisfied, and just planed off a tiny shaving here and there with his knife, his face one broad galvanic grin all the while. I, too, felt so pleased with his handiwork that I decided to try to get it for my collection of curios. Though Agali did not refuse my request I could see that he was not anxious to part with his bow. However, he quickly got over his loss when I presented him in exchange with a brand new penknife. Such little gifts often work wonders among the Bambuti. When Agali succeeded, after a few abortive attempts, in manipulating the mechanism of the knife, he literally giggled with hysterical delight like a schoolgirl. I had brought happiness to a primitive man !

But to go back to the morning camp scenes. Tired of play, and with keen appetites, the little community huddled round the simmering pots. The preliminaries to breakfast were simple, and they started eating right away. The mothers spread green phrynium leaves on the ground which did duty as plates. On these were placed the boiled bananas. Sharpened sticks served as forks. With wooden spoons other women ladled out the stewed vegetables and the gruel, and all set to with a zest.

The pigmies pound the oil palm fruit after the fashion of the negroes, and squeeze out the oil, which is a favourite seasoning for all kinds of dishes. After this extraction of oil, the residue, a yellowish fibrous mass, is never thrown away, but is eaten with great relish. Boys and girls pounce on it, and everyone grabs a lump and crams it into his mouth. The pigmies are decidedly to be envied for their digestive apparatus. Such a feed of crude stringy stuff would have put an average European stomach out of order for days.

In the morning everyone in the camp stuffs himself with as much as he can. They are then fortified fairly well for a tramp into the forest, or whatever the day's job may be. There is no more food to be had until late in the afternoon.

Simple as was their breakfast, it gave the young men new life. They grabbed their bows and arrows and started playing. Bananas were thrown into the air, and to the accompaniment of crazy capers and grimaces the lads started shooting at them. There was a frenzied pushing and shouting in the contest for the award for the best marksman. I was an absorbed onlooker at the competition between the youths, who showed an extraordinary

dexterity. Sometimes a banana would be pierced simultaneously by three arrows.

Ear-splitting yells from the other end of the camp
brought a sudden end to the competition. All rushed
towards the group of boys who had been having a similar
game. Bad luck or carelessness had led to one lad wounding another in the eye. A man was by the side of the
little victim in a flash, and had plucked out the wooden
arrow. The child was carried into his mother's hut, and,
while some held him down, the juice of a fruit, called
tondoro, was poured into the wound. The boy roared
with agony and laid about him with hands and feet. It
was only my intervention that saved him from further
torture, for the fruit juice, which apparently was intended
as a sort of antiseptic, caused a terrible burning pain.
At the touch of my hand the little fellow became somewhat calmer, and I managed to bandage him up. Luckily
the eyeball itself was uninjured, so for the time being
there was no danger of his losing the sight of the eye. His
face swelled ominously, however, and the pain from the
wound must have been fearful. A little later I called in
again to see my little patient, and found that he had torn
the bandage off. There was no point in reprimanding
him for it. By this time the eye was much worse, and my
bandage was blamed for this, which was his reason for
removing it. Well, that was pigmy logic, and I had to
acquiesce in its deduction. I now relied upon the vigorous
constitution of the pigmy race, and was not disappointed.
Only a fortnight later the little fellow was sizing me up
with two healthy, but rather mistrustful, eyes.

In addition to bows and arrows, one usually sees the
children using the domestic and working implements of
the adults as toys. The young girls play " mothers,"
with real babies as dolls. They take toddlers and nurse-
lings from their parents and fondle them with the greatest
affection.

The bows used by the boys are smaller and lighter than
those of the grown men, and are made by themselves.
Even at the early age of four they start fiddling with their
fathers' weapons. Their arrows are made from the fibre
of palm leaves. It is only on the rarest occasions that one
sees a boy with an iron arrow, and is as unusual a sight

as one of our own babies with a real watch. The boys use their thin wooden arrows to kill birds, and they are almost the same as those employed by the men in monkey hunts, although the latter are tipped with poison.

The games played by the boys with bows are extremely practical, as they train them for hunting. It is at his play that the pigmy child learns all that is needed for the battle of life. I was always amused at the sight of an excited crowd of pigmy boys setting off for a day's hunting, prattling gaily and boasting of what they would bring back. Generally they returned with a bird or a composite bag of snakes, frogs and caterpillars!

One afternoon, as we sat in a group by the river bank, I promised to give the youngsters some fish hooks. I had brought a large assortment with me, but as I had never seen any of them fishing, I had not, so far, distributed them. Contrary to the custom of the negroes they seemed to use neither hooks nor fish-baskets. Accordingly I was greatly astonished to see the immense glee that greeted my promise. Straight away the boys started making fishing tackle from guseliana threads and fibres. They rolled the thread in the palms of their hands until they made a strong twine, which they attached to rods. The resourcefulness of the wee fellows fascinated me. I was still more astonished when I saw them split open the coils of the injoka-liana, from the pith of which they extracted grubs, which apparently are splendid bait.

Equipped with their tackle the youngsters lined up in front of my hut and held out their little hands. The moment I gave them the hooks, they vanished in the direction of the river. Not a word of thanks for my gift— the pigmy has no use for such conventions!

The news that "Muzungu" was doling out fishing hooks spread through the camp like wildfire, and in a few seconds all the grown-ups brought their children to my hut. The mothers dragged along tiny babes, who, screaming with terror and with averted heads, were made to hold out their wee hands towards me. Marriageable boys and girls brazenly posed as children in order to get hooks! It was lucky that I had plenty for them all!

My remarks on the discourtesy of the pigmies should not be taken too literally. Their behaviour is the outcome of their uncouth habits, which in turn are due to their fierce battle for existence. Their minds, consequently, are primitive and rugged, but, fundamentally, they are sound and plastic. Children of nature, they are too sincere to indulge in the superficial lip courtesies on which we civilized men lay such stress.

On their way home from the fishing, the boys halted in front of my hut. They joyously showed me their afternoon's bag : little parcels wrapped in leaves. For the most part these contained tiny fishes, while some of them had fragments of a snake that they had apparently dispatched with a cudgel.

" Aren't you going to give me some ? " I asked jokingly. Immediately the little fellows swarmed round me with their little parcels. Each one wanted to present me with his fish. I naturally refused to take any of the gifts thrust upon me, but this cordial generosity delighted me. It had far more genuine worth than any perfunctory " Thank you."

Once I surprised a gang of boys marching to and fro through the camp with a sedan chair. Now, the pigmy never rides, either on horseback or in a vehicle of any kind. On the other hand, negro chiefs, following the Wangwana customs, are sometimes carried by their subjects in sedan chairs, and it is quite possible that the boys may have seen them. With their innate inventiveness and drollery they manufactured a rather crude, but, nevertheless, a useful chair. In lieu of upholstery they had used boughs and twigs, skilfully interwoven with liana. The framework was so ingeniously put together that I was really astounded. While two lads in front and two in the rear carried the improvised litter on their shoulders, the most crafty of the bunch lolled back on the seat playing the pasha. I got them to halt and pose for a photograph.

It would be the greatest mistake to picture the pigmies, young or old, as a dull gloomy people. They are the most alert and temperamental race that I have ever met. Their keen and impulsive nature finds expression even in the games of the children. The lads are fond of wrestling, and their keen competitions often wind up in brawling and squabbling, which only the intervention of the grown-ups can end. They frequently have pitched battles, which open with mutual taunts and end with cudgelings and mud-slinging. Occasionally I witnessed fierce arguments between the young men. However, it is not in the pigmy nature to nurse grievances for long or to bear malice against one another. I had feared that the lad with the injured eye would seek vengeance against his playmate, and was agreeably surprised when I saw them playing together peaceably a few days later.

" Os, Os, Os ! " It is the call to the huntsmen ! The cry echoes and re-echoes through the camp. The pace becomes wilder and wilder as the sun mounts higher in the heavens. Its fierce rays, penetrating the dense foliage of the tree tops, weave fantastic flickering figures of light and shade in the undergrowth, while the huge tree trunks assume an eerie ghost-like aspect.

" Os, Os, Os ! " The jungle reverberates the call of the leader, who stands ready, with his bow in hand and packed quiver on his back.

At length the cries cease, and the man looks round until his hunting dog, an utter mongrel, comes bounding up. Rapidly he fixes the wooden collar round its neck, which operation, incidentally, seems to drive the animal into a fury. The fastening is barely done up before it disappears into the forest. The young huntsman dexterously attaches the thong to his left wrist and starts after his dog.

Once more " Os, Os, Os ! " rings through the camp, as the other youths, slinging quivers over their shoulders, follow him. The cry echoes fainter and fainter into the forest. At last it dies away and leaves the little camp in comparative silence.

For a long time after the youths had disappeared old Asangwa crouched over the fire, on which he had cooked his breakfast of nuts. At length he rose stiffly, clutched a bow and arrow, and with slow uncertain steps tottered out of the camp. The call to the chase had lured even him, on the verge of seventy, into the forest. Had he an idea that he might overtake those young fellows who had gone ahead of him, or was he following some private trail of his own, in quest of small game or honey ? He told nobody of his purpose, and nobody asked him.

At first I used to wonder why the huntsmen moved off so late in the day. On dull days or after a prolonged spell of rain they start very late, or they may not go out at all. I soon found out their reason—not a difficult one to guess. The pigmy dreads rain, dripping trees, wet or cold in any form. He prefers to wait until the sun has drained up all the moisture before he ventures out.

Other gangs of young men, accompanied by swarms of boys, had followed the first group into the gloomy undergrowth. By means of shouting, singing and the shrill notes of the hunting whistle, which pierced the air every now and then, they kept in touch with one another. Wooden whistles, about eight inches long, are hung around the necks of the huntsmen on untanned hide thongs. Their note is high-pitched and shrill like that produced by schoolboys blowing into the bore of a key. Later we shall learn their magic import.

As band after band vanishes into the forest, the camp becomes more and more silent. The women throw their baskets to the children and the growing girls, who wait in front of their huts until the mothers are ready for the tramp into the forest. The entrances to the huts are crammed with branches and twigs. The nursling is adjusted against the mother's hip, in such a manner as to enable her to put her arm around it with comfort, or in some cases the babes are slung in a sort of sash, which hangs from the parent's shoulder. Two of the bigger children, with empty baskets on their backs, form a vanguard. A long train of women and children set off in step for the jungle. All have one objective : the quest of vegetable food for the general larder, just as the men are on a communal hunt for meat.

Another band of women, escorted by a still larger number of children, sets out for the nearest negro village, to purchase bananas, manioc roots and oil palm fruit, or to barter any meat that may be available in return for them.

The camp is now almost empty. Only a few lads, who feel that they have a roving commission in connection with my kitchen, loaf around, waiting for any odd job that may turn up. They disembowel any kill that my huntsmen bring in ; the intestines and, as a rule, the hide are their perquisites. Monkey skins are especially prized, as apron flaps, made from them, are fastened to the girdles of dandies for their dancing garb. The fur of the Kema monkey's tail is carefully separated from the cartilage, and rolled round bows so as to cover them partially, or, if possible, entirely. Hunters are particularly proud of bows decorated in this fashion.

I had a half-witted, but harmless, pigmy half-breed, Pembereko, among my kitchen staff. His father was a village Musua, his mother a Mombuti. He was a few inches taller than the tallest pure-bred Bambuti, but his features were pure pigmy. Pembereko was of a very simple and childish mentality, and, owing to his limitations, the Mombuti made fun of him. Although my servants treated him as a fool, I always found him very loyal and hard-working. He liked to sit near me, promptly executed my orders, and could read my wishes in my eyes.

Once at my request Pembereko began setting traps, as I wished to study their mechanism. Although the pigmies do not catch game with traps, they are very clever at constructing them in several different ways. It is a knack that they acquired from the negroes. When Pembereko was setting one with a strong spring, the latter shot back prematurely and struck him full in the face. In a rage he hurled the thing far away, scowled at me, and walked off, grumbling to himself. He appeared more angry with me for bidding him to set the trap than he was with himself for his clumsiness. A few leaves of tobacco soothed his ire right away, and he sat down again by my side. Squatting down on the veranda with his rush cap on his head, he watched every movement that I made.

" Pembereko ! " I addressed him.

" Baba ! " he replied. He always called me " Baba " (" Father ") while everyone else in the camp called me " Muzungu " (" The White ") or, even more curtly, " You."

" Why do they call you Pembereko ?" (" Chimpanzee ")

" Because they gave me that name at birth, Baba."

" So you are a chimpanzee by birth ? " I bantered.

Pembereko protested laughingly, then spat with feigned disgust.

"I am not a chimpanzee. That's just my name. Chimpanzees live in the forest."

"And don't you?"

"No, I live in the camp."

"Very well, then you are a village chimpanzee."

"The Baba says that I am a Sheko Chimpanzee," he shouted to the servants, who forthwith seized upon this new chance of pulling his leg.

Pembereko was in a peculiar position in the camp. His father lived in the negro village, to which he was actually attached, although he very rarely showed up unless he wanted a meal. As his mother was now dead, Pembereko had nobody in the camp to care for him, except a few women of his mother's family group, who very charitably allowed him to share their scanty provisions. Normally his father's relations should have been responsible for this, as in the case of every child.

Although he was the eldest of the young men in the camp—he was about twenty-five—he was still unmarried. I hardly think that this was because the girls did not care for him, although such may have been the case, for he seemed to have no idea of marriage. The fact remains that poor Pembereko was an outcast. I never saw a bow and arrow in his hands. Nor, during my two months' stay in the Bafwaguda camp, did he take part in a hunt. But he was by no means sullen. On the contrary he was always an ardent patron of the dance, and was always one of the merriest revellers.

Pembereko was decidedly not the ideal *vis-à-vis* for a sustained conversation, but time and again I sent for him for a chat, through lack of anyone better when I wanted to jot down notes about the local dialect. My questions always eventually bored him, when the conversation became too prolonged. I found the same thing with all the Bambuti : they are incapable of any sustained effort.

In moments like the present one, when the camp was almost empty, a terrible atmosphere of desolation descended on me. Something vital was missing ; maybe the vigour and the alertness of youth. After sitting for awhile in my arm-chair, reading my notes, I strolled through the camp to examine the huts.

As I was descending the steps of my house to have a

look around, with Pembereko at my heels like a dog, a
woman laden with phrynium leaves entered the camp.
It was Bambina, Alianga's wife, who was building a new
hut close to her own, for her eldest son, who was now
grown up.

It was an ideal opportunity to observe, at my leisure,
how these primitive men built their huts. I sat down
facing the plot, so that I could see everything, while my
cicerone made a running commentary on every movement of the woman.

A Bambuti hut is like one half of a huge egg, that has
been bisected through its longer diameter, and placed on
the ground. Then, if you can imagine the narrower end
of this mammoth half-egg cut off for the doorway, you
have a fair picture of what a pigmy's home is like.
Occasionally you find huts abnormally longish, and in
such cases they are proportionately higher, and tend
rather towards a cone shape. A pigmy hut is actually a
branch-propped roof that has been thatched, lying arch-
wise on the ground. As the building of the huts is
exclusively the woman's job, she also collects the building
materials, which consist of thin branches and phrynium
leaves.

Bambina threw the huge bundle of leaves on the ground,
and rubbed her hands a few times on her body to clean off
the dirt and perspiration. Then she sat down and split
the top part of the stalks of the phrynium leaves for
about four inches. In this way she spliced one leaf to
another. It was delightful to see how dexterously leaf
after leaf slid through her fingers. Only through long
practice could the woman attain such nimbleness with her
fingers. How many huts must she have already made
during her lifetime! Every time camp is struck the
housewife has to build a new home.

She had erected the framework of the hut days before.
She started by ramming a thin branch into the ground
with the thick end downwards, and another of similar
length opposite. They were joined, not by attaching a
third one horizontally, but by plaiting the thin ends to
form an arch. About six inches to the rear, this process
was repeated with two more branches, just a little bit
longer. This was to be the entrance to the hut. The

A PIGMY'S BED
(*Page* 65)

FRAMEWORK OF A PIGMY HUT
(*Page* 64)

DISTRIBUTING THE SPOIL—CUTTING UP MEAT
(Page 67)

ON THE WAY HOME AFTER A SUCCESSFUL HUNT. AN ASUNGUDA
CAMP SCENE
(Page 67)

longest sapling that was to be used was then planted in the centre of this arch, but much farther back, and was bent towards the arch, bow-wise, until both met and were fastened together. This was the ridge of the roof. Then branch by branch was pushed into the earth, to form a semicircle on each side of the ridge. From the arch, the branches used were graduated until the two longest were level with the centre of the ridge. From that point, they diminished in length until each semicircle ended at the base of the ridge that was stuck into the ground. The thin ends were next attached to the ridge, and the framework was complete.

Thatching a pigmy hut is a real work of art. Starting from the ground, Bambina placed leaf over leaf, exactly as tiles are laid on a roof. She fixed each leaf to the thatch frame by bending the split stalk and twisting it round a branch ; next she pushed it back through the next leaf's stalk. Thus each leaf was, so to speak, held fast with a pin. One woman, unaided, can have her hut ready in two hours, providing the building materials have not to be fetched from too great a distance.

Doors are unknown to the primitive man. They appear to have been invented later on in capitalistic eras, when the householder had to guard his movable pro-perties ! The utmost the pigmies will do is to barricade the entrance with branches and twigs when they leave the camp, merely with a view to keeping out unwelcome fauna, or during the night as a protection against storm and rain.

For our European dwellings the question of furniture is a serious one, but for the little men of the forest, the essential equipment of his hut is just the bed, which consists of three, often only two, smooth pieces of wood, placed side by side on the ground. By wedging a lump of wood underneath, the end destined for the head is raised somewhat. That is the Bambuti bed, which every one of them makes for himself. The pigmy has no knowledge of mattresses, blankets, or of all the other things which we regard as necessary for a night's repose, and yet he is perfectly satisfied. He stretches himself on the hard timber, facing the fire to keep himself warm during the chilly night. The pigmy always sleeps on his

E

side with his knees huddled up, and his arm under his head in lieu of a pillow. He is in exactly the same position in the morning as he was when he lay down to sleep the evening before. He never changes his garb during his lifetime.

In addition to this " bedstead " you will find in the hut the barest essentials in the matter of pots. Frequently there is also a crude wooden mortar and a basket. A knife is stuck in the thatch, where you will also find the man's bow and his quiver. A bachelor has nothing in his hut but his weapons and the bed.

When there are several children in a family there is a departure from the normal form of the hut. A niche is built on to it, which, seen from the outside, looks something like a hump. That is the bedroom of the growing children. There are also tunnelled huts when two structures have openings facing one another. Windscreens are rare. I only remember having seen one once, and, to judge from its structure, it was really a beehive hut with a very wide entrance extending over its entire front.

Pembereko sat silently by my side and stared vacantly into space, when a din in the distance made him prick up his ears. I was fully convinced, in my early days in the camp, that the pigmies had not only far keener eyesight than I had, but that their sense of hearing, too, was far more acute. From the direction of the Asunguda River we heard cries that came nearer and nearer.

" Nama! Nama! " (Game! Game!) shouted the lads in the kitchens, and darted into the forest. The chase swept on furiously, passing close to the camp. For a considerable time we still heard the calls and the whistling of the hunters. Then all was silent. " It has escaped," said Pembereko, and squatted again. He was referring to the quarry.

When I came to know the pigmy huntsmen better, I understood their method of hunting, and realized that almost every animal they pursue is bound to fall before the arrows of the hunters, unless a river or a stream destroys the scent, and the hunting dog fails to pick it up again. And this was to all appearances the case now.

Judging by the position of the sun, it must have been

three o'clock when the first hunting dog, with the rattling
wooden collar around his neck, came bounding into the
camp. Hunger drove him from hut to hut, where he
sniffed at each ash-heap for refuse. The rattling of the
wooden bells was an indication of a successful hunt, for
the pigmies, when they have to return empty-handed,
usually silence the bells with leaves so that the dog may
reach the camp without making any noise. Then too,
in silence, the weary and dispirited huntsmen come into
the camp after a disappointing chase. You have only
to reflect on the terrible strain that an intensive hunt
through the dense undergrowth of the forest of six hours
or even more puts upon these little chaps, to understand
their depression.

Even after a successful run, the huntsmen returning
home make very little noise. It takes an exceptionally
good bag to induce them to express their joy by singing
and shouting, and that is a signal for general jubilation
throughout the camp.

A long time had elapsed from the time of the dog's
return before the hunters showed up. One youth after
another came trailing sore-footed into the camp. The
rear was brought up by a boy who panted under his load
—a baby antelope which he had suspended from the
crown of his head with a liana sling. He had stuck a
sprig of green in his belt, by way, I presumed, of jubilation.

The eldest of the tribe, or his deputy, disembowels the
game on clean leaves, and sets about the distribution of
the carcase. The hunters sit aloof, as though the affair
were no concern of theirs. The heart and liver go, on all
occasions, to the man who has shot the game. I noticed,
however, as I was watching from very close range, that,
first, a fragment was cut from the heart and thrown into
the forest. Later I learned the meaning of this strange
custom, for the incident that I had just witnessed stirred
my curiosity. When I made closer inquiries into the
religious rites of the pigmies, I found that they always
sacrificed the first fruits of their labour to their god.

The peculiar customs prevailing at the division of the
spoil revealed to me the clue to the social and economic
code of the pigmies. The kill belongs to the entire family

group, but the first claim goes to the narrower family group of the marksman whose arrow has given the quarry its final wound, irrespective of whether that wound was a fatal one or not. If, however, he has killed the animal with another man's bow, then the owner of the weapon has the first claim. The owner of the hunting dog has also a claim on the game, and the head is his special perquisite. As you can see, the division becomes rather complicated when several family groups join in the hunt.

As the afternoon wore on the camp once more became animated and relieved the depressing atmosphere I had felt, as an ever-increasing number of men and women reappeared from their daily tasks. The women were the last arrivals. They came in two groups, one singing and laughing, the other silent and dog-tired.

The women with their swarms of children are the very life of the camp ; they radiate an aura of friendship everywhere. Panting under the weight of the heavily-laden baskets perched on their backs, they totter—in a long line of them, the children leading. The baby reposes in the mother's shoulder-sash in the same position as when they set out. The huge wide-meshed basket is suspended by a liana bandeau from the crown of her sweat-bathed head. Bowed down like a beast of burden, she struggles towards her hut. Possibly, perched on top of the basket, there is a little one who, weary after its long ramble, cannot walk any farther. And yet not once did I hear a Bambuti wife complain about this daily " penal servitude."

They have barely laid down their burdens, before some of the women feverishly rush to fetch water, others fan the smouldering camp fire into life, while a third batch sets off at a run in search of firewood. Meanwhile some of the nurslings start yowling, but are quickly soothed by the younger girls, and lulled to sleep. And now at last the mothers are free for their biggest job in the daily round—the preparation of the evening meal.

The sun's last rays, gleaming obliquely through the branches, brighten the camp. Dusk is drawing on. What an atmosphere of domestic happiness there is about these evenings in the pigmy camp ! How much more soothing and snug than its morning look. A comforting,

"IN THE REAR A LAD PANTED, LADEN WITH A
BABY ANTELOPE WHICH HE HAD SUSPENDED
FROM A LIANA BAND TIED ROUND HIS HEAD"

(Page 67)

THREE BAKANGO YOUTHS FROM THE
ASUNGUDA CAMP

WOMEN BRINGING FIRE-WOOD TO THE CAMP
(*Page* 68)

BAKANGO CHILDREN
(*Page* 58)

genial quiet broods over this corner of the virgin forest. Nature and man are resting; the day's task is done. They are sure of their food till to-morrow; in fact, to-day's bag will probably last for two days. Can you imagine the feeling of a pigmy community that has sufficient food for two days? To do so you must first bear in mind what toil and sweat, what risk to life and limb the procuring of their simple food costs them.

It is very unfair to assume, as some do, that the pigmies are an indolent and slovenly race. The civilized man and the primitive man have alike to bear life's burden; but the burden is undoubtedly heavier for the primitive man, who has to battle with elemental conditions. Luckily the burden lies lightly on his shoulders; for he bears it with a smile and with the stoicism of a philosopher. On the other hand, how miserable we civilized people are compared with these children of nature! It is true that they earn their poor food by the sweat of their brows, but they have no unemployed, no workhouses and no hunger-marchers. The spectre of absolute want is never before their eyes. It is always before ours!

Around the fire are scattered roots, bananas and vegetables, and the stew is simmering in the pot. All have keen appetites, but they wait patiently for the evening meal. All, that is except the little ones, who with querulous cries of hunger, hang on to their mother's aprons. Some of the more boisterous among them rummage about among the roots and the fruit, and capsize a pot of water. And then one mother who is busy attending to the cooking and has several other petty annoyances, spanks a particularly troublesome little brat, who runs off howling. Whereupon the father, who has been holding the nursling in his arms, flies into a passion and blames his wife for her cruelty. She makes no reply, and goes on with her work. A few minutes later husband and wife have forgotten their quarrel, and the child returns laughing, the dried-up tears channelling its dirty little cheeks.

At last the women begin to pour out the contents of the pots and to divide the food. Each family eats in front of its own hut. The bachelors eat in community fashion with their family group brothers and sisters,

When the meal is finished the exhausted pigmy wife has not finished her evening's toil. She has no rest until her youngest is fast asleep against her hip and the others in her arms. Then she subsides gently on the hard wooden bed near the fire in her hut. At last she is free.

The evening meal is by no means a quiet affair. The joy of the hungry men, as they tackle their food, finds vent in merry chatter and in comic facial gestures. I never saw them squabbling over their meals. And to-night they have an excellent menu : boiled bananas, roast meat and oil palm sauce. They do not always fare so sumptuously ; frequently they have nothing but a handful of stewed vegetables.

Look at this group squatting close together, the very picture of happiness and contentment ! Each one picks up a banana and dips it in the sauce. Then he bites off a large mouthful of his portion of meat, which he masticates with slow, appreciative movements of his powerful jaws. Observe what really excellent, though primitive, table manners they all have. There is no greedy looking for choice bits. Everyone is anxious to help his comrade to food. Look at those little girls handing round the portion of bananas and roots to each one. The meat and the stew are, of course, divided in accordance with definite community rules.

In cleanliness at table, the Ituri pigmy is sadly lacking. His fingers which he dips into the stew he washes neither before nor after meals. He just rubs them with leaves or against his own body.

The table is the bare ground and the table cloth is a layer of fresh phrynium leaves. When the meal is served, they all squat around as best they can, or perhaps they sit on the low reed bench, which is placed before practically every hut.

" Boom ! Boom ! Boom ! " Listen to the thunder of the camp drum, beaten by an unskilled childish hand. Some little nipper has finished his food, and is starting his monkey tricks. Yes—it is little Maduali, who is squatting beside the mammoth drum, and hammering away on it with a cudgel. With loud yells the other children join him, and they all start pounding on the drum with fists and sticks, The din is deafening. But here comes Abiti, the cleverest drummer among the Bafwaguda, lurching along with slow, swaggering steps towards the gang of children. Note the grace with which he rubs his greasy hands on his buttocks two or three times ! Now he seizes the drum, and a jubilant overture thunders forth on the evening air.

Watch Abiti's facial contortions closely ! He prides himself that they interpret the motif of the melody. Incidentally I have noticed that, throughout the Congo, the pigmies accompany song and dance with bizarre grimaces. But Abiti is an expert, a virtuoso in his flair for this method of exposition. His mouth awry, his head sunk between his shoulders, he beats the drum with magical tempo and force. Now the dancers start singing, keeping time with the thunder of Abiti's drum. Their spirits, their movements, their *élan* are attuned in precise harmony to his. With his eyes rigidly fixed on the drum, he thumps the skin with his left fist, while his right hand flourishes the drum stick, with which he alternately strikes drum and frame. He springs lithely from one foot to the other, his face working convulsively, like an epileptic in the throes of a fit. He holds all the dancers in a rhythmic spell. His face becomes bloated ; sweat exudes from every pore. He is very unlovely to look upon, but he rivets the attention of every individual. A magnetic aura seems to radiate from the drummer. He holds men and women under his sway, like the figures of a marionette show. The movement of their feet is in exquisite accord with the beat of his drum and the tempo symbolized by his capers and contortions.

As soon as he stops playing the dance flags and grows listless ; but at the first beat, when he starts again, or if he transports the revellers to rhythmic frenzy by his gestures or voice, a galvanic thrill vibrates through the entire camp. All the dancers turn, as though obeying a word of command, and sway in symphony with every boom of the drum. The effect that a skilled drummer has on a group of dancers is almost incredible. For this reason the most able exponent is always put in charge. If he is only a second-rate performer the dance drags wearily and grows monotonous. Sometimes a drum is not available, and sorry substitutes are improvised in the form of rattles or clappers, which are either manipulated by hand or tied to the leg or arm.

Abiti was a genius as a drummer ; as I have already said, he was the finest performer among the Bafwaguda. In the course of my wanderings I met others who perhaps surpassed him in vigour, but not in virtuosity.

Maseru and Arao were, of course, there, but at first merely tentatively ventured a few gyrations in various dances. After a while, however, they became bolder, and reacted to the beat of Abiti's drum with verve and abandon. I noticed this peculiarity about every camp dance. At first, both men and women seemed listless, nervous and, in fact, almost self-conscious, but invariably, one after another, they would, sooner or later, come under the mesmeric spell of Abiti and his magic drumstick, until at length practically the entire population of the camp swayed and swirled in perfect unison.

A dance always begins with the men and women, and boys and girls, marking time in serried ranks. Even the children lined up for the fun. The dancers were marshalled according to age, with the men and women in separate rows.

Alianga headed the procession. He wore his rush cap with its swinging plumes of blue feathers, and in his right hand he waved a fan. Some of the men swung green branches to and fro. The dandies decorated their hair with tufts of wild boars' bristles. They nodded their heads in time to the beat of the drum, and the bristles moved in symphonic rise and fall.

The women deployed round the files of men, and encircled them with measured swaying movements. All the while, they beat time with their hands raised on a level with their faces. They sang so loudly from the beginning, that they completely drowned the voices of the men. Presently, one woman after another left the ranks to pluck green branches from the surrounding undergrowth with which they adorned their hips.

Mothers, with their infants strapped to their hips with sashes, hurried up to join the circle. If a baby fell asleep during a dance, it was quickly thrust into the arms of some young girl who was looking on, so that its mother could dance with greater freedom.

The three-year-old Maduali had sneaked up close to the drummer, and was pounding the frame of the drum with his little fists. He danced out of time from one foot to the other, and twisted his little body into all sorts of contortions. From their earliest years little boys and girls join in the dance, and thus, later, attain that grace in rhythmic movement which the negroes admire so much in the Bambuti. All the local negroes invariably turn out for the show when the Bambuti dance in a village.

If a dance starts with real enthusiasm, it is a difficult job to bring it to an end. Should the drummer's strength be exhausted, there may be a very short interval for rest. Sometimes a dance goes on all day and continues late into the night. I have been present at Bambuti dances in pitch dark, when a man could scarcely see his neighbour. Indeed, I am sure that I have never seen people so crazy as the pigmies about dancing.

CHAPTER III

THE PIGMIES IN THEIR GREY DAILY ROUND

THE shades of night gently spread over the dreaming forest, and darkness stretched its veil across the little camp. Dance and song had come to an end. Bathed in sweat, the pigmies crouched over their fires, or lay on their beds, and chatted in subdued and drowsy voices, which, after a little while, died away altogether. I had stretched my weary limbs in my armchair on the veranda of my hut, and filled my lungs with the cool night air.

Absolute silence reigned, and a wave of homesickness swept over me. In moments like these, my thoughts strayed back to my home. Detached from their immediate environment, they travelled in one precipitous leap over thousands of miles of virgin forest, sea and mountains to another land, where spring was just awakening, and intoxicating both man and beast. But here nature was overwhelming and terrifying in her wildness and primitive brutality. At home God made His presence felt in the soft whispering of the wind and in the beauty of the flowers. Here He spoke in thunder, amidst the roar of the storm, among gnarled, sinister trees of the woods. There was an eerie stillness about these nights in the tropical forest. Black magic seemed to call when the wail of an owl thridded the air, and the pigmies, huddled together in their huts, terror-stricken, said it was the voice of God. The distant growl of a leopard smote ears, strained for every sound, and made the black uncanny night still more unearthly.

I knew that in the sky above, millions of stars twinkled, but only with great difficulty could I catch the gleam of one or two through the dense roof of leaves.

The pale moon, kindly night friend of the lonely man

74

in the wilderness, had not yet risen. How I longed to see its silver rays flooding my veranda ! Even the faintest glimmer of light has a cheerful, reassuring effect amid the palpable ebon blackness of a forest night.

I made up my mind to watch for the rising of the evening star and sat up straighter in my chair. A gentle gust of wind in the tree-tops, caused the branches and leaves to murmur and whisper. My spirits rose and the breeze brought a refreshing coolness in its train.

Had I heard aright ? What was that dull booming in the distance ? I listened intently. There was no mistaking the ominous sound. A thunderstorm was brewing. A flash of lightning showed that it was approaching from the west—the rainy direction. From experience, I knew that it would only be a matter of a few minutes before the hurricane burst over our heads. I had barely stuffed everything inside the hut, when the storm was upon us in full fury. The huge trees creaked and moaned ; withered branches crashed to the ground and were whirled like matchsticks on to my veranda by the force of the wind. I lay back in my chair again, and watched the lightning, which lit up the camp with a fitful ghostly glare. Flash after flash zig-zagged down with intermittent deafening peals of thunder.

A terrific thunder-clap made me leap from my seat. I heard a sudden chorus of pigmy yells, followed by dead silence. I stepped out in front of my hut. The rain was coming down in buckets, and the giant trees, which grew in rows quite close to my hut, groaned aloud, swaying to and fro before the fury of the storm. I thought how easily lightning might strike the tree, over a hundred and twenty feet high, which overshadowed my hut, and send it crashing down. I immediately decided that I would have those mammoth trees felled the very next day.

Like most tropical storms, this one passed over the camp very quickly. For a long time the thunder still reverberated in the distance, like a lion baulked of its prey ; and for hours the rain kept up its monotonous downpour.

The pigmies, who had kept remarkably quiet during the storm, soon showed renewed signs of life. I heard people talking in loud tones, and there was a good deal of squabbling and screaming in the two huts opposite mine. Snatching up my lantern, I hurried out, in spite of the rain, to find out the cause of the noise. When I reached one of the huts I saw the inhabitants crouching helplessly on their wooden beds in a puddle. The hut had stupidly been built in a hollow, towards which the rain was bound to drain, and it had been completely flooded. The occupants, mainly women and children, were whimpering and snivelling as they baled the water out of the hut with their hands. I quickly dug a drain with my jungle-knife and drew off the water. The hut was now habitable again, and in a few minutes the fire was crackling merrily, and the bed fixed in its position on the damp earth. Unpleasant though the incident had been, it did not prevent the pigmies from dropping off again at once into a sound sleep.

As I knew that the pigmies were incapable of felling the menacing trees unaided, I sent to the village for help. Both the negroes and the pigmies cut down their trees, not from the root, but at a height of two to three yards from the ground, where the circumference is smaller.

For this purpose they erect a simple scaffolding, made of boughs which are fixed at one end into forked uprights or attached to small trees. The other end is then fastened with liana to the tree that is to be cut down. On this swaying platform the tree-cutter stands, and swings his axe untiringly. Frequently hours pass before the first movement in the tree-top warns the cutter to be on his guard. After about ten more blows the man flies to a safe distance, while the tree falls with a crash into the forest—crushing everything in its course.

It was a difficult day's work, but had to be finished. Two iron-wood trees, the highest of the lot, gave us the most trouble. When late in the afternoon the second of the two had been cut half through, a storm suddenly broke on the camp, which might easily have brought disaster, as the tree was in imminent danger of collapsing on the huts. Adzapori, who had been plying the axe, leaped from the platform in a flash and fled howling. All the bystanders took to their heels. In a few minutes my belongings were brought out of the threatened hut in safety, but the tree showed no sign of falling. Adzapori

A PIGMY WOMAN "TREKKING"

FELLING A TREE IN THE ASUNGUDA CAMP
(*Page* 76)

PEELING OFF THE BARK OF TREES FOR
LOIN-CLOTHS

A PIGMY SOUNDS THE HORN
(*Page 94*)

once more ventured towards it with timid steps, to give it the death-blows. The rest of us stood in breathless silence, staring at the topmost branches. At that moment, Agbendu, the young medicine-man of the camp, emerged from his hut, holding a fan in front of him, which he kept waving in the direction of the tree, although I noticed that he stood a very safe distance from it. Through his magical powers he was to make the tree fall into the forest in the opposite direction, despite the tempest. He was remarkably successful! One more blow with the axe, and the giant fell into the undergrowth with a terrific crash. Just as silently as he had appeared, Agbendu vanished into his hut again. And that was the only time that I saw a pigmy magician in action.

My continual dodging about the camp, now at this hut, now at that, and chatting with the pigmies, helped me greatly in my research work and enriched my collection of curios. Owing to this community life with my hut alongside those of the pigmies, I saw and heard things that I could never have discovered through the medium of random questions. I penetrated into the tiny huts, frequently crawling through the entrances on all fours. I talked with the little people, and asked them about their cares and worries. All the time I never forgot to observe the interiors of the huts as closely as possible. Every strange article, no matter how insignificant, was examined by me with the greatest care. On one of these occasions, when I was in Asangwa's hut, my attention was drawn to a little hollow reed of quaint shape. I picked up the thing to examine it, but I had hardly done so when the old woman, who was crouching by the fire and watching every move, suddenly screamed. I barely managed to get out into the open with my spoil, before all the women of the camp swarmed round me with loud wails, and tried to snatch it away from me. They shouted to Adzapori, who diplomatically intervened, and advised me to give it back to them if I wished to avert a disaster. An incident, trivial in itself, was assuming a mysterious aspect that piqued my curiosity. I had already opened one end of the reed which was packed with clay, and discovered inside a shred of cloth, a piece of the very material that I had brought with me as a present for the pigmies. Needless to say there was no risk of my precipitating a quarrel with the Bambuti over such an article, and I gave it back, but made it a condition that they should make another one for me exactly like it. This Alianga gladly agreed to do.

Alianga and Adzapori then gave me a detailed account of the mystery surrounding the little reed. From the point of view of the pigmies, very vital issues were at stake, and the commotion of the women was thoroughly justified.

The thing is called a " pikipiki," and is very well known by, and is in use among, the negroes of the forest, under this name. The Bakango call it " ungbe." The pikipiki is in reality a kind of whistle, about the thickness of a man's finger, and is cut out of a round piece of wood. In both ends holes are made, or rather burned, with a red-hot spike. It can then be used as a whistle like a hollow key. Pikipikis often have one hole only, and may be decorated with spiral metal ornamentations. This type is used by the hunters, who, as mentioned previously, hang it round their necks on pieces of hide. The particular one that caused such a hullabaloo was a crude piece of work with two openings, but quite undecorated. Presumably as the women made such a fuss and begged so earnestly for its return, it was their property.

The pikipiki is used for making magic, not only by the huntsmen, but by every member of the pigmy community. It is an article of extreme significance—a sort of amulet, which, when held in accordance with ritualistic prescription, is an effective protection against enemies, or against strangers about whose mission the pigmies are not quite certain. The latter was the case in this instance. The Bakango deemed it prudent to protect themselves against any risk of hostile intent on my part. To ensure this they put a few shreds of my cloth into the pikipiki, and sealed the opening with clay. Thus I was in their power, indeed their prisoner. In their view the cloth was a part of me, and I was no longer in a position to do them any harm, even if I wished to do so. Here was magic—fetichism with a vengeance for you !

In war time the pikipiki plays an especially important part. Sometimes it may save the whole clan, particularly if they manage to get hold of something belonging to the enemy and put it into the reed. No matter how fierce the foe may be, he won't fight. You fare forth with your stuffed pikipiki, and blow through it until the forests resound. Immediately the enemy forgets all his hostile intent—and the war is over ! What a simple and effective means of attaining peace ! What a boon a pikipiki would be to civilized nations !

One morning I noticed a pigmy, who had left the camp previously with the hunt, come hurrying back, snatch a brand from the fire and set off again in great haste. I stopped him, and asked where he was going. The hunters, he said, had " tree-ed " a wild animal, a " Djiko," and they could only get at it by means of fire. This struck me as something rather peculiar, and, spurred by curiosity, I accompanied him. At the foot of a hollow tree the rest of the hunt were resting and patiently waiting for the fire.

After the roots had been partially cut away, the hollow, which went deep into the tree, was clearly exposed. The hound whimpered excitedly and scraped and burrowed round the hole, which was stuffed with twigs and leaves. The hunters then lit a fire, which blazed up, but soon smouldered into heavy clouds of smoke that filled the hollow in the tree.

In a few moments growls and a scratching noise were heard coming from the hole, followed later by squeals and crying. Then suddenly there was dead silence. The animal had been stifled. I was anxious to find out what the bag would be. After the fire was removed one man after another poked his head in the hole, but it was too deep to get at the creature. At length by prodding about with a stick they located their prey. There was nothing to do but cut the tree down, when they found a porcupine ! Hardly was it pulled out before they all pounced on it and plucked out its quills, which are highly prized as ornaments. The young men and women love to push them through the cartilage of their noses.

While the hunters were roasting the porcupine over the fire, I returned to the camp with Mengito, who had injured his foot. The others set out in quest of a second porcupine hidden in a similar way in a tree, whose scent had been picked up by the dog.

It may seem surprising that the pigmy went all the way back to the camp to fetch live embers, but the explanation, although somewhat surprising, is quite simple. The Bakango, alone of African aboriginies, know absolutely nothing about lighting a fire by striking sparks from a flint or other similar devices. Though they know how the negroes kindle a fire, they will not imitate them. It seems puzzling that they have never made an effort to acquire a knowledge of this absolutely essential craft. I was so amazed myself at their seemingly wilful ignorance in this respect that I spoke to them about it.

" How do you manage," I said, " when you are far from the camp and need fire ? "

" You saw what we do. We either take it with us or get it from elsewhere."

" But supposing that it were quenched *en route* or that the rain put it out during the night—what then ? "

" It is never quenched," was the constant answer to every possible contingency that I suggested.

" But what if it goes out when you are far away in the forest ? "

" Somebody returns to look after it, or goes to the village and fetches live coals."

It is just possible that the Bakango possessed the knowledge of striking fire at some distant era, and lost it later. It seems unlikely, however, that a people could forget such a vital art. We are more likely to be right in our second assumption that they never learned it. It is significant, apropos of this, that their negro neighbours and all the other pigmies understand the use of fire-whirls.

For the benefit of the uninitiated I will describe briefly the mechanism of the fire-whirl. A few round holes are drilled in a block of dry soft wood. The operator sits on the ground in such a way that he can keep both ends of this block firmly wedged between his feet. He packs dry leaves or bast, both of which are highly inflammable, into one of the holes, and afterwards inserts a fire-whirl twelve inches in length. He then proceeds to spin the whirl between the palms of his hands at such a speed that the friction starts it smouldering and the bast ignites. He carefully piles more bast around the flame and blows on it. This comparatively quick and simple method of striking fire is unknown to the Bakango, and therefore they are obliged to keep their fires constantly alight. Both hunters and women, when they go into the forest, usually carry supplies of live coals.

Once in the Nduye camp of the Efé pigmies I picked up a significant legend about the way in which the Bambuti came by their first fire. Incidentally I do not know whether the Bakango are familiar with this particular myth. As will be seen, it is really a somewhat elaborated version of the banana saga.

In the course of his long rambles a Mombuti, while out hunting one day, happened to hit upon a chimpanzee village. It should be mentioned incidentally that the chimpanzees were men formerly, but exasperated by the thieving and trickery of the Bambuti, they withdrew into the heart of the forest, went wild among the trees, and, in short, became what they are to this day. Formerly they lived in villages, owned extensive banana plantations, and were acquainted with the use of fire. In other words, they were to the original Bambuti, what the negroes are to their descendants at the present day.

The chimpanzees received the pigmy with princely hospitality, and gave him bananas, the taste of which he found delicious. When evening came he squatted by their fire to warm himself. The pleasant glow and the warmth of the dancing flames fascinated him, and from that day onward our pigmy was a frequent guest in the chimpanzee village.

One day he arrived in the village dressed in quaint garb. The old chimpanzees were busy in the plantation, and only the children were present. The latter had a lot of fun at the expense of the pigmy, who had a long tail of pounded bark hanging from his loin-apron, and trailing along the ground. When as usual they gave him bananas, he squatted with them so close to the fire that his tail was in danger of catching alight every moment. " Look out, Mombuti," the chimpanzee children shouted to him, " your murumba is catching fire ! " " That doesn't matter. It is long enough as it is," replied the pigmy, with apparent indifference, as he chewed up half a banana, at the same time glancing furtively at his tail,

F

which began to smoulder. Then suddenly he sprang to his feet and made off at full gallop.

The dumbfounded chimpanzee children started to scream, whereupon their parents came rushing in from the plantation. When they heard what had happened they guessed at once that the pigmy had stolen the fire by means of a trick. They started in pursuit of him at once, but he was far too nimble for them. When at length the chimpanzees reached the pigmy camp, fires were blazing merrily everywhere. " Why did you steal our fire, instead of buying it from us honestly ? " they shouted reproachfully to the pigmies. The latter, however, were not intimidated by the abusive language of the chimpanzees, who returned, completely outwitted, to their village. They were so enraged at the gross ingratitude of the Bambuti, who had also stolen their bananas from them, as the other legend tells, that they abandoned everything and withdrew to the forest, where they live now without either fire or bananas, and feed on wild fruit.

It was a lucky day for the Bakango when they killed the porcupine. They had lost the scent of the second one which they were trailing, but to compensate for their loss, an antelope and a wild boar were brought in. As the young men laid down the wild boar an intolerable odour spread over the entire camp like a heavy cloud. I sniffed around to see what was the cause of this poisonous stench. Not till then had I the faintest idea that the Bambuti would eat carrion ! I glanced at the putrefied corpse lying at my feet, and held my nose, to the delight, I noticed, of the pigmies. The hunters had found the wild boar dead in the forest and had carried it home as first-rate game.

This time they had reckoned without me. As a rule I would not dream of meddling in the culinary affairs of the pigmies, but that intolerable stench had aroused a feeling of nausea in me. I made a vigorous protest and demanded that the carrion should be shifted out of the camp with all possible speed, and I warned the people against eating it.

At first they were all dumbfounded. There were loud growls of protest, but at last they picked up the pole on which the dead beast was slung, and carried it out of the camp. Asangwa's whole family, to whom the boar belonged, escorted it. Why they did this I was soon to find out. Alianga's group remained standing loyally by my decision. They even made some malicious remarks indicative of a certain hostility to Asangwa's group. I explained to those around me the reasons why they should not eat putrid meat. My statement seemed to sink deep into the minds of the pigmies, who listened to me open-mouthed. I could see, however, that what worried most of them was the fact that I had done them out of a dainty banquet.

In this connection Alianga complained to me that Asangwa's group usually did not share their spoil with his group, but ate it alone. They did not even give a share to him, the " Ndiki," a thing that was always done. When I asked him what were his duties as an " Ndiki," he said that he had at certain prescribed times to act as director of the ceremonies at the initiation of the boys into the tribal code. For this reason he had a special claim to respect and to certain privileges with regard to the distribution of meat. He was genuinely furious at the slight inflicted on him. Even before he mentioned it to me I had already noticed that his family group and Asangwa's did not hit it off at all well together.

So Alianga's people consoled themselves by rallying to my side, while the others were apparently doing themselves proud on the dead wild boar somewhere in the undergrowth. My surmise proved correct. It was already pitch dark when the same all-pervading reek hung anew over the whole camp. I could imagine the sly pigmies, as they divided the carrion, laughing heartily at the sensitive nose of their white guest, then carefully wrapping their respective portions in leaves, and smuggling them into the camp under the cover of darkness. I was powerless, and tried to drown the smell as best I could with cigarette smoke. I dared not proceed to extremes. But retribution was to come—and that soon !

Next morning the aged and feeble Asangwa called on me complaining of stomach-ache and begged for " dawa " (" medicine "). I felt almost sorry that the old man should be the victim, and would have been far better pleased to hear that his two sons, who had brought the carrion into the camp, were ill. But, as on the other hand, the fathers are responsible for the sins of their children, I gave the old ruffian a sound lecture. It never occurred to me to make a thorough inquiry into the cause of his trouble. I arbitrarily put it down to his feed of carrion, and told him that all his children would be ill, if nothing worse happened.

My lecture had no particular effect on Asangwa, however ; in fact, it seemed to bore him slightly. All he wanted was " dawa." So I gave him a strong dose of purgative, and he toddled off contentedly to his hut.

No further reports were made to me as to the after-effects of the feed of carrion. Evidently the stomachs of the pigmies had successfully combated even greater risks than the putrid hog.

The great confidence that the Bambuti had in me was shown by the fact that they frequently called on me for medicine. They preferred tobacco to quinine and aspirin as a drug. They used to come to me, too, to dress their wounds, and the mothers always brought their ailing little ones to my hut.

Mengito's three-year-old child was dreadfully disfigured with buba eruptions. His little body was covered all over with sores, which gave him intense agony. All that I could do was to attempt to alleviate the agony of the little chap, for I was not familiar with the method of treatment for this complaint. Soon, however, I gave it up, and allowed the parents to try their primitive method of healing. Twice a day they smeared the acid juice of the apoka-liana on the sores, while the child yelled with pain and struck out on all sides. This got so much on my nerves that when the treatment of the child started, I used to flee from the camp to get out of earshot of those screams of agony. I do not believe that a European child could have stood the shock of so strenuous a cure. After a prolonged treatment with the juice of the apoka-liana the little fellow's sores slowly healed.

One peculiarity in the attitude of the forest pigmies regarding the treatment of the sick is that they go to their work with absolute indifference, and are in nowise affected by the moans or complaints of a patient.

Framboesia (" Buba sickness ") is very common among

the pigmies, and especially among the children. Negroes assured me that the Bambuti deliberately inoculate their children with buba virus in order to make them immune in their mature years, as seemingly the illness does not recur.

Apparently Asangwa's reason for asking me for medicine was his belief that he would get a drug which would have a soothing effect. The pigmies are quite competent to deal with colics themselves, and they are acquainted with the use of the enema, in a very primitive form of course. For its administration the patient lies face downwards on the ground and a reed which is firmly fixed with gum into a hollowed gourd, is inserted in the rectum and a decoction of gorogoro bark injected. So we see that these primitive little people are not absolutely bereft of ways for fighting against sickness. Let us just take stock of a few of the specifics in their medicine chest.

To an aching tooth they apply an infusion of the root of the adamba-plant, or they rub dzandza-liana ashes into the gums, if they cannot get it down into the tooth cavity.

As a salve for eye trouble they use tondo-fruit extract, as we have already noted. The Efé pigmies prefer the juice of the leka herb for this purpose. If a child comes into the world with its eyes sealed, they smear them with the mother's milk.

As a cough syrup they use piripiri water. They cure diarrhœa with an injection of tebvo-liana via the rectum. Rheumatism they treat by making an incision in the skin with an arrow and rubbing in powder made of dried leaves of the gutse tree.

The pigmies are, unfortunately, quite helpless to cope with many ailments. Fever, for instance, makes frequent inroads, simultaneously with epidemics of influenza and pneumonia. Colds are the most common ailments of the Bambuti, and they claim the greatest number of victims, if we except the periodic epidemics.

I never met a case of sleeping sickness among them. The virgin forest provides a natural rampart against this scourge.

To sum up, however, the general standard of health among the pigmies, both adults and children, allowing for periodic epidemics, is very good.

I had no illusions that my lecture on decomposed meat would have any lasting effect on Asangwa, and I knew perfectly well that my admonitions would never make Alianga and his family group abstain from indulgence in carrion in the future. They ate indiscriminately pretty well anything they came across. Of course it is not to be inferred from this that certain specified foods are not taboo among them.

One night after a heavy fall of rain, frogs croaked from all sides of the camp, and hosts of toads selected the puddles as concert stands and created an infernal din. Immediately the pigmies went for them wholesale. By the gleam of pine torches they made fierce onslaughts on the disturbers of their sleep. The women and children regard frogs and toads as dainties, but the men never touch them.

The luxury esteemed most among all the Bambuti is honey. At the very mention of the word the pigmy will lick his dirty fingers.

One afternoon Alianga went into the forest in quest of suitable wood for arrows. As he strolled along in his usual thoughtful manner, peering anxiously in all directions and examining the trees, he saw a swarm of bees. Forgotten were wood and arrows. Alianga rushed back to the camp with lightning speed and beat up three of his family group, who hurried out of the camp equipped with a hatchet and a blazing brand. I decided not to miss such a favourable opportunity of being present at the collection of the honey, and followed them into the forest accompanied by Adzapori. After half an hour's tramp through the marsh along the Asunguda River we came upon a giant tree, which, encircled with liana to its very summit, looked as if it were adorned with a veil. It was evidently in its hollow trunk that the bees' nest was to be found. Alianga forced his way through bushes and brambles to the trunk, which he smote with his axe, while he intoned :

" Aja, wa, wa, wa, wa, wa, papa mekweti ! "

Translated, his invocation runs thus : " Father, permit me to find honey ! " A prayer to the deity for abundance of honey.

A moment later the youngest of those present clambered up the liana with the agility of a monkey. The others squatted on the ground and lit a fire. Alianga moved off and returned soon with long trails of rattan. Agbendu was busy making a basket out of liana. The blazing fire was raked inward and covered with leaves, with the result that a dense cloud of smoke arose. The rattan-liana trailing from his shoulders, Agbendu climbed far up into the tree, the grey-haired Alianga following close on his heels with an agility that I would never have thought the old man capable of. Meanwhile Mengito had located the bees' nest and clambered on to an immense horizontal bough, just as I looked up. His exuberance of spirits nearly cost him his life. He reeled and was on the point of toppling headlong. Luckily just in the nick of time he managed to grab hold of a branch, barely saving himself from a fall of some sixty feet, which would have certainly proved fatal.

As soon as the three men reached the nest they fumigated it thoroughly. Alianga tried to insert his hand, but the hole was too narrow. They widened it with a few strokes of the axe.

Standing underneath, I kept looking upward, taking everything in. Near me old Dzaka crouched on the ground. I thought the moment favourable to elicit from him some of the taboo secrets that are associated with the rites of the initiation of the young men, but to no avail. Dzaka refused to give me any information, and hinted that it was imprudent to talk on such a subject there. A woman or some other unauthorized person might be listening. I laughed at him, and asked how could anybody possibly be listening to us in that wilderness. The idea was absurd. Nevertheless he still remained silent. Then suddenly he stared with dilated eyes into the undergrowth ahead of us. The morass was so overgrown with shrubs and phrynium bushes that one could not see a yard ahead.

" A Kango ! " shouted Dzaka.

I jumped to my feet in amazement, and peered in the same direction, but could see nothing. Not a twig moved. Then suddenly the phrynium leaves parted, and a youth with a bow and arrow stood right under my nose, as if he had been conjured by magic out of the earth !

A leopard could not have slunk up so noiselessly. A few minutes later a second and then a third young man stood before us. All three belonged to Asangwa's family group. I was astounded both by the incredible agility and by the acute senses of the pigmies.

The three sudden apparitions had just squatted near us by the fire, when something came whizzing down from the trees and came flop on Dzaka's clean-shaven head. The first honeycomb! Others followed, falling in all directions. Such a method of collecting honey struck me as strange. I learned afterwards that the honeycombs I had seen falling, seemingly at random, were thank-offerings for the god which were cast into the wood for him. God had permitted the pigmies to find honey; in fact, had presented it to them, and consequently he was entitled to the first combs as tokens of their gratitude. It is an invariable rule that no one touches the honey before the god has been given his share.

Although their day's harvest of honey was not particularly abundant, they gave me a share, apparently thinking that by my presence I had brought them luck in their quest.

One morning a tattered Mubali negro, who had married a pigmy woman, came into the camp to settle amongst us. Without much ceremony and without asking for permission to do so, he started to build his hut. He took no notice of me whatsoever, but his wife presented me with a little pot of honey.

The pair were exceedingly unobtrusive. The negro adapted himself in general to the daily routine of the pigmies, but his hut was built on a rather larger scale with a gable-shaped roof. We were soon to learn that his residence in the camp might easily have proved disastrous to us. As it was, he was the cause of a riot that might have had very nasty complications. Early in the morning of the third day after the arrival of the pair, the normal drowsy quiet of the camp at dawn was rudely broken by a fierce wordy battle. At first I just listened to the brawling from a respectful and safe distance. A negro policeman wearing a red cap richly decorated with braid and brandishing a hippopotamus whip, had arrived from the negro village of Lipongo, and was doing his best to arrest our negro guest. The latter, however, resisted for all he was worth and punched the policeman with great zest. The punching and cursing and yelling became more intense every minute. The whole camp was in an uproar. The pigmies sided with the negro, and feeling ran very high. The women came tearing along armed with cudgels and belaboured the policeman, who, abandoning his prisoner, backed away in a nervous fashion. His faintheartedness only increased the frenzy of his attackers. The mob that pressed round him became bigger and more menacing, until at last I deemed it discreet to step forward in the interests of peace and come to his aid. My well-meant advice was, however, utterly disregarded ; in fact, the women became even more bloodthirsty and more voluble. At last I lost my temper and charged into the howling mob, knocking them in all directions. I even had to threaten to give one of the amazons a hiding. This ended the squabble, and a sullen silence fell upon the panting mob.

The policeman had arrived at the camp with orders from his chief to arrest the negro, who had fled from his village, because he was in arrears with his tax payments. So that was it. Taxes ! The pigmies could see no justice in arresting a man who had not stolen anything. They did not even know the meaning of the word " taxes." About the negro himself they were not so much concerned. Only through his marriage with one of their folk had he a bond with them, and for the sake of that bond they were resolved to defend him by force of arms if necessary.

I succeeded in persuading the negro that the more prudent course would be to accompany the policeman, and as I gave him a personal letter to the tax controller, together with a sum of money covering the last instalment of his taxes, he placed himself under voluntary arrest.

After he had gone his wife burst into such a torrent of sobs that her neighbours flocked around to comfort her. Her tears were really touching, and it seemed clear that she was very devoted to her negro husband. The poor creature refused to be consoled. For two days she mooned about the camp, and as there were still no tidings of her husband forthcoming, she packed her poor belongings in a basket, and set out for the station of Bafwasende, to make inquiries about him. From that day to the end of my stay, the big hut remained empty and desolate. I never saw the couple again.

CHAPTER IV

A TEMPERAMENTAL PEOPLE

ALTHOUGH I frequently gave the pigmies presents and partially accepted responsibility for their food, they felt themselves in no wise tied to me by any sense of duty or honour. I had always to be prepared for the possibility of their striking camp at any moment and clearing off. That this did not occur was attributable with good reason to the supplies of bananas which the negroes of the outlying districts brought twice or three times a week to the camp. In an earlier chapter I have already referred to this arrangement.

On certain days a gang of negro women appeared in the camp, laden with bananas and manioc, which they arranged in rows, exactly like the stalls of a market. Adzapori undertook the details of purchasing their produce, paying either in coin or in the coveted salt. The distribution of the food among the pigmies was, however, not always an easy matter. Many of them were of an exceedingly jealous nature, and felt slighted if once in a while their share was just a trifle smaller than a neighbour's. As again and again squabbles on this score arose between the various family groups, I gave instructions to have each hut's portion delivered at the door, instead of getting the women to line up for the share-out.

The banana days were festive occasions. On such days very few women went into the forest, as they were amply provided with food for the day. And when they had disposed of their wares, the negro women would squat for hours before the huts of their forest sisters and gossip animatedly with them.

Sometimes a family or individual members of a family vanished from the camp for days, without giving any clue as to their destination. Asking questions, on such occasions, was absolutely futile. The answers I got were meaningless to me, as I had as yet only a very superficial acquaintance with the geography of the neighbourhood.

One morning " Policy " turned up in the camp after an absence of several days, accompanied by an old pigmy, the chief of the Bafwasengwe, as I heard. The young man had summoned the veteran to the camp, as various matrimonial differences between the Bafwaguda and the Bafwasengwe had to be settled with his aid. Gradually they initiated me into the genesis of those disputes. It took me quite a while, however, to get a proper grip of the matrimonial customs of the Bambuti.

Policy had brought back with him a bundle of Sambali liana, from which arrow poison is prepared. It is by no means known to all pigmies, or more strictly speaking, not universally used among them. The Bakango frequently use it on their wooden arrows. It is not prepared by each individual hunter for his own use, but by the community for common use.

A crude trough is hollowed out of a fallen tree, in which the poisonous plants are pounded into pulp. I was very emphatically assured that the process is never carried out in one of the few cooking utensils that the pigmies possess. While one man sees to the pounding, another makes a press of rattan reeds, one end of which he makes fast to a small tree. A stick is inserted at the other end, which is twisted rapidly round until it squeezes out the soft succulent mass so thoroughly that its juice drops into a vessel placed beneath it. The hunters with their arrows are quickly on the spot and light a fire. The arrow points are dipped in the poisonous extract and held over the fire until the sticky stuff adheres to the wood. Then they place the arrows in the sunshine until the poison has thoroughly dried. Before the arrows are collected their poisoned tips are carefully wrapped in leaves and bast, to minimize the risk of accidental wounds from them. The process of preparing poison is not of frequent occurrence, and the hunters always equip themselves on these occasions with sufficient arrows to last them for some time to come.

Wooden arrows are not tailed with feather flights. The Bakango adopt a much more simple device. A special leaf, whose texture is exceptionally tough, is folded in

MAKING LOIN-CLOTH

After being soaked, the tree bark is pounded with a ribbed mallet.

PREPARING ARROW POISON. EXCAVATING A TROUGH IN WHICH
TO POUND THE POISONOUS SAMBALILIANA

THE ARROWS ARE SMEARED WITH POISON AND
HELD OVER A FIRE

(Page 92)

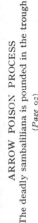

ARROW POISON PROCESS
The deadly sambailiana is pounded in the trough.

(Page 92)

two, and an ellipse cut out of it the shape of an arrow
head. This ellipse is then divided into two, and one half
is inserted in the right and one in the left end of the
arrow, where a narrow slit has been cut. Care is taken
that the two halves meet in the middle of the slit. The
pigmies have great faith in this style of " flighting "
arrows, and state that it makes them very accurate in
the air.

The arrow heads made of iron come from the negro
smithy, where they have to be purchased with money or
by barter. Usually there, too, they are shafted and
feathered, although sometimes the pigmies see to the
latter processes themselves.

Through my own personal observations I was
thoroughly convinced that the Bambuti are very skilful
in the manufacture of their primitive weapons. They
were always quite willing to sell me bows and arrows
for cotton, knives, etcetera. Occasionally I paid money,
with which they would purchase new iron arrows from the
negroes.

As a rule the pigmy is very devoted to his humble
belongings. This is especially noticeable if they are
keepsakes of members of his family who are dead.
Apropos of this, here is an incident I witnessed, which
shows how bitterly they lament the loss of any such
pathetic little tokens.

An old widow, who lived with her three grown-up sons,
was standing in front of her hut haranguing them with
frenzied gestures. The men stood dejectedly a few yards
away, and silently listened to their mother's tirade. At
last the old woman, who carried a grandchild in her
shoulder-sash, turned into her hut, whence presently were
heard heart-breaking sobs and lamentations. Inquiring
as to the cause of her passionate outburst, I was told that
for a long time the poor woman had treasured, as a
memento, a belt which had belonged to a son of hers who
had died some years previously. One day one of her sons
had worn this belt to the hunt, and had lent it to another
who had either lost it, or thrown it away as worthless.
All efforts to recover this little link with her dead son
proved unavailing. Hence the prostration of the old
woman. She was not even appeased when a girl brought

her a bow, which had also been the property of her dead child. She only glanced at it and threw it away, bursting anew into a tempest of weeping.

Some days later another affliction befell the poor old lady. A hunting horn, likewise belonging to the same dead son, had also been carefully treasured by her. Unaware of her sentimental attachment to the thing, I had seen it in the hut and asked her sons to sell it to me for inclusion in my collection. Day after day I tried to induce them to part with it, but in vain. At length, when I offered them a mouth-organ for it, the temptation proved too great and they fell. Hardly was the deal concluded before I heard another outburst of lamentations from the interior of the hut. The widow had just found out that the horn was missing. Naturally, immediately the sons told me what was wrong, I returned the article to her.

The thoughtlessness of these young men in stealing this little memento from their mother should not create the impression that young pigmies are lacking in filial affection. On the contrary, the love for their parents is a very strong trait, and manifests itself not only among the little ones, but even among the stalwart youths. In fact, this struck me as one of the most marked characteristics of Bambuti family life. The youths invariably took the coins or other trifles that they got from me to their mothers to mind for them. And it is the custom for a young man returning home after a long stay away, to seek his mother at once and to fondle her bosom as he was wont to do as a baby. This little act is regarded as a special token of affection and tenderness.

I have never seen a pigmy man weep, but I have noticed that their womenfolk are very prone to tears. Typical of their emotional nature is the following incident which I saw one day. On returning to her hut a young pigmy matron noticed that during her momentary absence, someone had eaten the food she had prepared for her family. She rushed out and poured forth a stream of violent invective. When, however, nobody showed any sympathy for her, she crept back into her hut and sobbed for hours as if her heart would break.

The pigmies are an extremely temperamental little

folk, liable to passionate outbursts of rage or sorrow. It must be remembered, however, that such unrestrained demonstrations are quite natural among unconventional primitive people, and, incidentally, are indications of a profound depth of emotion.

I must admit that the explosive, quarrelsome disposition of the pigmies got on my nerves after a time. It is all very well to put it down to the strong primitive streaks in them, but I often wished that they were not quite so primitive. The infernal din and the clamorous wrangling of the Bambuti jarred all the more when I mentally compared them with the pigmies of Malacca, for I had learned to esteem the latter especially for their quiet, peaceful, I might almost say, pensive temperament.

What I have just said will appear, no doubt, to clash very glaringly with the idyllic pictures that I previously drew of the quiet and soothing scenes of pigmy camp life. Alas! Those fleeting tranquil hours were only in the afternoon and evening, before and after the chief meal of the day. Then it was that the pigmy showed himself at his very best. At other times almost continuous shouting and bickering prevailed. The unbridled wanton disposition of the pigmy showed itself on the slightest provocation. The instant that they are up against any difficulty they fly into a passion. Every other minute you see women abusing their little ones in frenzied screaming tones when they do something to annoy them. Once I saw a four-year-old child fleeing into the forest, pursued by its mother, yelling and brandishing a cudgel. For a long time after I heard the wails of the little one in the undergrowth and the unremitting scolding of the mother in her hut. Eventually, however, one of the neighbours rounded up the child, soothed it and brought it home. Such scenes might incline one to think that the pigmy women were neurotic, ill-balanced creatures. Such an impression regarding a healthy stock like theirs would be, however, incorrect. They are merely giving free vent to their unrestrained primitive animalism.

The following incident illustrates the pigmy's passionate, volubly clamorous method of conducting negotiations which other people would carry through with decorum and restraint in solemn conclave. Very early one morning I

was roused from my sleep by voices raised in fierce alter-
cation. By this time I had been accustomed to all kinds
of impromptu bickerings, but had never previously had
my night's rest disturbed thereby. The screams came
from two opposite ends of the camp, and amidst the
tumult I could clearly distinguish the voices of Alianga
and a woman. The din waxing louder and louder, I
stepped into the open, and insisted that they should stop
their squabbling. Immediately there was dead silence.
Hardly, however, had I disappeared into my hut when the
wrangling started afresh. This was a bit too much for me.
I lost patience, snatched my gun from the peg and
strolled in front of the huts. Again there was silence, but
this time it lasted until the normal waking hours.

In the morning I inquired into the cause of the brawling.
It is nothing unusual for the different family groups to
come to loggerheads and attack one another, frequently
with fatal results. Pigmies themselves assured me that it
sometimes happens that whole groups wipe each other
out in such disputes. The efforts of the older men to
restrain the impulsive youths and to stop the mischief in
time are not always successful. Once they are thoroughly
aroused, the passions of these primitive men are often
uncontrollable.

The early morning disturbance on this occasion, however, was not caused by a fight, but by an animated discussion among older people as to the proper method of
bringing irresponsible youth under the control of reason.
And it was this ponderous debate conducted in a high-
pitched key that I had ended abruptly with my gun,
incidentally winning thereby more thanks from the
young people than from their elders. To the latter I had
unwittingly done a disservice.

I opened my inquiry by sending for Alianga. The old
man turned up, but refused to make a statement. He
said that I should also send for the woman, who had
kicked up a greater row than he had. He was obviously
annoyed by my unwarranted intervention. Hardly had
the woman sat down in my hut by Alianga's side, when
the quarrel threatened to break out afresh. They kept
up a mutual competition in invective, until I bade them
both to be silent. I ruled that Alianga was to speak first

and was not to be interrupted. After that the woman's turn would come. And in this way I eventually got a grip of the matter at issue.

Alianga stated that he caught his younger son spending the night in the hut of a " grass-widow "—an intolerable thing to do, as he had his own sleeping quarters in his grandmother's hut. He had absolutely no business there. He was no longer a mere lad. He was circumcised, and should have nothing to do with strange girls and women. His apron might quite easily come undone during the night. His nakedness would then be exposed and the woman would see that he was circumcised. The whole matter was intolerable.

The woman, an industrious decent poor soul and the mother of a numerous brood, now stated her trouble, which concerned her daughter Akandu, a girl just blossoming into womanhood, whose bashful retiring demeanour I had found rather charming.

" On several occasions," she said, " when I awoke in the middle of the night I have missed Akandu from the hut. Last night I went out to look for her, and surprised her in the ' grass-widow's ' hut. Her bed is by my side—not in that woman's place."

So this was the cause of the din which had rudely roused me from my sleep. The anxious and incensed mother at one end of the camp had just been expostulating with her erring daughter in such vehement tones that she startled all her neighbours from their sleep. Alianga had the very same reason to be annoyed, and started to lecture his son with a strident volubility that drowned the woman's harangue. And when they had both finished lecturing their own offspring, they inveighed clamorously against the loose morality of modern youth in general.

Apparently the two lovers had been keeping a " date " under the cover of night in the " grass-widow's " hut, which was an assignation place for the young bloods of the camp. Their romance was, however, abruptly ended by the intervention of their vigilant parents.

This incident and many others which I might cite do not tally with the impression conveyed by the American film, " Africa Speaks," regarding the moral code of the Ituri pigmies. The actual pictures are genuine enough.

G

The camera gives us no portrayal of lax morality. It is in the running commentary, given during the course of the film, that facts are grossly travestied. As well as I can recollect, one passage runs approximately thus : " These primitive people of the virgin forest have recognized for thousands of years the system of ' marriage on probation,' which we civilized folk are beginning to practise in a tentative fashion."

Only sensation-mongering film producers who during a motor tour via Buta-Nyangara-Kilo route happened by accident to come upon a group of pigmies and photographed them, could be capable of such a nonsensical statement. I wonder if they spent one full day in the company of the pigmies before they made this discovery ! As we go on, the reader will be able to judge for himself the standard of morality and the attitude towards the marriage tie among the pigmies.

Here is another incident which may help to explain the outburst of the two old people against the children.

In the early days of my stay in the camp of the Bafwaguda, I saw a comely girl who was pregnant. She was the daughter of Asangwa, and lived with her parents. As I never saw her husband, I casually inquired about him in the girl's presence. I was informed with the utmost sangfroid by " Policy " and the others that she was not married, but was pregnant by a negro. I accepted this explanation in perfect good faith, as I saw no reason to disbelieve it. It was only a few weeks later, as I was settling a series of disputes between Bafwaguda and the Bafwasengwe that I found that I had been told a lie. The girl was Policy's own mistress. He could not, however, marry her, as he could offer the Asangwa clan no other girl in compensation according to the regulations. The two young people seemingly had been in the habit of meeting at the " grass-widow's " hut, like the other two whose love affair I have already mentioned.

To this day I cannot quite make out why Policy and the rest of the Bakango thought it necessary to tell me a lie about the girl. It is probable that they wanted to conceal something from me that transgressed against their moral code. It certainly was not fear that made them tell a deliberate falsehood—it must have been shame.

The trust which the Bafwaguda placed in me increased from day to day. They always asked for my assistance in settling their matrimonial concerns with the neighbouring clan of the Bafwasengwe. For this purpose Policy had even brought the aged chief of the Bafwasengwe into the camp. He stayed some days with us, but no negotiations were entered into, as it was my intention to visit the Bafwasengwe camp as soon as possible, and to take those Bafwaguda who were concerned in the disputes with me.

Six young men from the camp came to me and urged me to assist them in getting wives ; they could not get married, they said, because the negroes had wooed and won all their marriageable girls. For the time being I could do nothing beyond laying the matter before Lipongo, the negro chief, and telling him emphatically that such a state of affairs must cease. I knew quite well that I was just talking to the wind, for the negroes regarded the system as based on ancient precedent. It is only the intervention of the white man that can remedy this state of affairs, for the negroes, as the more important economically, have such power over the pigmies that they can take their women as wives whenever they want to. Moreover, the pigmy girls are quite ready to acquiesce, for they live more comfortably and luxuriously in the negro villages, and can at any time they wish visit their own family groups in the forest. Thus, under this system the only sufferers are the young pigmy men. Sometimes marriage is made absolutely impossible for them, and it is of course quite obvious that in such a state of affairs laxity of the moral code must inevitably follow.

In other respects, too, my intervention was destined to prove helpful and effective. One day Agbendu, whom I had repeatedly interrogated on religious questions with very good results, appeared on my veranda, and told me a very gruesome tale of murder and cannibalism. He charged the chief of the village of Zongere and his clan with having killed and eaten his aunt, and demanded compensation for the wrong done to him thereby. He urged that I should compel the chief of Zongere to pay him for their misdeed. I was naturally absolutely astonished to hear that such a crime could be possible at the present day. I felt very reluctant, however, to have anything to do with such an unsavoury affair, and was even about to pass on the matter to the officer in Bafwasende, when I suddenly decided to hear both sides at the same time.

The inquiry revealed the fact that at the time when the Europeans were fighting against the negroes, in other words before the birth of Agbendu and the founding of Zongere, the Basua villagers had killed Agbendu's aunt, a pigmy woman. They charged her with witchcraft in connection with the death of her husband and her child. When they cut the body open in quest of the magic abscess which is always present in the entrails of witches, they found no trace of anything of the sort, and realized that they had killed an innocent woman. However, as she was dead they could not restore her to life, and, as her flesh was perfectly healthy they ate her and agreed that she tasted very nice. In their view it would have been sinful waste to have thrown away such excellent sound meat.

Agbendu admitted that this was an accurate version of the happening, and said that his father had told him all about the incident. He emphasized, however, that his aunt had been unjustly put to death and eaten, because, as the investigation showed, she was not a witch. Therefore he was entitled to compensation.

The chief of Zongere shrugged his shoulders contemptuously. What had wrongs done by his ancestor to do with him anyhow? Moreover, his ancestor had to carry out the negro regulations regarding witchcraft in vogue in his day.

I tried to console the pigmy by pointing out that it was an unpleasant incident of bygone times which could never occur at the present day. He made no reply, but I could see that he thought that I had not insisted as strongly as I should on the justice of his claim.

The present day Bakango will not admit to you that he would eat human flesh. And it is, of course, only on very rare occasions and in great privacy that the negroes indulge in cannibalism. Although the Bakango deny absolutely that they ever connived at cannibalism, their protest should not be taken too literally. I have been informed that some of them find it hard to resist the flavour of a fresh succulent corpse that has not been the victim of disease. The Bakango can scarcely be more squeamish in this respect than their overlords the negroes. All the other pigmy stocks are quite frank about their cannibalistic tastes. However, one thing is quite certain : they acquired this horrible appetite first by imitating the negroes.

The tattooing of the body, as far as it has penetrated into the Bakango code, must also be attributed to negro influence. I first noticed little scar tattooes, especially on the faces of the women. This art is, however, known only to the negroes, and the pigmy females have to resort to them for this beauty treatment.

Quite the opposite is the case with regard to pointing the front teeth. Alianga was a professional in this operation, and had both pigmy and negro clients. The dental operator's tools consisted of a little chisel and a cudgel. The client lay at full length on his back with a block of wood under his head. He either closed his eyes and played on a sansi-guitar or gazed dreamily into space. Alianga squatted on the ground in such a way that he held the man's head between his legs. Gently he chipped fragment after fragment from the tooth, until it had assumed the desired pointed shape. Frequently the teeth were made as sharp as a needle. This sharpening of the front teeth among the pigmies and a considerable number of the forest negroes is a form of beauty culture. They will gladly endure the pain of this treatment, and of the toothaches that follow in its train, in order to acquire " a beautiful mouth and beautiful teeth "—fashionable foibles dating back to primitive times which they have never given up. All protests that I made against this idiotic craze were of no avail. " The beasts have teeth like yours," a pigmy once replied to my onslaught against the habit, " but we sharpen our teeth so that we may not look like beasts." This reply was hardly flattering to me, although I can state with confidence that I have exceptionally fine and even teeth. The only result of all my arguments with the pigmies on this score was a definite conviction that our ideas on the question of dental beauty were hopelessly at variance. Even the warning that they would lose their teeth prematurely owing to this stupid system of dental culture, was of no avail. And they had only to look around them to see abundant proof of the truth of my words, for among the elder pigmies, both men and women, one sees huge disfiguring gaps between the teeth in almost every case.

Yet another type of disfigurement popular among the women is undoubtedly of negro origin. Negro women of different forest tribes deem that it enhances their charms enormously to pierce the upper lip and insert in it a huge round " saucer " of ivory. The result is bizarre, and in profile gives the appearance of a duck's bill, which the reader has no doubt frequently seen in films. The sight of a woman thus disfigured is extremely repulsive to us Europeans. The pigmy men have no particular liking for this custom, but, despite that, their women have their upper lips bored in several places, and insert bits of iron and sometimes rings in the holes. As kissing is unknown to the pigmies, the pegs inserted in the lips of the fair ones, frequently as much as four inches long, do not hamper them in any way, and although they look like a bunch of keys, they do not interfere in the slightest with their speech.

Even in their tenderest years girl's lips are pierced. What sacrifices for the sake of beauty are the vain humans of every race on earth prepared to make! On one occasion I shuddered as I witnessed a lip-piercing operation. Some women had formed a ring round a ten-year-old girl and held her pinned down so firmly that she could not stir, while an aged crone pierced her upper lip with the oiled bristle of a porcupine. The little girl screamed in agony. Hardly was the lip pierced through, when thin fragments of banana stalk were pulled through the hole. Then thicker and thicker fragments were drawn through it, until eventually a thick piece of arrow-shaft was inserted. A horizontal peg was then pushed through the end of the stick that was inside the mouth. This prevented the arrow-shaft from slipping out, and effectively ensured that the hole would be kept open. With this contraption in its mouth the child sat in the sunshine, writhing with pain, until the hole eventually healed and was ready for the reception of the decorating ring or peg.

In similar fashion women pierce the lobes of the ears

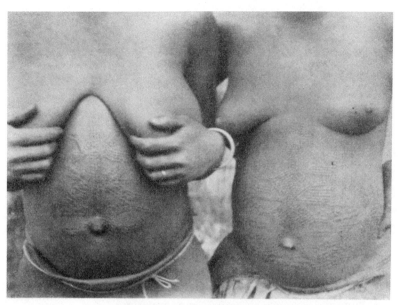

TATTOOING NEGRO-FASHION

(Page 101)

BIG BLOCKS OF WOOD ARE FASTENED ROUND THE NECKS OF
HUNTING-DOGS

(Page 60)

A BAFWAGUDA FIRE-DANCE
(*Page* 103)

PLAYING MUSIC-BOWS. AN ASUNGUDA CAMP SCENE
(*Page* 106)

and push rolled leaves through the holes as ornaments. Sometimes I met men as well as women with porcupine bristles driven through the cartilage of their noses.

Like the majority of the pigmies almost all the male Bakangos are circumcized. But to the most primitive and most racially pure pigmies circumcision is unknown to this day. Whence we may conclude that this rite was introduced among the pigmies indirectly by the negroes.

After I had spent almost two months in the Asunguda camp I felt it was time for me to take up my travels once more. The mighty expanse of the virgin forest swarmed on all sides with Bambuti, with whom I resolved to get acquainted.

My new friends volunteered to escort me themselves through the forest to Bafwasili, in the vicinity of which the Bafwasengwe, the allied clan to the Bafwaguda, were to be found. My objective was Avakubi, a government outpost and a mission station, from whence my expedition to the north-east was to be planned.

On a sunny morning the Bakango arranged a surprise for me by staging a fire-dance which I then saw for the first and last time. At dawn the camp was all agog with excitement. The young men, decked with leaves, ran up and down the camp to the beat of drums. Soon older men and women joined them. In serpentine lines the procession of dancers swayed now in this direction, now in that. Others collected dry wood and soon the flames of a brilliant fire leaped high, round which the dancers swayed and swirled to the accompaniment of singing and the beating of drums. And now with wild abandon they started leaping over the fire amidst loud laughter and wild screams when any one of them landed into the flames. Ever madder and madder were the frenzied leaps until the fire collapsed, whereupon the fun, if it was just fun and not a ritualistic dance, came to an end.

The camp was duly informed that the deliveries of bananas by the negroes were stopped. The news had an overwhelming effect. The faces of the pigmies grew longer and longer. The little fellows seemed to cherish the idea that they would be supplied with food for the rest of their lives. Some bolder souls called on me and asked where they were to get food in future. Even Alianga remarked sadly : " We shall all die of hunger."

I patted the old man on the shoulder in a friendly fashion, and repeated the advice I had again and again tendered, that they should start a plantation on their own account. I showed that I was deadly serious in making this suggestion, by distributing a large number of jungle-knives among the pigmies to help them to prepare the ground for planting. I had but scant hope that they would follow my very earnest suggestions, and my joy was all the greater when that very day I saw Alianga start cutting down the brushwood on the northern slope of the camp. Next morning he continued at the job and staked off a piece of land that he intended for his plantation. Some others, following his example, had marked off strips of land for themselves, without, however, as yet making any effort to dig them up.

About a year later when I returned to the neighbour-hood of the Asunguda River, I had the satisfaction of hearing that the Bafwaguda had actually started a banana plantation. Well, that was one good result of my stay among them.

I have very kindly memories of some of the pigmies with whom I daily came in contact during those first two months. Among them Alianga especially stands out most vividly. He was the leader of the Bafwaguda clan, at first in conjunction with Koko, the father of the present head of the camp. After Koko's death he ruled alone, as far as anyone could be said to rule the pigmies at all. And Alianga was only too conscious of the limits of his power. Consequently he preferred to give no commands or instructions. When I spoke to him about this he said that there would be no point in his giving orders, as nobody would heed them. When he gave instructions to strike camp, they all followed him of course ; apart from this, however, each one went his own way.

Even so he clung tenaciously to his post as chief of the Bafwaguda, and vehemently warded off any injury—internal or external to his clan. When in the first days of my stay in the camp the negro chief Lipongo appointed a young Mombuti, whose patron he was, as chief of the Bafwaguda, Alianga flew into a passion, tore his feather bonnet from his head, and asked the negro how he had the audacity to appoint as chief a young man who was only an infant in comparison with himself. He and he alone was the "Sultan." Alianga had worked himself up into such a fit of temper that he started to stammer, a frequent characteristic of his when he became excited. The effect of his outburst on this occasion was an obvious victory for him. Nobody— not even the all-powerful negro chief—dared to retort.

Alianga was of a quiet, I might almost say, shy disposition, and in this way contrasted very favourably with the others. And yet on occasion, if put to it, he could storm and bluster. He held an executive job that was in keeping with his dignity. He was the " Tata Ka Mambela " who undertook the initiation of the young lads in the tribal codes.

As a rule he was to be found sitting solemnly before his tent doing some odd job. He was a clever handicraftsman in many ways. He pointed the teeth of the negroes and the pigmies, and he made drums and collars for dogs. He no longer went hunting, but still occasionally took part in dances in the camp, and no doubt was an impressive figure at them. He had a short stumpy figure ; his broad wrinkled face, encircled with a beard which, like the close-cut crop of hair on his head was of a dirty grey colour, was not repulsive, as it was lit up by kindly eyes. His movements in the dance were grave and formal ; he never let himself go with the unrestrained, crazy abandon of the rest of the revellers. Here, too, he knew how to preserve that solemnity of mien which he found an invaluable asset in his dealings with people.

Alianga was undoubtedly very good-natured. I often saw him rocking little children in his arms or taking part in their games. And he was not a brazen, importunate beggar like most of the others. Naturally now and again he came to beg for some little trifle in a hesitating, shame-faced way. When I asked him to do some job in return for a present, he never shirked it. In everything he did he was slow and careful, and what he did he did well.

As master of ceremonies in the secret rites of initiation of the young men he had the custody of the sacred implements, the " whirring-wood " and the " ngbundure-flute." I begged him repeatedly to show them to me.

Once he was on the point of doing so and went to fetch them. When he returned a little later—perhaps after consultation with others—he started making evasive statements about them, and eventually sought refuge in lies. He told me that as Koko had died suddenly, he was not in a position to say where he had hidden the sacred implements. Since Koko's death they had been lost and his people had been obliged to carry out the ritual among the Bafwasengwe. It was possible I might be able to get them to show me the implements.

Some weeks later I found I was correct in my suspicion that this was merely a cunning evasion.

While Alianga was clever at craftsmanship, he was hopeless as an instructor and a raconteur. It was very difficult to get any clear information from him about his views on religion or about the social customs of his people. Yet this was not his fault ; he was naturally somewhat illogical and rambling in his speech. I found in this as in many other traits that he resembled my Semang friend Ramogn in Malacca.

Asangwa, a lean sickly little fellow, with very red-rimmed eyes and a grey scrubby beard, was older than Alianga. It was quite obvious that Alianga and he were not friends, although they belonged to the same clan. It was clear, too, that there were very strained relations between the two family groups. Asangwa was—perhaps as a result of his delicacy—if possible even more quiet and reserved than Alianga. I never saw him among the dancers, although he was very fond of wandering through the forest. Almost every day he set out, generally alone, either hunting or in quest of vegetables and wild fruit. I never heard him talking loudly or wrangling. When in the camp he used to sit quietly in front of his hut, almost invariably quite alone.

Often when I questioned the young men about something that puzzled me they would seek out the old man and ask him for the required information. And whenever I wished to have some particular tune played on the musical bow, they would lead me to Asangwa. Without making any comment, the old man would take the musical bow in his hand and start to play, while we all listened spellbound. He played any tune we asked him, but never suggested any particular one himself. He was as unobtrusive in this as in everything else.

Unfortunately it was very difficult to get him to talk. With him a wealth of pigmy lore will sink into the grave. On religious topics it is true he was very reserved ; but in narrating old myths and sagas he was much more communicative. When he began he was always somewhat stilted and a trifle ponderous, but when he warmed to his subject the tale ran on smoothly. Once his interest in the saga was thoroughly aroused, he went into exhaustive detail and illustrated incidents in his narrative with gestures and weird vocal inflections. Ever and anon, too, he would break into song. From his lips I have heard the only true traditional pigmy melodies, which were not merely dance tunes. He told me the following story on one occasion, in the course of which he gave me a sample of a touching little folk-song.

A woman gave birth to a girl-child named Mepimanza. As the child was extremely beautiful, the mother shut it up in her hut, and to guard it more effectively, she hung a bell over the entrance so that she could hear anyone going in or out. One day a Mombuti who was passing the hut saw the beautiful girl, and his heart went out to her at once. Returning to his camp he told of his discovery, and conspired with a comrade to steal the girl. When they reached the River Ituri, its flooded waters barred their progress. After holding a consultation with his comrade he cut down a tree on which the two paddled across to the other bank. By night time they reached the hut, silenced the bell over the entrance, seized the girl, and returned by the same route to their own camp.

When the mother awoke next morning and did not hear the bell, she looked round at once for her child. Imagine her dismay when she found that she was gone ! In her anguish she called out the girl's name again and again, but only the forest echoed her appeal. Then suddenly she noticed the trail of the ravisher, and immediately followed it up, breaking into a song of lamentation as she toiled away through the undergrowth :

> " Mepimanza ho, Mepimanza ho,
> Kpene, Kpene, Mepimanza ho,
> Mepimanza mokotabone, Mepimanza ho,
> Golie, golie, ziao ! "

A fairly literal translation runs thus :

> " Oh Mepimanza, oh Mepimanza,
> What have I done to thee ?
> Come back again and let me
> Rock thee in thy little swing ! "

Reaching the village she made inquiries about her child, and laid information before the chief about the outrage. The ravisher, one Mikandoro, went to his father, who immediately lectured him soundly for his rascality. The father also ordered a large load of bananas to be cut, which he presented to the afflicted mother, and he also gave her a girl from the village as compensation for her daughter, who remained with Mikandoro.

Another good example of Asangwa's gifts as a raconteur is the tale of the wild pig. Moreover, as, under the guise of a parable, it tells of conditions long ago among the pigmies and the negroes, it is perhaps worth repeating.

" A Mubali negro once worked very hard to make a clearing in the forest for a banana plantation. With the sweat of his brow he cut down the trees, and after he had burned away the dry undergrowth his wife planted the banana shoots. ' That is my field,' proclaimed the negro, ' let no one but you and me dare to touch its produce.'

" Day after day the wife went out to inspect the plantation. One morning, however, she returned to her hut, wailing : ' Our field ! Our field ! Wild pigs have laid it waste ! '

" The minute her husband heard this, he hurried to the plantation to kill the wild pigs. He took along rattan snares and traps which he cunningly hid in the plantation. During the night the wild pigs returned to get the rest of the bananas. Many of the brutes were caught in the snares and killed. Only three young pigs and a boar which was badly wounded escaped. With the aid of the youngsters the wounded boar managed to get back safely to the pigs' village.

" At dawn the negro followed the trail of blood to the village. As soon as the wounded boar saw him, he attacked him and mauled him terribly. Finally he bound him to a tree, and all the pigs took to flight in quest of another camp.

" The negro succeeded at last in freeing himself. Once

again he took up the trail of the wild pigs and soon over-took them. But again the wild boar attacked him fiercely, gored him and bound him to a tree.

" The negro extricated himself yet once more, and resumed the pursuit of his enemies. When the wild boar returned to the attack, his father stepped forward and said : ' Why do you attack the man so savagely ? Leave him in peace.'

" The negro now lodged his complaint against the wild pigs, and demanded compensation from the wild boar's father : ' Give me your son and I will take him back to my village.' The father seized his son, bound him and handed him over to the negro. The latter brought him to his village, but instead of killing him dressed his wounds. When the wild boar was fully recovered the negro said to him : ' Pack your belongings. We are going to your father's camp.' After they had reached the camp, the negro said to the old boar : ' This son of yours has laid waste my plantation, and attacked me several times. Look at all my wounds ! '

" Whereupon the old boar gave as compensation one sow for every wound on the negro, and the latter returned appeased to his village."

The wild pigs of the parable are, of course, the pigmies. There is a tradition among the negroes that in bygone days the little men plundered their plantations like the wild pigs. The upshot of every punitive expedition of the negroes was that they beat the Bambuti and seized their wives and daughters, until the pigmies, dispirited at last, begged for peace, which was usually granted on condition that they handed over the girls by way of compensation to the negroes, who married them.

And now just a few lines about a third old man in the same camp, named Maduali. I found him extremely uncommunicative, and hardly exchanged two words with him during my long stay there. He was even more reserved than the other two elders. The father of a large brood of children, he seemed extremely devoted to his family and took little interest in the general amenities and entertainments of the camp. He was only very occasionally seen among the dancers. On the rare occasions on which he did join them he was invariably adorned with waving plumes. I have an idea that he was somewhat henpecked. His wife was the woman I mentioned a few pages back who scolded her daughter so volubly. But I must confess that Maduali seemed to submit very contentedly to petticoat rule.

CHAPTER V

PRIMITIVE SOCIETY AND ITS LAWS

THERE was very little ceremony about my departure from the Bafwaguda. I warned the pigmies that I had heard the negroes contemplated seizing the camp site with a view to converting it into a new banana plantation. To forestall this, I presented my huts, which seemed the nearest approach to a solid structure in the camp, to the pigmies.

My bearers consisted of both men and women, who had volunteered to accompany me to the Bafwasengwe. They took charge of my belongings and we set off through the undergrowth to the village of Zongere. As I calculated that it would take me at least eight days to cover the forest district as far as Avakubi in quest of pigmies, I shed all my superfluous baggage, giving it to the negroes to forward via the beaten caravan track to Avakubi. My escort, carrying only the barest necessities for their nomad existence, now consisted merely of my poor little pigmies.

My residence in Zongere gave me an opportunity to investigate the outlying village communities, the Basua and the Babali, and especially to get a thorough grip of the initiation rites of the Mambela and to probe the mysteries of the Anyota secret league of murder and cannibalism. I have held over my experiences in making these investigations for a later book. They gave me an insight into the most sinister aspects of negro psychology and of negro social life.

The gloomy trail which joins Bomili and Bafwasili, led to Lipongo's village, where the caravan spent the first night, and where provisions were secured for the two days' journey through the forest.

Lipongo is a super-chief by the grace of the white man. He is officially known as " Chef de secteur," and has several villages under his sway. Supported by native police and with the authority of the white man to back him, he is a great potentate. But from the tribal point of view he is merely an ordinary negro like any other member of his tribe. As a tool of the colonial police he holds sway through a dread of imprisonment and the lash. He is not obeyed through any deep-felt conviction or reverence, such as is freely yielded to the elders, the genuine tribal chiefs. The latter, however, remain hidden from European eyes.

Lipongo himself was by no means a bad fellow. He was very intelligent, and had a great deal of personal charm. He and his family group were rich, and as, of course, their wealth had been acquired directly through his position, there were a great number who were envious of him. Lipongo greeted me courteously and effusively, and he occasionally visited me in the camp. Moreover, the official reception which he accorded me in the village was extremely friendly. He even brought the inevitable hen that is presented to every white man that travels through the negro villages, himself, and soon regular supplies of bananas were allotted to my bearers.

In a rather long private interview with the chief I gave him a detailed account of my experiences among the pigmies, drew his attention to several grievances which constantly cropped up in the dealings between the negroes and the Bambuti, and declared that I would appeal to the authorities for redress. Lipongo seemed to take it all in very stoically. Perhaps he took even less interest in the pigmies than many other negroes. With regard to most of the cases I quoted he thoroughly agreed with me, but with regard to some he pleaded old-time customs.

At the finish he took me round to see his farm, and after presenting me with another hen for my dinner on the next day, which I and my caravan were to spend in the un-trodden forest, he bade me farewell.

Shortly after I had returned to my quarters, an appalling din broke out in the village, of which I took no notice, until my cook raised the alarm. There was a fight in progress. I already suspected that my pigmies were involved in it, and snatched up my rifle in order to restore peace by firing a few rounds to scare the brawlers.

A glance towards the veranda, however, showed me that all the Bambuti were crouching in terror beside me. In order to escape unnecessary annoyances, which seemed in the offing, I was about to step among the mob with my gun, but on second thoughts I hung it up again, and picking up my heavy rattan cudgel, linked with memories of Malacca, I hurried outside.

A seething mass of humanity fighting savagely with fists and feet, greeted my eyes. Isolated groups were writhing on the ground, biting and clawing one another. Whips sang through the air and cudgels were flourished in all directions. When they saw me, some of the fighters fell back, while others flew at one another with all the more ferocity. And now my rattan cudgel crashed among the brown bodies. A large section of the bullies broke away forthwith, but there was still a mob of frenzied combatants who showed no sign of ending the battle. Suddenly the dull roll of the war-drum, suggestive of the menacing growl of a wild beast, was heard, summoning the men in the plantations to the fray. And now a swirling sea of savage faces surged in the background. Knives and spears were flashing. The position began to become menacing, while all the time I had not the faintest idea of the cause of the outbreak. This much I could see very clearly—Lipongo and his family group, who were acting in conjunction with the police, were hard pressed. Once more I charged in with my rattan cudgel, and simultaneously auxiliary forces from the chief's family group came up. It was lucky that the armed men, who had been summoned by the beating of the war-drum, kept their heads, and did not take part in the battle as yet. At length the police succeeded in arresting and removing the leader of the brawl. But still the mob fought with undiminished frenzy, and assumed an even more menacing attitude.

Lipongo brought the prisoner with a rope round his neck before me, and gave a detailed explanation of the squabble. Imagine my astonishment to find that the fight was about me—or rather about the hen I had got from Lipongo, and for which I was prepared to pay. Lipongo had demanded this hen from a neighbouring family group, but had been met with a blunt refusal.

H

Whereupon the chief just ordered a policeman to seize a hen. The negroes put up a stout resistance, not through personal hostility to me, whom they scarcely knew, but through a hatred of white men in general, and of their tool, Lipongo.

" At any rate, he is not a white man," the negroes had said to the policeman when he demanded the hen. In the view of the aborigines of the forest, only the colonial official with a badge on his helmet, who is escorted by police and soldiers, is regarded as a genuine " Muzungu " (white man), before whom all must grovel on their bellies. On the other hand whites who hold no official position are at the mercy of the favour or displeasure of the negroes ; they are absolutely thrown on their own initiative, and can only secure provisions in return for valuable presents with which they must not be niggardly.

The colonial authorities are, of course, very obliging and anxious to assist any white man, but their good will is of very little help to him when he is in the heart of the virgin forest far from their zone of effective intervention. It is indeed extremely regrettable that for some inexplicable reason a hostile racial feeling towards the white man in general is implanted and fostered in the heart of the negro. The incident I have just described of the brawl over the hen should not be regarded as an isolated instance. I had numerous similar experiences during the course of my wanderings, and again and again " white " friends of mine had complaints to make about racial bitterness among the black men. In my case, of course, the fact that I was regarded as an official of the Bambuti and travelled in their company may have somewhat affected the attitude of the negroes towards me.

As may be imagined, my stay in the village was anything but pleasant. I began to feel rather uneasy when Lipongo called on me to sell me another hen, and at the same time begged me to write to the authorities and inform them of the hostility shown to him by the villagers, which he said had been apparent for quite a long time, adding that they tried to thwart every move he made. He asked me to apply for military aid to restore peace and punish the disturbers, and said that he feared worse outbreaks during the coming few days.

The two policemen who brought the prisoner to the station that evening, took charge of the letter. Hardly were the three of them out of our sight, when the mob again became turbulent. Armed with cudgels, some of them hurried off in the direction in which the police and their prisoner had vanished. I was wondering whether they were planning to head them off and make an effort at rescue in the forest. Lipongo took no notice of them, but he counted the number of those who started out, by dropping a tiny fragment of wood on the ground for each man. It was dawn before the village became quiet once more.

The morning was wet and chilly, but, nevertheless, the pigmies packed their loads on their backs, and the little caravan trotted through the rank " tongo," a derelict plantation, towards the forest. Again and again we crossed the River Asunguda, which twists with innumerable windings through the undergrowth. Our trail was a gentle upward gradient for the most part, but now and again there was a rather steep slope to negotiate. For two long days we travelled through a seemingly interminable twilight gloom. Not once did we encounter a single clearing, nor could we see ten yards ahead of us through the greenish dusk of musty woodland.

During the course of the second day the little " Sultan," who kept running ahead of us, carefully picking out our course, suddenly gave a wild scream, and leaping madly through the undergrowth, rushed back towards us. At the same moment a decayed giant tree crashed to the ground with a loud roar and blocked our path. In how many strange ways does death prowl in the track of the forest dweller ! It was lucky that the young man's ear had detected in time the sinister crackling of the rotten tree, and that through his opportune warning we escaped with only a nasty shock.

Just after this incident we continued along a narrower trail, which for some reason I fancied had never been trodden save by pigmies. I was soon disillusioned. About noon our little company halted and listened attentively to an ominous murmur just ahead of us. What could it be ? I gripped my rifle at the ready, prepared for charging a wild beast. Soon, however, we heard human voices, and a troop of Babali negroes, wearing fur caps and decorated with trailing wild cats' hides, marched past us, brandishing gleaming spears and knives. Babali negroes in their war kit look impressive in a village ; in the gloom of the forest they look spectral. The giants swept on past our unimpressive pigmy caravan. They were Babali from Bafwasili, dancers who trailed from village to village, displaying their craft. Their objective at the moment was Lipongo's village.

The rain now became heavier, and our path became slippery and difficult. The wet shrubbery lashed our faces, and handicapped my pigmy bearers badly, who nevertheless preserved their good humour wonderfully. Maseru, laden with a heavy box, kept singing ceaselessly in a carefree style, heedless whether anyone joined in or not.

The eternal up-hill and down-dale trekking so utterly exhausted me that I was heartily delighted when at length we reached the camp. But my delight was short-lived. My heart sank into my boots when I saw the appalling squalor of the quarters that awaited us. How those three tiny, weather-battered, foul-smelling, un-speakably dirty huts nauseated me ! However, as no other shelter was available, the pigmy women started at once patching these foul little dens with phrynium leaves. A hasty superficial attempt was made to clean up my hut, and then I crawled into the musty hole. How glad I would have been to have been able to spend the night under the leafy roof of the giant forest trees ! Unfor-tunately the rain made it impossible to think of sleeping in the open. My pigmies shivered as they huddled over the fire and roasted the bananas that they had brought with them. The little camp was isolated in the very depths of the forest, far away from any link with human-ity. According to some of the pigmies a Bafwasengwe family group had pitched camp in the place, but later had taken up its abode on the other side of Bafwasili. The path by which we had come was the shortest to Bafwasili, but it was impassable for heavily laden caravans, as I could very readily believe. It certainly had been a very good idea to send my heavy luggage by another route to Avakubi. We never could have managed to get it through the dense undergrowth. Indeed, the pigmies assured me that I was the first white man to travel by this trail.

Uncomfortable though my quarters were, I slept fairly well during the night. Our journey next day was even more difficult than before. I always preferred quick going for about four hours to a slow journey of indefinite length which frequently continued for seven or eight hours. And such was the position now. We sank knee-deep in the morass, formed by the overflow of the River Sangani. Romantic vistas, however, were unfolded as we crossed the upper reaches of the River Apare, where it thundered downwards boiling and foaming over rocks and boulders. Hopping perilously from rock to rock, I reached the opposite bank. The crossing was a much more difficult job for my carriers. They were very nimble at climbing, however, and crossed by the very narrow bridge-way afforded by a giant tree which had fallen across the stream, its topmost branches resting on the very steep bank on the other side. At last we were able to take a short rest. When we resumed our march, we found that the path led downwards, towards the River Mulinda, along whose banks we travelled for a good while. At midday we reached the first " tongo," and soon after came upon a second and a third one. For hours we wandered among the bushes of the abandoned and ruined plantations, after which we climbed a steep gradient and suddenly found that we had reached the village of Bafwasili. To our left lay the valley of the Ituri. My eye could not trace the course of the river itself, but the negroes and the pigmies saw its silvery thread along the horizon. Before us spread the swollen expanse of the Mulinda, whose waters flashed back the rays of the tropical sun.

I took up my abode in the rest-hut, as I always did in the negro villages when one was available. The bearers cast their burdens on the ground and scattered through the village, where many of them had their patrons—their " waschenzi "—on whom they could call for provisions.

Our fourth day's march was through less rugged and drier territory and along tracks laid by the negroes. But the pigmies were already quite exhausted—obviously they had undertaken more than they had bargained for.

Pembereko, who was carrying the cooking equipment, was suffering torments in his efforts to keep pace with the other bearers. His courage, however, revived whenever he thought of the coming payment, which was to be made not in cash, but in fabric. Maseru stuck it out bravely to the end. All the time she was singing. I found it very hard to understand the psychology of this enigmatical young woman. Never before or after did I meet her parallel among the pigmies for care-freedom and good humour. And she was eternally on the go. She was equally enthusiastic about work and play. Her voice was never silent. When alone she sang or hummed to herself.

This journey she was now making was fraught with portentous consequences for Maseru, for at its end her tangled matrimonial affairs had to be arranged. And yet to look at her or to hear her, you would imagine that she had never a care. Perhaps such was the case ; perhaps temperamentally she took everything in a light-hearted way. When not singing she was joking or laughing or chatting animatedly. Her jolly way and her abandon made many a weary bearer forget his heavy burden, and when she exchanged her comparatively light load for Pembereko's heavy box, in order to relieve the poor devil, I felt that she must be unique among the lowly people of the forest.

After a six hours' march, we reached the village of Ischumi, near which were two settlements of the Bakango-Bafwasengwe. We got rather a miserable reception in the negro village. I did not concern myself about the question of getting quarters and food, and was sitting on a tree-stump at the entrance to the village, nursing my sore feet when Adzapori, accompanied by a sullen, lowering negro, came towards me with the news that we could not spend the night in the village. My cook butted in to say that the negro had said I was not a real " Muzungu "—I was the " Muzungu " of the pigmies. My blood rushed to my head—I sprang from my tree-stump and shook the insolent negro by the throat. The effect was magical. When I released my grip he wheeled round, and pointed out a hut which he said was available. It had been available before I half-choked him, and he knew it !

Not only did the negro give me the hut, but with

extraordinary speed he set off down the village, called the inhabitants together, and ordered them to supply me at once with the usual day's rations. In the absence of the chief, the man whom I had half choked was his representative, and one of his duties was to see to the comfort of myself and my bearers. Incidentally the fellow's face and carriage were those of the inveterate hemp-smoker. There are numerous addicts to this vice in the more remote negro villages.

The dwelling which he placed at my disposal being a newly built hut without any window, as is the custom of this neighbourhood, I got one of my servants to bore some holes in its mud walls. I put my bed in the club hut which served as a smithy, and was swathed in a very heavy coat of soot. The place pleased me, however, as, like all the club huts of the Babali, it was open on all sides.

My pigmy bearers scattered in quest of sleeping quarters, with the exception of Pembereko, who remained to look after my food. The others vanished into the Bafwasengwe settlement just opposite, where I paid a visit the same evening.

The Bafwasengwe are definitely a progressive tribe of the Bambuti, and I was very agreeably surprised to see their two camps surrounded with large banana plantations. It was only a few years ago that they made a move towards making a permanent settlement. This must have been the outcome of the initiative and energy of the head of the clan, who came to me with a request to make him super-chief of all the Bakango, including, of course, the Bafwaguda. The earnestness of the old man impressed me very much, but I had to turn down his proposal right away, because the pigmy code does not tolerate anything in the nature of a super-chief. Moreover, I was perfectly well aware that the Bafwaguda had many complaints against the Bafwasengwe and their leader. I had not the faintest doubt, however, that the old man had the stuff in him to make a leader of all the Bakango. He had already proved this by freeing his clan from the sway of the negroes, on his own initiative, and making it economically independent. The plantations, to be sure, were rather wretched ones, but, for all that, they sufficed for the nourishment of the inhabitants of both camps.

I could not quite determine during the brief period of my stay the precise scope of the old man's influence over his people. But he knew how to get his own way whenever he was fully determined, as will be clearly seen from an incident which I shall narrate later on.

The dwellings of these pigmies were made on the pattern of those of the negroes. There was not a bee-hive hut to be seen. They were all tiny gable-roofed huts, such as are favoured by the Babali. They were built, however, on a very wretched plan.

The old man was the one whom " Policy " had brought a little previously to the Asunguda camp to unravel some matrimonial tangles. The greatest obstacle towards a settlement of these disputes was the old man himself, as he set himself above all customs and usages, and hoped that his strength of will would override the wishes of the whole tribe. But he found he was trying to bite granite.

It was interesting to observe how in this primitive community an individual who far surpassed his fellows in shrewdness, will-power and ambition, made use of these personal endowments to set aside old-established customs to suit his own interest, while on the other hand the community adopted a defensive attitude against him, when the social, nay, even the moral principles of their little cosmos were menaced by him. The domination which he obtained in economic matters comparatively easily, he either secured only with the greatest difficulty in social and moral spheres, or failed utterly in every detail. They all stood up as one man against him ; but owing to his pigheadedness, he neither yielded to the representations of others nor to his own better judgment. At length, however, he found in me one who was stronger than himself.

And now a few explanatory remarks are essential before we examine the matrimonial code of the pigmies.

The sketch I am giving in these pages of the social system, the morals and customs of the Bakango and of their families, family groups and clans is a replica in the main outlines of the conditions existing among the pigmies, and is all the more fascinating as it undoubtedly portrays in a general way the organization of primeval human society.

It should not be inferred that the principles of social
organization among the pigmies are obvious at a superficial glance. Even the studious explorer, who spends a
long time in a camp, sees nothing but a medley of huts
clustered close together, each of which shelters a larger or
smaller family—in other words he just sees families.
Consequently the family as the social unit immediately
grips his interest. The observant eye will probably soon
notice that there are isolated groups of several huts
huddled close together. This system of detached groups
of huts will be attributed by the explorer, and with
apparent logic, to the configuration of the ground,
because hollows are very bad sites for building, while
elevated patches are ideal for the purpose. A protracted
stay in the camp will reveal to him the real cause for this
grouping. He will notice that batches of families cling
together in groups. These groups consist of families
joined by kinship, and they appoint the oldest of their
members as a sort of overlord. In the family the father
is the head and his authority is recognized by the children,
as long as they remain in the bosom of the family ; so
likewise, but in a lesser degree, the senior of the family
group holds sway over all the members of the group.
Actually any given family group consists only of the male
kindred, as they remain permanently members of it,
whereas its women-folk marry into a different family
group, and thereby, though still tied by blood to their
parent group, they become foreign to it from an economic
point of view. Still access to their parent group is always
available to these female members who have married
outside it, and they will always get protection and aid
from it, should they need it. They even have as much
claim on the parent group as those women who never
leave its fold. They are always known as the " sisters "
of the rest of the parent group, and are called "mothers"
by the little ones of that group.

How great is the economic loss caused by a girl marrying
into an outside family group will be realized when it is
remembered that it is the women who for the most part
are responsible for the housing and feeding both of the
family and the family group. I have already pointed out
that the women bring in all the fruit and vegetable food

to the camp, and it is on this diet that the pigmies mainly depend. At the present time meat constitutes only thirty per cent of their food. Consequently the family group feels the loss of a girl very severely, and cannot, and will not, put up with that loss without compensation. A possible solution of the difficulty would be marriage within the family group, which would entail inbreeding. Such a thing is, however, unknown. Among this primitive people, a marriage of blood-relations is considered so unnatural, that it would not be tolerated on any account. A girl must always marry into an outside family group—frequently even into a strange clan.

In order to compensate for the economic loss to a family group caused by the marriage of a girl an ingenious arrangement is adopted. A family group will permit the marriage of one of its girls into a strange group, only on condition that the latter can supply a girl in her lieu, who is then incorporated by a marriage and consequently automatically takes the place of the girl who has left. They call this system of marriage " head for head." It should not be inferred from this, however, that the pigmies barter their marriageable girls, and interfere with their freedom of choice in selecting husbands. On the contrary, every girl can follow her own natural inclinations in this matter, and select the boy of her heart from the family group decided upon. Of course it is quite possible that a young man may exercise a certain amount of pressure on his sisters to induce them to marry into a certain family group, should he have his eye on a prospective bride from that group and have to provide a girl in place of her. In a primitive form of society, in which no monetary indemnification can be given for the economic loss entailed by a marriage, I think that the matrimonial system of " head for head " is absolutely ideal.

Exceptions to the system occur more or less frequently according to the neighbourhood. In the case of a marriage between a negro and a pigmy girl, of course, there could be no question of giving a girl by way of compensation. Special regulations are made with regard to such marriages so as to prevent economic loss to the girl's family group.

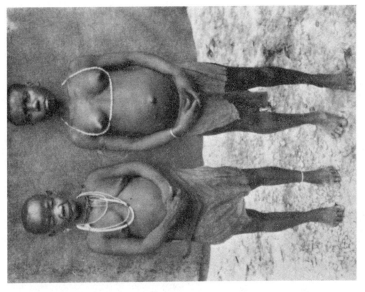

ITURI PIGMY WOMEN

THE OLDEST MEN IN THE BAFWASENGWE
CAMP

(Page 123)

THREE PIGMY "TYPES"

THE AUTHOR AMONG THE ITURI PIGMIES

I have already frequently referred to the " clan," a social grouping which apparently is of negro origin. At the present day all pigmies are grouped in " Totem clans." Each clan, as a rule, erects one camp. Only very rarely have I seen a clan divided into two camps.

To the " Totem clan " belong several family groups, which, owing to their common totems, are closely allied and frequently linked by ties of kinship. Their origin is lost in obscurity. It is possible that the family groups, which lived with a specified negro clan, united so as to form a pigmy clan, and that they took over the totem of the negroes, or chose a new one for themselves. However this is merely surmise. Totem animals and the " tabu " system are recognized by all the clans, but I was unable to obtain details on this point.

Clan-exogamy, i.e. marriage of girls into a strange clan, frequently occurs. On the other hand, family-group-exogamy is a definite and binding regulation. The elders of the clan enjoy a certain influence, which depends upon their own personality, but which is generally of very little account. Alianga's retort, " Why should I give orders, seeing that everyone finally does what he likes ? " is significant apropos of this. As umpires in disputes between different family groups, however, the clan-elders have the best chance of getting a hearing.

While we must consider the riddle of the origin of the clan system among the Bambuti as insoluble, we can definitely affirm that tribal fusion is absolutely unknown to them. Moreover, they completely lack any sense of national solidarity. Consequently, the existence of a tribal chief is an impossibility. On the other hand the pigmies are quite conscious that they are an individual race, absolutely distinct from the negroes. They pit themselves against the negroes, just as a race, but not in a national or tribal sense.

Let us take, for example, the Bakango, who lead a nomad existence over a clearly defined territory, and are divided into various clans. You could look in vain for a trace of tribal unity among them. It simply does not exist.

An elder of the Bafwasengwe apparently had some

vague idea of such a tribal fusion, and strove to set himself
up as a chief. His ambitious project was wrecked by the
folly of his confederates. He then invoked my influence
to help him in his aim. There is no scope, however, as I
have already pointed out, for a tribal chief in the social
structure of the pigmies. The real tie among the Bakango
is the fact that their clans are bound together by a series
of marriages. Bambuti clans that live far apart have
far less in common with one another than with the
racially different negroes with whom they are linked
economically.

In fact, it is this community life, in conjunction with
the racially different negroes, whose local dialect they
have individually adopted, which prevents the national
or tribal cohesion of the scattered nomad pigmy clans.

Every clan has a clearly defined home territory, in
which the individual family group, or families, hunt and
collect the produce of the forest, while each family has its
ant-hill, which it alone exploits. Every family group
and every family has an equal claim to the entire territory, and neither a family group nor an individual can
call a patch of land his own. Everything is common
property, even the ant-hill and any game that is captured
or killed in the course of the day's hunting.

Economically the clan is of no account, except in the
case of net-hunting, for which a large number of men—
consequently all those in the clan, are requisitioned.
Apart from this the members of the clan have very little
to do with one another. The family group is the real and
only economic unit. The members of a family group are
in constant touch with one another throughout the daily
round ; they form an entity which aims at the welfare of
the group as a whole. The proceeds of the hunt and the
fruits of the forest are common property. The day's
game is cut up by the family group elder, and is divided
among the individual families. The man who killed the
animal has no say in the actual division. And even an
outside family group, in the same camp, can come in for a
share of the spoil if it has any claim on the grounds of
kinship by marriage.

Vegetables are rarely shared out in this fashion owing
to the fact that all the women of the family group who

set out together in quest of food, usually bring home approximately similar quantities. But when members of a family group, from whatsoever cause, have brought nothing home, the others come to their assistance.

From the economic point of view the individual family does not count for very much. And yet in order to forestall false deductions on this point, I wish to emphasize that such a thing as whole-hog communism does not exist among the Bambuti. Your pigmy is fundamentally an uncompromising egoist. Old Asangwa gathered nuts in the forest, roasted them in the camp, and ate them alone, unless by chance somebody sat beside him and joined him in the feast. But he never invited a guest to tuck in. And a pigmy woman who finds snakes in the wood roasts them in her own hut and gives them to her own children. The individual family attends to all its own petty wants, as far as it is able to do so. But the moment there is a question of produce that is the outcome of a common effort, the whole family group joins in the share-out.

The life of these forest nomads makes it impossible, taking everything into consideration, for an individual family to provide its means of livelihood unaided. For the battle for existence a larger unit is needed—the family group. The family group therefore represents the nucleus of primitive social and economic life. The family is the ant on the ant-hill, bustling hither and thither, toiling zealously for the community, while incidentally it is battening on all that comes its way. An ant that is ejected from its community, inevitably goes under. Individual pigmy families, if left for any length of time to their own resources, would meet with a similar fate. But the question whether, in this primitive social organization, the family preceded the family group, or vice versa, must remain unanswered.

When the Bambuti appointed me as umpire in their matrimonial disputes, the condition of their social organization was only known to me in a very hazy way. But owing to the allegations and complaints that were advanced by one batch of disputants, and either refuted or admitted by another batch, I got a good insight into their system of community life.

Late one afternoon I had just returned from a visit to

Ischumi village, when I was suddenly surrounded by a
group of pigmies and negroes. Adzapori placed my
camp-stool in front of the hut, and informed me that the
Bambuti wished me to settle their disputes. And so
there I was elevated to the status of a judge in Bambuti-
land.

At a distance from the crowd Akapura, the oldest man
of the Bafwasengwe, wearing his feather cap, crouched
with his back against his hut. His shrewd eyes staring
straight ahead, he remained silent. Adzapori led before
me Mengito, a man of forty, who had followed our caravan
all the way from Asunguda. He had left at home a wife
and also two children by another woman. This other
woman, Mamuti, I now saw for the first time. She had a
more attractive face than one usually finds among
Bambuti women—a face that was mobile and expressive.
She was Akapura's daughter, and had been living for
years in happy wedlock with Mengito. Beside her stood
Maseru, Mengito's sister, who, as was her wont, glanced
about with indifference, as though something utterly
trivial were at stake. She was married to a son of
Akapura, who now remained in the background and took
no part in the discussion. In this matter, too, it was a
case of conjugal infidelity, with the venerable ruffian
Akapura himself as the villain of the drama. It was a
misdemeanour, which not only caused complications and
annoyance to the two family groups, but brought about
strained relations between the clans of the Bafwasengwe
and the Bafwaguda.

It was a sordid tale. Akapura had seduced Maseru,
his own son's wife. It was not clear whether the hoary
sinner had secured Maseru's compliance through threats
or whether she was a consenting party. As soon as their
guilty relationship became known, the family group protested against it. Mamuti, who lived among the Bafwaguda, heard of the outrage to her brother. She decided
to stand by him. She left Mengito and her little children
abruptly, and returned to her parent family group. And
now the poor fellow was left alone ! In accordance with
the prevailing custom, the husband who has been deserted
by his wife has a right to claim back the married girl who
had been given as a substitute. Consequently Mengito

demanded the return of Maseru. It was a matter for herself whether she decided to obey the call of her family group. Normally women married into an outside family group remain loyal to their parent group, and rarely forsake it when it is in trouble. And so Maseru obeyed the summons, left the Bafwasengwe, and lived during the two months that I spent among the Bafwaguda in our camp as a merry grass widow. However, before she left the Bafwasengwe, old Akapura had taken some blood from her breast, and sealed it in a pikipiki, threatening her at the same time that he would kill her by magic if she married another man. It is possible that the old man terrified the woman to such an extent with his threats of vengeance by magic that she obeyed him. He could not, however, prevent her returning to her family group.

Inquiries among some Bambuti and negro elders who were near me, showed that the conduct of the old man was regarded as an absolute offence against the moral code of his people. Whereupon I pleaded with Akapura, but he remained mute and stubborn. The old negroes also spoke to him, but got no answer.

As the preaching and scolding had no effect, I took the old man aside, as well as Adzapori and an aged pigmy, and once more appealed to the veteran sinner with all the eloquence I could command. My admonitions, coupled with the caustic taunts and threats of Adzapori, at length brought him round. He agreed to all our proposals. We returned with the good tidings to the waiting group, and everybody looked relieved. Mengito took Mamuti by the hand, and led her away, while Maseru walked up and down through the crowd, talking to herself. Later on, however, I saw her with an earthenware pot on her shoulder, an indication that she was once more reconciled to her lot as a loyal wife.

But a wife does not always obey the call of her parent family group. When on the sundering of a marriage the girl, who had been given in compensation, declines to dissolve her marriage, because she feels that she is more tied to her husband and children than to her parent family group, efforts are made to arrive at a compromise. The aggrieved family group demands full indemnification —that is to say, another girl. Should this be impossible, the first-born boy of the marriage, as soon as he is grown-up, must spend some months in his mother's family group, during which he has to assist in the pursuit of game. Sometimes compensation in the form of presents is accepted.

But even among the Bambuti love breaks through the barriers of morals and customs. The pigmies told me that it sometimes happens that a couple become so devoted to one another that they will not be parted even if the youth cannot provide a girl in exchange for his beloved, or cannot buy out the latter. The girl then takes the initiative by fleeing to her lover, and living in his family group. Anon come emissaries from her family group to the camp, and demand her return home. Sometimes violence ensues. The girl goes with them, but soon returns to her husband's family group, and once more the other group demands its rights. At this stage the husband's own group usually urges her to return to her people. Still the last word lies with herself. Should she refuse to leave her lover, her parent family group must be satisfied with some little presents—in many cases a dog, a spear and some arrows will suffice—and the trouble is amicably ended. If the youth cannot even make the little presents, they both live for a certain period with the wife's family group, for which they must work until they have ransomed themselves, whereupon they return to the husband's group.

The anxiety of a family group not to lose such an important economic asset as a girl can be thoroughly appreciated, when one remembers that the standard of comfort of a group depends on the number of women who cater for it. The more women available, the more food.

Speaking of them in general, the pigmies are a monogamous race. From my knowledge of them I should say that only one per cent of the Bambuti is polygamous. That this should be so considering that they live in the midst of the polygamous negroes, seems very extraordinary. Doubtless the rough nomad existence of the pigmies induces greater continence in sex than we find among the negroes. This is, however, not the only explanation of their monogamy, and probably it is not the chief reason for it. Economic grounds would, more logically, account for it.

I have noticed that even in the few cases of polygamy among the Bambuti, there is no open evidence of it. One would never hear of such cases if one did not make inquiries. A polygamous pigmy continues to live in his own camp with one wife, while his other wife lives in another camp. This is always the case, save in places where the pigmies have succumbed to negro standards of life and morals.

The second wife of a polygamous pigmy has to live with her own family group because, I presume, no individual pigmy could sustain life if isolated from such protection. It might be inferred from what I have said, that a family group would deem it advantageous to itself to supply every one of its male members with several wives. Such is not the case, however, because there are no superfluous women among the pigmies, and, as all members of a family group have equal rights, one man cannot have two or more wives at the expense of other men, who must then remain wifeless. There are always the negroes, who frequently prefer to marry pigmy women. The result is frequently, as I saw among the Bafwaguda, that pigmy youths were unable to get wives. The negroes had snapped them all up.

There is yet another reason why it would not be to the interest of a family group to assist its members to get several wives. As I have already mentioned, the second wife continues to live in her parents' family group. The main family group would thereby have no economic advantage, and would take care not to give one of their own girls in exchange in connection with such a union.

While it is true that a woman becomes economically the property of the family group into which she marries, I have never seen anything savouring of communism of wives within such groups. I may mention, however, that the Efé pigmies informed me that misconduct with a woman on the part of one of her own family group does not entail such penalties as would be the case if he belonged to another family group—or, worse still, another clan. In the latter case the death penalty was inflicted formerly—either that or bloodshed ensued

between the family groups or clans, often culminating in
their mutual annihilation.

As I have already, said the woman does not sever connection with her parent group through her marriage.
Visits are frequent, and you would only need to observe
the beaming faces of the women, when one of their
group returns to them, to realize what intimate ties exist
between married women and the homes of their parents.
Her family group always holds a protecting hand over a
married woman, thereby ensuring that she is well treated
by her husband and his family group. Any insult, any
ill-treatment may be countered by the wife by running
away, because she knows well that she will be received
with open arms by her parent group. The group undertakes under such circumstances to reconsider the whole
issue of the marriage. It should not be inferred from this
that divorces are easily obtainable. Such a solution is
adopted very rarely and only in exceptional cases. The
" head for head " exchange system of marriage definitely
precludes any mere arbitrary sundering of a union, as the
other woman concerned has also something to say in the
matter. Her family group always tries in the first instance
to persuade the runaway wife to return to her husband.
As a rule she follows this advice. I think I am not
mistaken in my view that the links that bind family
groups together are, for the most part, stronger and more
lasting than those uniting the members of individual
families, and that, on the other hand, individual family
ties are strengthened by the marriage regulations between
family groups.

To prove this, let us take the second case I was called
upon to decide. It concerned Abiti, the celebrated
drummer of the Bafwaguda, who had for a long time been
begging me to use my influence to get him back his wife
who had left him.

When Abiti married his wife, who had previously
borne him a child, he gave his sister in exchange to the
Bafwasengwe. Abiti's sister subsequently died in childbirth, with the result that the Bafwasengwe demanded
the return of his wife to her parent family group. She
hearkened to the call and departed home to her family.
In accordance with pigmy code and custom, I decided

that Abiti should either give the Bafwasengwe another girl, or ransom his wife with gifts to them. The latter procedure alone was open to Abiti, as his family group at the moment had no marriageable girls at their disposal. Abiti immediately expressed his readiness to ransom his wife with gifts, with which the Bafwasengwe were eventually satisfied.

And now came another dispute for me to settle. Babali negroes, taking advantage of the helplessness of the Bambuti, had taken for themselves wives from their women folk without paying the purchase price. The pigmies demanded compensation. I insisted that the negroes should pay them the usual indemnification money. I was resolved as far as I could to check the bad habit the negroes had, of snapping up the Bambuti girls.

More complicated was the case of my friend " Policy," who was very annoyed, because for a long time he had failed to get a solution to his own love problem. It was only now that I learned all the details of his romance with Asangwa's daughter, who had become pregnant, and not for a negro, as I had been told previously. He could not marry her, however, as he could not offer her family group any girl of his own kith in exchange for her. He had, it is true, a marriageable half-sister, who lived with his stepmother among the Bafwasengwe. Strictly speaking, she belonged to the Bafwaguda, and to Policy's family group, as the child always follows the father in this matter. But, as frequently happens in cases of this kind, the mother took the girl with her and simply refused to part with her. Policy was in despair. At first he had been hoping that his sister would listen to his pleading that she would go with him and marry Asangwa's son. The girl hesitated for a while, but eventually obeyed her mother and stayed with her. The mother was really to blame for the trouble, as the girl was not disinclined, so Policy and others assured me, to marry the handsome, strapping youth. The tangle was still unsolved late in the evening, when the pigmies were already starting to dance in the village. Policy was beside me. I asked him where his sister was, and he pointed out a girl who was among the dancers. Stepping up to the little one I caught her by the hand, whereupon she screamed with

terror, as if a snake had bitten her. I had just started to
plead Policy's case with her, when a scolding woman
broke into the ring of dancers, gripped the girl by the
wrist and dragged her away. It was the girl's mother.
Exasperated by her rudeness I rushed forward, gave the
woman a gentle push, and brought the girl back. Policy
greeted his sister and led her to his group of friends.
After a little while I approached her again, and learned
with satisfaction that not only was she reconciled to the
prospect of going to the Bafwaguda camp to marry
Asangwa's son, but was quite eager to do so.

I was thoroughly satisfied with this denouement, and I
could see that the Bafwaguda were very grateful to me
for what I had done in the matter. The Bafwasengwe
and their patrons, the Babali negroes, who were always
out to exploit the Bafwaguda, were not so pleased with
me for my intervention.

Next morning the caravan set out to Avakubi. The
pigmies who had hitherto been my bearers stayed behind
and were replaced by Babali negroes. Scarcely twenty
minutes had elapsed after our leaving the village when
two Bambuti came rushing up to me with the Job's
tidings that the Bafwasengwe and the Babali had attacked
them and taken back again the women who had been
awarded to them the evening before.

As owing to the soreness of my feet I could only
manage to hobble along with difficulty, I sent Adzapori
back with my gun to settle the matter. It was only late
in the evening at our next halting place that he turned
up again and made his report. There had been another
fierce fight, he said, but he had succeeded in rescuing the
Bafwaguda, who afterwards had branched off by a
circuitous route towards the Asunguda camp, to prevent
the risk of being taken by surprise again.

With regard to another matter I had unsuccessful
negotiations with the Bafwasengwe. Following Alianga's
advice, I tried to persuade the elders to show me the
sacred utensils for the initiation of the youth into the
Mambela rites. The men deliberated with one another.
At one moment they were prepared to take me with
them, at the next fear got the better of them. They
pleaded that they were doomed to death if it were known

that they took me with them. Whether this was just a pretext to extort still bigger presents from me or real anxiety, I could not say, but at any rate I was weary of parleying with them, and said farewell.

Two days' march brought us to Avakubi, on the Ituri, which was the old headquarters of the Wangwana. On our way we neither saw nor heard of any kind of pigmy camps. It is possible that long ago pigmies might have lived in this region, and have trekked along with the negroes, because the place is so overrun with elephants that plantations are out of the question.

We next travelled to Kabura's village through derelict quarters of the Babeyru negroes, consisting, for the most part, of a few battered and tumble-down huts. At length our route swerved towards the south-west, and a dull roar, that momentarily increased in volume, smote our ears. The Ituri, the river of my dreams, gleamed through the dense growth of bush on its banks. Its mighty waters thundered majestically through the rapids. An excellent path, which sometimes led through plantations and villages, wound along the river bank towards Avakubi. We passed slowly through the village of Wangwana, built on sun-kissed rocks, crossed the bridge which led to the shady path among mango trees, passed the government buildings, and arrived at the mission house of Avakubi, which was surrounded with shady palms.

CHAPTER VI

ON THE BANKS OF THE ITURI

AVAKUBI! The very name, for me, had a ring of romance and mystery. Avakubi is not a mere station : it is the heart of the civilization of the entire primeval forest—at least so it was ten years ago. To-day it may be eclipsed by Wamba, which lies north of it, but which cannot compare with it, either for scenic or for historic association. Situated in the heart of the forest, Avakubi dates back to those days of horror and bloodshed when black slave traffic was rife.

Perched on the left bank of the Ituri, protected on the upper and lower reaches of that river by foaming rapids, it was a stronghold firmly buttressed by its environment. It was for this reason that the Wangwana, the notorious slave-hunters, the successors of the Zangabarites and the fanatical Mohammedans, had selected it. Indeed, from a strategic point of view, no outpost in the Ituri forest region equalled it in bygone days. To-day, however, it has lost much of its pristine glory, chiefly owing to the decline of the Wangwana themselves. Of course, they are still, numerically speaking, a force in Avakubi, but their days of power and their martial prowess are long past. Venereal disease is sapping them, and, as their race can no longer acquire new life from the blood of the quondam serfs, they are doomed to extinction.

During my stay of several months by the Ituri, Avakubi made an excellent headquarters for me. The missionaries were not only very friendly towards me, giving me many valuable hints, and making things as easy as possible for me, but owing to its position in the very heart of the forest, their mission was an ideal centre for dropping into, as I frequently did, to store my belongings and the specimens I collected. The numerous negro tribes, all

with varied local characteristics, whose villages were
situated in a ring around the station, were comparatively
easy of access, as well as the numerous hordes of pigmies,
who were attached to every village, particularly to the
east and north.

Babali to the west, Bandaka to the east and Babeyru
to the south, encircled Avakubi. Approximately a three
days' march to the south-west brings one right into the
heart of the Babira tribe, while with a five days' journey
northwards you come to the Wabundu. Not to mention
the hordes of Bambuti, who are the most interesting
people in the Ituri forest, the explorer finds a host of
novel attractions in this region.

The vast tracts of virgin forest, which surround them
on all sides, have so thoroughly protected the natives
against European influences that one comes upon tribes
that are utterly unspoiled in their old-world primitiveness.

This tract of the Ituri forest has an added interest
from the fact that it is a kind of central basin, in which all
types of the most varied stocks meet, including the Medje-
Mamvu and Balese forest-dwellers from the north-east.

In this comparatively small area I found converging
representatives of all the main languages of Africa. A
salient of the Bantu, who live to the south of Avakubi,
has been driven northward, and their vanguard, the
Babira-Bakumu, have advanced along a seven-hundred-
mile front into the forest, from Stanleyville to Lake
Albert. They are far more primitive than the Banande,
who are now absorbed by the eastern Bantu, the last-
named having overrun them completely in the Beni
region on the verge of the forest.

To the north of the Babira, numerous tribes, closely
resembling the Bantu, surround Avakubi. They have
come, in many ways, under the influence of the northern
Sudanese tribes. These Sudanese tribes have penetrated
mainly in a south-easterly direction into the forest
region, and their vanguard, the Babeyru, have driven a
wedge, the Bantori clan and the Babira, to the station
of Makala.

In the east we have the Mamvu–Balese, a branch with
a peculiar dialect of their own, and bordering on them

are the Nilotes, whose teeming numbers spread to the very edge of the forest.

We are not dealing just now with the customs and morals of these negro tribes, but with the pigmies who are dotted throughout this extensive area, everywhere alike in their main characteristics, yet everywhere with distinct local traits. Racially they are all alike as one egg is to another, but in customs and in speech they are always strongly influenced by their negro patrons, and hence the extraordinary divergences of language among the scattered pigmy stocks.

Although, broadly speaking, the pigmies are racially similar, one can clearly discern two distinct types of facial formation among them. You find some of them with shapely oval faces and abnormally broad brows, while others are relatively round-faced. In both types the brow is rather prominent, and stands out like a ball over the huge indeterminate nose, devoid of bridge and with wide nostril wings. The most unique trait of the pigmy face, however, and one common to both types, is the wide expanse between the eyes.

I had not been quite two days in Avakubi when a horde of pigmies from the other side of the river turned up to greet the " Baba wa Bambuti." And this was not the only gang that visited me, for my name was now familiar to pigmies in remote regions of the forest which I had not touched. As at the moment I had a great deal of business of all sorts to look after, these intermittent visits were frequently extremely inopportune. However, I had to make the best of it, even though it meant considerable waste of time.

I was particularly keen on measuring the physical proportions of the pigmies and getting a clue to their vagaries of dialect. I had paid always for my information with salt and tobacco, which never failed to make the little fellows very communicative. An unpleasant feature of their visits was the retinue of negroes that usually accompanied them. Negro patrons always thought they were conferring a great favour on me by rounding up their vassal pigmies and dumping them before me at their own sweet will. And although my interest in the Bambuti had not waned, I often felt that it would be a great relief to me if none of them showed up for a few days. I had called up ghosts from the forest, and could not lay them.

There was a market held in Avakubi on certain fixed days every week. Among the long ranks of half-naked women, who, with their backs laden with heavy baskets full of bananas, panted along the forest tracks to the market, I saw some strange tiny golden-brown creatures, who, as soon as they caught a glimpse of the " white man," suddenly dived sideways into the undergrowth with their loads. They were Bambuti women and girls, who were carrying produce to the market for their patrons, for which service they would be paid with food supplies in the usual way. After my experience among the Bafwaguda, I was astonished at this dread of me. I had found that pigmies can gradually become accustomed to such a queer thing as a white man, and can overcome their proverbial shyness with regard to him. I also found it strange that I could not induce any of the Bafwaguda pigmies to accompany me to Bafwasengwe.

I undertook two minor journeys of exploration from Avakubi with the object of confirming my impression about the linguistic versatility of the Bambuti of that region. Although the missionaries paid no appreciable attention to the Bambuti, as they were fully occupied with the teeming negro population, they had a fairly good idea as to the whereabouts of their camping grounds, for they frequently met them during their travels. Father Faszbender had an unpleasant recollection of the little men. Once when he was travelling with his caravan through the forest to the nearest village, their arrows whizzed around his head, and he was forced to abandon his journey and return home. The reason of this ambush by the Bambuti was never discovered.

So far no Christian missionaries have made serious efforts to approach the Bambuti. Two years ago three pigmies, who have since died, were baptized in Avakubi. Their baptism was the outcome of a misunderstanding. At any rate the difficulties that missionaries who try to convert the pigmies have to encounter, are almost insuperable. This is not due to any preconceived pre-judices whatsoever on the part of the pigmies against

Christianity—it is merely the result of their ways of life and their mental make-up. If missionaries made any serious efforts to adjust themselves to the nomad existence of the Bambuti, they would have to face hardships with which no European constitution could cope. On the other hand any attempt to make the pigmies settle down in definite patches of land would, in my opinion, imperil the existence of their race. They are still, to-day, in their inmost fibre, wanderers ; they are just forest gypsies, ever spurred onward by an insatiable wanderlust bequeathed to them by their remote ancestors. They have, since time immemorial, become accustomed to a humble standard of comfort and to the casualness of their daily round of existence.

Sometimes I mentally compare the happy-go-lucky, improvident and casual pigmies with the tribes of forest negroes, agricultural folk who have penetrated into the heart of the inhospitable undergrowth. They came equipped with the experience acquired in their previous environment ; they were acquainted with the devices for exploiting nature, and all they had to do was to adapt themselves to their new surroundings. And they never rested until they forced the forest wilderness to do their bidding. They became acclimatized to their new environment, and evolved into forest peasants.

Not so pigmies, who for thousands of years have wandered at the behest of sheer hunger in small gangs, probably only in family groups, through the gloomy virgin forest. Owing to their unsettled life they never knew what leisure meant, and their scattered gangs were too small to do battle with the forest with their clumsy primitive implements. Yet they did not absolutely submit to the cruelty of nature in the raw. Even they refused to descend to the level of the beasts, which live on what they can seize with their teeth as they shuffle along. The intelligence of the pigmies led them a step higher in the scale of life. It enabled them to invent implements for the purpose of gathering the produce of the forest with greater ease and in more abundance. It aided them in discovering weapons to kill game at a distance, poison to slay fierce animals with tiny arrows, and fire to make meat and fruit more palatable and digestible. But in the main the pigmies have ever dwelt and ever will dwell under the spell of the forest, and are forced by it to wander to and fro, to hunt game and seek new sites where roots and edible vegetables abound. And so the Bambuti remain to this day children of the wild, primitive creatures in the strictest sense of the word.

It seems exceedingly strange that the pigmies who have lived so long with the more civilized negro peasants have not imitated them, and improved their standard of living. There is no insuperable external force that prevents their doing so. It is my view that the pigmies have become so thoroughly accustomed to the method of existence which they have had to lead for centuries, when fighting absolutely on their own against cruel elemental forces, that it has become second nature to them, and that, even if they were inclined to do so, they are temperamentally unable to settle down. And yet, we can see indications that by systematic, slow and patient endeavour perhaps even here at least a partial improvement might be produced, and that if a mission were definitely established for the purpose of bringing these little fellows in closer touch with civilization, it would probably prove successful.

Their nomad life and haphazard outlook have left a permanent impression on the mentality of the pigmies. They completely lack the power of introspection, and they are very easily affected by the varying external influences with which they are constantly brought in contact in their nomad existence. Moreover, they have no organization to enable them to assemble in large numbers—and this is absolutely essential as a preliminary to any kind of mass instruction. In conversation they quickly become weary, listless and absent-minded. Sitting on a school bench would be the very acme of agony to these temperamental little folk. And for this reason a mission sent among them to convert them to Christianity or to civilize them would encounter extraordinary obstacles.

Physically, as well as mentally, the pigmies form a distinct race on our planet ; they are definitely specimens of the " dawn " man. It is absolutely absurd to regard the forest pigmies of Africa or Asia as degenerate types of a primitive race, who were driven from more congenial surroundings into the crude environment of the wilderness, and gradually shedding all traces of their former civilization, became atrophied both in body and soul. Experience teaches us that quite the contrary is the case. Take, for instance, the negro peasants we referred to just recently. They adapted themselves so thoroughly to the conditions of the forest that they became the masters of the wilderness—in short, they not only succeeded in doing this, but they retained the culture acquired from their ancestors, even in the crude environment of the forest. And even apart from all this there are absolutely no grounds for the assumption that the Bambuti are a degenerate race.

My first journey from Avakubi, which kept me away from that station for ten days, was upstream. The Ituri, which the Bakango call the Itiri, runs through the heart of the forest from its source to its estuary. One gets the impression that it feeds the forest. A strange aroma of romance hangs around its banks. Fierce and turbulent in its upper reaches, where it is known as the Ituri, in its lower reaches, where the negroes call it the Lohali, or sometimes the Aruwini—a name given to it by Stanley in error, it is a wild roaring torrent, which, swollen to colossal size at Basoko, pours its waters into the Congo or Lualaba. The Bambuti are to be found all along the region where it is called the Ituri, but no pigmies live nowadays on the banks of the Lohali.

Though muffled by the heavy foliage of the forest, the thunder of the river is heard from a very considerable distance before one approaches it, and gives one an impression of its might and its magic. Near Avakubi there are numerous rapids, and the seething foam of the tumbling masses of water floats down-stream for hundreds of yards. Mud-tinged wreaths of spray languidly dancing on the sluggish waters constantly warn you of the vicinity of a waterfall before you hear its thunder. The Ituri is a treacherous stream and thousands of boats and men have perished in its swirling cascades. A pigmy will never venture out in a boat on its waves, and negroes and white men will only trust themselves on its surface when experienced Wagenia boatmen, who know the Ituri as well as they know their own sleepy village on its banks, take the helm.

Sometimes we walked, sometimes we cycled along the well-trodden path, skirting by which, sixty years previously, gangs of slaves travelled past Pengi towards Mawambi-Irumu or Beni. It is to-day just as it was in those far-off days, comfortable for walking, but in parts impassable for the cyclist.

Kero, a Bandaka village, was our first halting place, where Father de Leest, who accompanied me on this trip, offered me very comfortable quarters in the mission school. Kero lies on the elevated northern bank of the river. From it one gets a splendid view of the famous Kero cascade, which thunders and roars eternally, and can only be crossed when the river is in full spate after heavy rain.

The negro teacher in this station, a Munande from Beni, gifted with a vein of humour, told me of the whimsical fate that had torn him many years previously from his home, and after many perilous adventures, gave him a peaceful anchorage at last in the Avakubi mission. His vast fund of information about the Bambuti of the outlying territories and the Beni pigmies, which he generously placed at my disposal, proved extremely helpful to me in following up my research work.

On the same afternoon that we reached Kero the first hordes of pigmies came marching in. There were in all three clans, each led by its patron. What a bizarre outfit! The roll of drums and singing heralded from afar the approach of the pigmies. Then there appeared a flag of multi-coloured check design, borne by a Mombuti at the head of the procession. It definitely was not the Belgian flag, but what it was supposed to represent I have not the faintest idea. I suppose it was carried at the instigation of the negroes, who had a mania for imitating European ways.

Next morning over a hundred pigmies, both men and women, swarmed round me—sufficient material to make an excellent film. Unfortunately they made a louder din than I ever heard before in any market place in Africa. The Kero-Bambuti were in every respect, even in their speech, exactly like the Bakango, although they had absolutely no intimate dealings with the latter. In conjunction with the groups who lived farther up-stream they formed a league, whose name I could not discover. As a rule they either referred to themselves as Bambuti, or Basua, for short, or they gave the name of their clan. It was out of the question at the moment to make any closer inquiries with regard to this region, as in addition to the Bambuti the entire population of the village as well as numerous negroes from the vicinity surrounded our dwelling.

A fair, to the accompaniment of song and dance and unspeakable clamour, was in full swing. Again and again the pigmies stepped forth in measured tread into the fierce glare of the foreground, to vanish momentarily into the shade of the trees or of the overhanging roofs of the negro huts. I devoted my attention chiefly to recording measurements for my anthropological inquiries, and to taking photographs, as the constantly emerging and disappearing figures and faces were excellent pabulum for my camera. I was particularly struck by a very tiny emaciated dwarf, four feet four and a half inches in height, with a long pointed oval face. His body seemed on the verge of collapsing beneath the weight of his massive head. He was not a child, neither was he a freak. On the contrary, he was a genuine normal pigmy. My camera riveted its cyclopean eye hungrily on him. When I picked him out at last, close by a negro hut, he promptly crouched against the wall. My camera came nearer and nearer to him, for I was resolved to get as good a " close-up " of him as I could manage. The closer my apparatus came towards his saddle-nose, the greater was the panic of the terrified Agomu. His eye rigidly focussed on the lens, he dodged, now to the left, now to the right, to get out of the range of the horrible white eye of the camera. Round about stood grinning negroes who punched him and yelled at him, when in a sudden paroxysm of terror he tried to break away. They kept shouting at him not to be afraid and laughed heartily at him. Sweat ran from every pore of Agomu's face and body, and there was a look of mortal terror in his eyes. But for all that he kept up a constant unconvincing, quavering protest as he dodged furtively to right and left : " I am not afraid ! I am not afraid ! " My camera clicked. Agomu was indemnified for his spell of mortal terror with a piece of

BASA PIGMIES HAVING GOT IN TOUCH WITH CIVILISATION

FATHER AND SON WITH BOW AND ARROW

CHILDREN OF A NEGRO FATHER AND A
PIGMY MOTHER

AGOMU PRESENTS ME WITH A CAPTIVE BABY
ANTELOPE

(*Page* 143)

cotton, with which he immediately wiped the sweat from his face. Then he vanished among the dancers. I really think that the ordeal he went through made the poor little fellow give me a wide berth, for the time being at all events, because he never showed up the next day. I inquired about him from some of his friends, who said that he had gone hunting.

Two days later, however, Agomu put in an appearance again, accompanied by his entire family group. He presented me with a live baby antelope, for which I gave him another piece of cotton. And now I was about to take his measurement, when once more he started to dodge from side to side, and again beads of perspiration stood out on his brow. I did all I could to put him at his ease, but to no avail.

During our midday meal Agomu was an object of envy to all the negroes and Bambuti around, when they saw him squatting on the ground close by our table, nursing a large plate of rice and meat. How the tiny chap chewed his food, smacked his lips and cast a self-satisfied look all around him, full of pride because he had been permitted to sit with the " Azugu " (white man). With a patronizing air he handed the remnants of his meat course to his comrades, and tucked into the sweet. His brothers and comrades got none of the tinned apricots. As far as he was concerned they might die there and then of sheer envy. Agomu licked the inside of the tin thoroughly, wiped his mouth a few times with the palm of his hand, and looked up at me with inquisitive eyes. And now we gave him wine, sweet Samos wine which I only produced on special occasions. Agomu seemed to appreciate its bouquet, and cast a sidelong greedy glance at me to see if there was any more forthcoming. When he realized, however, that we had all finished our meal, he arose looking quite contented. The whole camp, old and young alike, swarmed round him admiringly. He was the hero of the day.

Early next morning I said farewell to Father de Leest and to Kero, and struck inland towards Makutambiri. I cycled ahead along the forest track, my camera following in the rear. Suddenly a little man trailing a big hen behind him, dived out of the undergrowth right ahead of me. The ringing of my bell made him leap nimbly to one side. It was Agomu—my new friend. He looked up at me with a puzzled expression.

" Where are you going with the hen ? " I inquired as I dismounted.

" Io iako " (it is for you) answered the pigmy, his eyes full of fear. Whether it was my bicycle or my sudden encounter with him in this solitude that terrified him, I cannot say.

When I explained to him that I could not possibly tie the hen to my bicycle, he volunteered to follow me to Makutambiri. And then he ran after my bicycle, swinging the hen pitilessly to and fro. In Makutambiri he handed me the half-dead bird, which he no doubt had stolen from some negro village. To what lengths a pigmy will go to show his gratitude to a friend ! I gave him a jungle knife in recognition of his present.

There was a great dance in Makutambiri. The pigmies had again streamed in from the surrounding districts to greet me. Agomu beat the drum with such zest and kept such perfect time that the dancers swayed and swirled in a delirium of rhythm. He seemed to act under a spell, pounding the drum skin with frenzy, and yelling to the full capacity of his lungs, his huge mouth so abnormally agape that it seemed in danger of splitting from ear to ear. And ever and anon he would rub an arm with lightning speed across his face to brush off the dripping perspiration, while he kept hopping from one foot to the other. This was his farewell performance. Never again did I see this prince of Bambuti drummers, whose technique was considered by some to be superior to Abiti's.

The Bambuti in this region were somewhat reserved and uncommunicative. They were, however, by no means nervous of me, which struck me as somewhat strange considering that this was the first time they saw me. I noticed this especially when I was measuring the physical proportions of the men and women. There were just a few individuals who looked somewhat terrified as I put the measuring tape around their heads, but even they stuck it out. A few, however, refused to submit to the operation at all.

In Kero a young self-conscious pigmy brought a com-

plaint before me against the negroes. He announced
himself as the chief of his clan ; whether such was really
the case I could not find out definitely. However, he was
the spokesman of a group, who stood by in silence. Formerly, he said, their liberty was not hampered in any
way, but at the present time every Bandaka chief thought
he was entitled to abuse them and to impose all kinds of
tasks and burdens on them, which they never had to
perform in the past. They would not put up with such a
state of things any longer, he went on. They wanted to
live as freely as their fathers had lived. In conclusion he
begged me to aid them in attaining their rights.

The young man was referring to the enforced labour
which the negroes imposed on the pigmies—tasks such as
road-cleaning, which was the negro's own special job.

Unfortunately all I could do was to report his complaint
to the proper authorities, as I had absolutely no influence
in this region to secure the redress he requested. I must
say, however, that I was very much impressed by the
candid, manly bearing of the young fellow.

I had the pleasure in Makutambiri of supplying the
pigmies with meat, as my excellent hunter always brought
in a very good bag. He had to requisition sixteen pigmies
to fetch a wild boar from the forest to the village. And
yet within the space of an hour this colossal carcase was
divided among a hundred Bambuti who had assembled.

There were also about a hundred Bambuti in the
neighbouring Bandaka village, which was ruled by the
chief, Kaitschui. As all these pigmies bore a general
resemblance to the Bakango on the Asunguda, there was
no reason for tarrying among them. Consequently I
turned further inland, and crossed the southern bank of
the river, where I waited for the pigmies in the huge
settlement over which the chief, Kayumba, held sway.
Kayumba, a great hunter and a pasha who owned an
extensive harem, was away in quest of game when I
arrived, and I had to await his return. Kayumba, I may
mention, is a Mohammedan, like his neighbour, Kaitschui
—Mohammedanism, incidentally, is the cachet of the
superman along the upper reaches of the Ituri. A mighty
chief he was, and nobody had any right to move hand or
foot in his domain without his consent. After I had

K

waited for a considerable time, the great chief came along in his sedan chair. Later in the evening the pigmies came trailing in.

The skill of the pigmies as linguists impressed me very much. Some of them spoke Kibango (Kibira), while others spoke Kilese, the language of the far-off north-eastern region on the other bank of the Ituri. Of course there were also just a few Mombuti in Avakubi who could speak Kilese. The versatility of the pigmies of Kayumba was also shown in the wide range of melody which their songs exhibited. This characteristic I noticed especially in their performances on the flute, of which I took gramophone records. Their extensive musical repertoire is probably due to the influence of the negro tribes, the Balese and the Babira. Speaking generally, I noticed that all pigmy songs and dances, in all parts of the Congo forest region, have definite common characteristics which keep recurring and which mark their individuality.

I heard repeatedly from negroes that these Bambuti were inveterate hemp-smokers, but I think this is a gross exaggeration. Of course there can be no doubt that some of them occasionally smoke hemp, although during my long stay among them I only saw one of them do so. Perhaps they do it in secret in the negro villages where they can buy the hemp.

Banana beer and palm wine (malofu) are both either prepared or procured by the negroes exclusively. The pigmies very rarely get an opportunity of indulging in either beverage, and, when they do, it is only in very small quantities. Now and then I have noticed intoxicated pigmies, but I have never seen even one stupidly drunk. Quite the reverse has been my experience with regard to the negroes. I may remark, however, that I think that the pigmy's temperance is due merely to lack of opportunity. The pigmy has an absolute craving for tobacco, and will greedily swallow any banana beer or malofu that comes his way.

I had reached the goal of my journey when I arrived at Kayumba's village, and I returned down-stream to Avakubi in a huge canoe, which with his oarsmen, the negro chief had placed at my disposal. After the baggage had been taken ashore, we shot the Kero waterfall in our

canoe. But no boat ever ventures to face the second
waterfall, and neither did ours. The inhabitants of the
village are bound to fetch the baggage to a spot at the
base of the roaring, foaming cascade, where other boats
are ready to do the rest of the journey. It was late at
night when we reached Avakubi.

My next excursion was to the camp of the Bambuti
dwelling by the River Ngayu, which flows into the Ituri
below Avakubi. The Ngayu is a small, but sinister
tributary stream. At one of its cascades, which has a
sheer drop of three hundred feet, spray, foam and spume
shoot high up into the air. Its steep canyon-like banks
are the most awe-inspiring that I have seen in the Congo
forest. They have a striking resemblance to those of the
Ibiena, a tributary stream which joins the Lenda above
Kayumba's village, and flows into the Ituri on the left.
One might say that along its entire coast the Ngayu is a
" pigmy " river ; along its upper reaches the Efé live,
while pigmies similar to the Bakango in appearance dwell
along its lower banks. The Ngayu pigmies are neighbours
of the Bakango of the Asunguda and the Apare, but they
are separated from them by the Ituri. In speech and in
customs they are allied, but they are more in touch with
the Kero pigmies, as they have the same patrons, the
Bandaka, while the Bakango are attached to the Babali.

In Ischumi's village I pitched my camp for some days
in order to study the Balenga, an offshoot of the Bandaka,
with Ischumi as their chief. A pompous negro chief,
proud of the warlike tribe over which he held sway, a
firm upholder of his ancestral code and customs, Ischumi
was an exact replica in every respect of the great Munza,
the ruler of the Azande, whose praise Shweinfurth sang
when he met him decades ago during the course of his
expedition. Ischumi's pigmies lived at the end of the
negro plantation ; their huts stood on the forest verge,
facing the blazing tropical sun. Nowhere did I find the
subjection of the pigmies to the negroes so marked as I
did in this place, where they were virtually serfs of the
great negro chief, and by serfs I mean serfs in the real
sense of the word. They lived in the chief's plantation,
and provided his household, which consisted of twelve
women and seventeen children, with game. The Bambuti

chief was an aged, emaciated little man, who looked a
real dwarf as he stood beside fat Ischumi. Ischumi
strutted about girt with spear and shield, his towering
headgear adorned with boar's teeth. The little old
Bambuti had a rush cap adorned with feathers, and his
withered little hand grasped a bow and arrow. A funny
pair they looked as they stood close together, lord and
vassal, the tiny, restless, skinny little nomad hunter and
the heavy, corpulent peasant and warrior chief.

This aged little chief told me that the Bambuti were
driven from the east towards the west, and then had to
trek back again, until finally they settled in their present
location.

I had repeatedly heard that the Bambuti and Bandaka,
in contrast with the Bakango of Asunguda, used to hunt
with nets. Here in Ischumi's realm and later in Majalla,
I found this statement to be true, and I even saw the
hunting nets. A considerable number of the pigmies
know nothing about this method of hunting ; many
authorities, on the other hand, including the majority of
the little people, contend that it originated among them,
and that they taught it to the forest negroes. It is
significant that the negroes themselves attribute the
discovery of net-hunting to the pigmies, and it is the
pigmies who make the nets from liana coils, which they
twist into thin cords. The nets are about thirty feet long
and three feet high.

According to reliable statements by pigmy elders their
ancestors neither used nets nor bows and arrows. Their
original method of hunting was a rounding-up, in which
the entire camp, men, women and children, took part.
They all set out together ; the men, armed only with
cudgels and torches, formed a long ring, and hidden
behind trees and bushes waited for the quarry. The rest
of the crowd, mainly composed of women and children,
went ahead and formed a huge semicircular cordon, which
then closed in, and yelled and beat the bushes and trees
in order to drive the terrified brute towards the line of
hunters, who hurled their torches at it to blind it, and
then dispatched it with their cudgels.

The modern net-hunting is based on a similar plan,
with this difference, that long nets are substituted for

READY FOR NET-HUNTING
(*Page 148*)

SUSPENSION BRIDGE OVER THE NGAYU

ISCHUMI, THE BALENGA CHIEF, AND HIS PIGMY VASSAL

Page 148)

blazing torches. You rarely see clubs in the hunters'
hands ; they generally use short spears. Women and
children act as beaters, while the men take cover in the
bushes behind the nets. One net is joined to another, and
as sometimes anything from ten to twenty nets may be
used, according to the number of hunters, a long composite net may run into the length of several hundred
yards. It is fastened at the top and bottom to branches,
so that the quarry that runs into it gets immediately
enmeshed. And at this point out steps the hunter. If
he has to deal with a baby antelope, he extricates it alive,
and pinions its legs with liana. Big antelopes and wild
pigs are despatched with spears or very occasionally clubs.
I have frequently noticed at these hunts that antelopes
get scared at the last moment, wheel round and break
through the cordon of beaters. Sometimes the hunt ends
in bloodshed, if by chance a leopard runs into the net.
This happens, however, very rarely.

It was from Ischumi's pigmies, too, that I first heard the
word " Okapi " ; the Bambuti pronounce it " Okwapi,"
with the accent on the last syllable. The word belongs to
the dialect of the Efé pigmies, in whose territory those
animals are most plentiful. This timid creature of the
giraffe family is not so scarce in the Ituri forest as might
seem on casual observation. It lives in remote and
inaccessible places, and shuns the vicinity of human
habitations and forest paths. It prefers the hilly region
in the heart of the forest ; consequently it is unknown
along the Asunguda and the Apare, where the land is flat.
It is found, on the other hand, in the region of the Ngayu
and in the hunting grounds of the Efé and the Babira-
Bambuti. Isolated squads of pigmies spend several days
at a stretch trailing the creature, and hunt it with bows
and arrows. From the large number of okapi girdles one
sees worn, it may be concluded that the shy little animal
is frequently tracked to its lone retreat. The Bandaka
negroes call it " Ndumbe," and catch it in pits, which
they dig deep in the heart of the forest.

At every halting-place during my Ngayu journey I
encountered numerous hordes of pigmies. On one icy
cold morning at dawn my caravan left Ischumi's village
for the nearest Bandaka village, which was approximately

a five days' journey distant. Our route lay through a stretch of the darkest and most sinister-looking forest land that I ever saw in the Congo. We passed a gang of negroes, who, under the guidance of a white man, were constructing a motor-track through the forest, and descended a slope into a stretch of woodland which was momentarily getting darker and darker. The path was loamy and slippery, and cold rain dripped steadily from the trees. In short, it was the most dismal weather one could imagine for a forest trip.

A few Bandaka and pigmy women, who some days previously had brought up provisions for the road-makers, attached themselves to our caravan, which now consisted exclusively of Wangwana men, in order to get back to their homes.

Depressed and only speaking in monosyllables, we jogged along through the quagmire, until at length the path followed rising ground, and we began to feel a somewhat firmer grip for our feet. The little troop of about five or six women—four of them pigmies, that walked right behind me, started a melancholy sing-song. It was a sort of litany in the Bandaka dialect of which I did not understand a word, and it fascinated me by its persistent monotony. I was just listening to the tune, when a pigmy behind me whispered : " Muzungu, do you understand what they are singing ? " I caught the word " Asobe," which cropped up again and again in the chorus. One of the women sang alone for a bit, and then the rest joined in the chorus. The song lasted for a very long time. When it ended I asked what it was about. Apparently the precentor always kept varying the same theme in different tones. She kept calling " Asobe " (God) to protect them and see them safely home. The gist of the song was that morning had come, and that if God protected them against all harm during the day, they would reach their village in safety.

This primitive, sincere and simple morning song chanted in such a desolate elemental environment, impressed me very much. From a psychological point of view, I could appreciate the emotion which prompted the song. There they were—just a mere handful of tiny women, alone and unprotected, travelling through the gloomy dripping forest with utter strangers, most of whom belonged to the dreaded Wangwana tribe. It was a situation calculated to stimulate an eerie feeling!

Thus we plodded along, our feet slipping every now and then on greasy patches, while occasionally the tired moan of a bearer as he shifted his burden from one shoulder to another, smote our ears. The only people we encountered were a gang of women and children, some of them frail little creatures, who panted under heavy loads of bananas, and gave our caravan a very wide berth. A black policeman wearing a red cap and swinging a rhinoceros whip, accompanied the gang and snarled out his commands. There was not a single negro woman among the group, although the onus of supplying the road-makers with provisions had been undertaken by the negroes alone. But in the Congo forest, as elsewhere, it is the strong man's fist that rules, and, when he can, he will make his weaker brother carry his burden.

As the weather improved, so did our spirits. After a few hours the sun shone again and gleamed through the tree-tops. The village with its extensive plantation nestled in the brilliant sunshine, as our caravan emerged from the forest. When they came within view of their camping ground, the spirits of my Wangwana bearers became exuberant, and they sang their marching songs, the same songs to which decades before the great slave gangs marched through the dark forest tracks.

Accompanied by the pigmies and a few negroes from the village, I branched off the same day to see the Ngayu waterfall, which is the theme of many eerie legends. Its waters fall some ninety feet down beetling crags, over which hangs an eternal misty drizzle, spanned by exquisitely beautiful rainbows, where the sun gleams through the haze. My companions halted in terror at the verge of the forest, and would not venture to look into the abyss, in which, so the legend runs, gigantic snakes lurk and drag down into the seething waters anyone who dares to approach too near. And so I had to go alone to take a film of this magnificent phenomenon, getting thoroughly drenched in the process. The Bambuti and the negroes, both of whom are equally superstitious, attributed my escape from destruction in the coils of the monstrous snakes to the mere fact that I was a white man. The snakes they speak of with such terror are the rainbows, and according to the legend, they get ample supplies of meat, rice and bananas to glut their insatiable appetites.

In the village I met a negro who was married to a Mombuti woman who had already presented him with four children, and who remained loyal to him and carefully attended to his banana plantation. I never met a negro so loud in praise of his pigmy wife. The tendency with a great many of the little nomad wives is to weary of the village life after a few months—maybe weeks, and then to vanish for days or weeks at a stretch. The nostalgia for the nomad life and their own folk is too much for them.

As housekeepers most pigmy women are not nearly as adept and neat as negresses. Many negroes have two wives—a pigmy for child-bearing purposes, and a childless woman of their own race to run the home.

I had already read a great deal about perilous elephant hunts by pigmies, and had heard European colonists tell blood-curdling tales about the courage with which the little fellows tackled those monsters. Consequently, I was all the more surprised to hear from the Bakango themselves that they never hunted elephants. The reason was that they had no spears, and their arrows were absolutely useless for attacking the thick-hided brutes.

When I came to Ischumi, however, the chief told me that my impression that pigmies never hunted elephants was incorrect. Some of the Bambuti, he said, were expert elephant killers. He added that in Majalla, my last stopping-place on that trip, I would meet those hunters of big game.

I found that there are two ways of attacking elephants in the Congo. The negroes slay him from a distance with spears, while the little pigmies, also using spears, pluckily come to close quarters with their quarry.

The Efé pigmies, whose territory stretches from Majalla inland towards Baleseland as far as the steppes in the east, when elephant hunting, use short spears about four or five feet long, with strong heavy heads fitted into the shafts and made fast with cord. Every hunter has his own spear, which he treasures with the greatest care. Frequently the negroes force the Bambuti to take the initiative in the battle with elephants. Incidentally I wish to point out that the negroes appropriate for themselves the greater part of the carcass and the valuable ivory tusks in every case, while the pigmies, who have to take most of the risks, just get a pot of beer, some bananas and perhaps a piece of cloth when the chase is ended. They are lucky if they also get a few scraps of elephant meat. In the course of my wanderings through the forest I have seen negro villages whose inhabitants had grown enormously rich from the proceeds of sales of ivory to European dealers.

On the eve of an elephant hunt all the women in the camp hold a magic dance, in the course of which they squirt water from their mouths with a view to bringing luck to the hunters.

At early dawn the hunters have a silent, hurried meal, pack up some provisions, mainly consisting of bananas, and, equipped with spears, start for the forest on the trail of the elephants. Usually they go in batches of two or three, and they spend days at a stretch in their quest. As soon as they see fresh elephant dung, they smear themselves with it, to camouflage their own particular stench from the pachyderms.

Cautiously and noiselessly they dodge among the giant trees until they see their prey. Then one of them steals up as close as he can to the monster, and using both hands, aims at the knee-joint of one of its back legs, and in a flash leaps back into the shelter of the undergrowth. Maddened with pain, the elephant emits its fierce trumpeting cry, and is just starting in pursuit of its fleeing assailant, when another hunter sneaks up behind it and drives his spear through the knee-joint of its other back leg. If the second spear has struck home, the elephant collapses, as its leg sinews have been cut through.

And now the pigmies approach the wounded brute cautiously, and hack off its trunk, thereby causing it to bleed to death. Then they start off for the camp, and also send tidings to the negro village. Negroes and pigmies are around the dead elephant with lightning speed, hack the carcass to pieces, and return to the village, when a great feast is held. The programme starts with an elephant dance by the Bambuti, while the negroes hand round copious draughts of beer and palm wine. Then the feast starts, and the elephant trunk is eaten by the negroes and grown-up pigmies. Children and pregnant women are debarred from this delicacy.

The hunters keep the elephant's tail hairs for themselves, and treasure them with superstitious awe. I recollect on one occasion the loud protests that were made when I ventured to ask for a few of the hairs as souvenirs. The hunter was doomed who gave away those hairs, I was told. He ran imminent risk of being trampled to death by an elephant the next time he encountered one.

A potent charm against hunting fatalities is made with these hairs. They are always burned to ashes, which are then smeared around the region of the heart and stomach of the hunter. On no account must the hairs be kept until the next hunt. If they are, the elephant will avenge its brother's death and kill the hunter.

The method of elephant-hunting I have just described is an extremely risky one. Despite the extraordinary agility and the splendid marksmanship of the pigmies, they sometimes miss their aim, or do not get clear of the stampeding brutes in time. In many camps I have heard of numerous cases where the hunters were pounded to pulp under the feet of wounded elephants. Hence the anxiety of the superstitious little fellows to protect themselves with magic balms and amulets against the risk of such a dreadful death.

Father de Leest, who had rendered first-aid to a pigmy hunter who narrowly escaped being killed by an elephant some years ago, gave me a vivid account of the incident. Two Bambuti, armed with spears, had for hours been trailing an elephant which they had just wounded, up hill and down dale, when suddenly the animal became infuriated and charged them. One of the pigmies fled in terror, but the other stood his ground and dodged the elephant, and proceeded to stalk it again ; when he got it within range, he aimed his spear at the brute's back leg, missed his aim and tripped. Immediately the

elephant pounced upon the sprawling pigmy and tried to
gore him with his tusks. The Bambuti, however, with
great presence of mind, gripped a hold of one of the tusks
and climbed up along it. The elephant swung the little
fellow to and fro a few times, and then suddenly hurled
him into the air. The pigmy landed on the bough of a
tree with his belly ripped open. But he did not give himself up for lost. He waited until the elephant had gone
by, managed to scramble down from the tree and, while
pressing back his protruding entrails, dragged himself to
the nearest village, where Father de Leest happened to
be. The missionary stitched the wound with ordinary
thread, and made bandages out of newspapers, as nothing else was available. Ten days later the pigmy was
running about again, perfectly restored to health. Yet
both he and his comrades thought the wound had taken
a terribly long time to heal! But then, the pigmies are
an extremely tough race, with tremendous powers of
resistance and recuperation.

It was the second type of elephant-hunting is practised by
the Babira Bambuti on the left bank of the Ituri. They
use longer spears, like harpoons. The spear-heads are
fixed loosely in the shaft, and they are either indented, or
provided with barbs like fish-hooks, and are attached to
the shaft with numerous coils of strong cord. The
Bambuti, who are just as cautious in their methods as
their cousins, the Éfé, approach the elephant from the
rear, and having hurled the spear at his belly, dart for
cover immediately. Maddened with pain, the elephant
stampedes furiously ahead, and the shaft becomes detached from the barbed head which sticks fast in the
animal's belly, but is trailed along by the long coils of
cord until finally it gets stuck fast in some shrubbery.
The elephant plunges about to free itself, until at last the
barbed head comes away, bringing the animal's intestines
with it. The elephant may still stagger about for some
time, but the Bambuti trail it until it collapses at length
from loss of blood.

It was among the Bambuti of Majalla that I first saw
the heavy, short elephant spears. The village negroes
tried to persuade me that the pigmies lived a long
distance away, and could not be brought in easily or

speedily. Whether they wanted to keep the dwarfs away from me, or whether their aim was to extort presents from me, I cannot say. It is significant that in the neighbouring village I had been assured that a considerable number of pigmies were attached to Majalla, and so I was determined to see them. Perhaps the aloofness of the negroes was due to the fact that I omitted to give a present to their chief's " principal wife." However, in spite of all the tricks and wiles of the negroes, the pigmies flocked to see me. In a short time there was a swarm of the little people around me, who offered me all kinds of articles in exchange for salt, cloth and beads, so that my hands were quite full.

Meanwhile my bold hunter turned up with a buffalo's tail—a token that he had killed a buffalo—and asked for people to bring the meat into the village. All the pigmies who had surrounded me set off immediately. To my astonishment I learned then that a bearer was keeping guard over the kill, which was lying close to the pigmy camp, quite near the village. It was then that I realized how the negroes had lied to me when they tried to persuade me that the camp was very far from the village. However, I let it pass, and I joined the mob. And presently I saw, at a short distance from the village, the big pigmy camp, over fifty huts in all, on the forest verge. A grey forest buffalo, the hunter's most formidable foe, lay dead in a dense undergrowth of bush near a marshy stretch, with a well-aimed direct hit. After we had dragged the carcass into a clearing, the hunter and the pigmies started about dismembering it. Needless to say, there was great jubilation in the pigmies' camp.

My present hunter was not only brave and resourceful, he was also persevering, and he almost always returned with big game. Monkeys, of course, he considered as mere minor items in his day's bag.

When I stayed in Ischumi's village I spent the first night in the big club-house. About midnight some dozen negroes came up to me in a state of panic and begged for help, as they said that buffaloes had broken into their plantations and were destroying them. Immediately my hunter ran to their assistance, and scarcely half an hour had elapsed before I heard a shot. The animal, however, had escaped. Next morning my hunter followed up the trail of the wounded beast, only to find out that it had not been a buffalo, but an elephant. Towards midday the news arrived that at a short distance from the village, the road-menders had found a wounded elephant, which their white overseer claimed as his. My hunter wanted to claim his share of it, but this I would not allow, as I had no licence for elephant-hunting. To be sure this particular elephant had been shot by mistake, and incidentally, had been doing damage. Still, the law was the law, and had to be obeyed.

I stayed a little while longer in the pigmy camp, just to have a look around, and was rather astounded to see six elephant spears propped against a tree. Their shafts were short and slender, and their heads broad and heavy. I was very keen, needless to say, on acquiring some of those spears, but my efforts were fruitless. The pigmies made all kinds of excuses. One time they said that the owner was not about, again they said that they belonged to the negroes—and so on. I went on further into the camp and returned to the same spot half an hour later, only to find that the spears had disappeared and that not a trace of them could be found. This annoyed me very much, and I gave full vent to my feelings. My words frightened the pigmies, who forthwith fetched the spears out of the bush where they had been hidden. After a little parley I then succeeded in getting two spears for my collection, in exchange for a few big pieces of cloth. I was quite convinced that the pigmies could never turn out such well-wrought weapons, and that they must have paid a good price in the form of big game for them. Consequently I too was quite prepared to offer a good price for them. But if I had had an idea that in the course of my subsequent travels I could have got similar spears comparatively easily, I would not have made such a fuss about obtaining these particular souvenirs.

The occupants of this camp belonged to two different groups, Efé pigmies who spoke Kilese, and Bakango. The Efé alone possessed elephant-spears.

A newly-made grave, surrounded by a bamboo paling, in the middle of the camp, aroused my curiosity. It proved conclusively that not all the Bambuti have

superstitious notions that they should strike camp
immediately on account of a death in their midst. A
child had died a few days previously, and they had buried
it in accordance with negro custom.

It was here that I saw net-hunting for the first time.
Some twenty men with nets hanging around their heads
and necks were marching along. I was very sorry that
circumstances prevented me from accompanying them to
see what their bag would be.

In this camp, too, I saw the smallest pigmy I had ever
encountered. It sounds almost incredible that a fully
grown and normally developed woman with a healthy
six-year-old child, could be only three feet eleven and a
half inches in height. And yet this tiny creature looked
far more self-satisfied than the peevish, wrinkled " head-
wife " of the negro chief, Majalla, beside whom she was
standing.

Although it occurred to me that the huge pigmy camp
attached to Majalla's village afforded ideal headquarters
for a student of Bambuti life and ways, circumstances
would not permit a more prolonged stay there. Moreover, my Wangwana bearers had only been hired for a
space of ten days, so that we soon had to move on.

A rather lengthy day's march through shady forest-
land along a well-kept broad path brought us face to face
again with the foaming Ituri, after we had taken a great
semicircular route through the forest to the north-east
of Avakubi. And it was once more Kayumba's boat that
carried us down-stream to Avakubi.

On our route we passed a large number of canoes,
manned by negroes. We called out to the crew of the
boats and asked where they were going. Kayumba had
shot an elephant, we were told. Hence the rush of negroes
in boatloads to get a share of the meat. With incredible
greed the mob swarmed over the carcass, as soon as they
landed, and in a very short space of time only the bare
skull and the huge ivory tusks gleamed ghost-like through
the trees on the river-bank.

We hoped to reach Kero before night, but in vain.
Although the boat shot like an arrow along the water,
darkness came on suddenly, and we had to land at a spot
that nobody knew, with the result that the vessel nearly

foundered. It was just shooting the rapids near the bank in the dark, when it hit a tree-trunk lying in the water with such force that all its joints strained and creaked. The stern of the boat was caught by the current and dragged with a great semicircular sweep right into mid-stream. Only with the greatest difficulty did we succeed in running her into the bushy bank a considerable distance below the landing-stage, and in rescuing our baggage.

CHAPTER VII

MY FIRST GLIMPSE INTO THE RELIGION OF THE BAMBUTI

THE fact that the Bambuti belonged to the lowest grade of human civilization could not make me believe that they had absolutely no form of religion of any kind. Basing my faith on my experience among other primitive people throughout the world, I was convinced that I had grounds to expect at least the fundamental principles of a religion among the pigmies, and I was delighted to discover at last that my surmise was correct.

I made an earnest effort to get an unclouded view into the inmost recesses of the pigmy soul, and to probe its depths. I knew that, psychologically, the gulf between these " dawn men " and civilized people was, in reality, not very wide. And therefore there was at least a possibility that I might be able to make a study of the pigmy soul. And yet I felt that this was to be the hardest task I had to face as an explorer.

The study of the externals of religion, which are very undemonstrative among primitive peoples and frequently remain in abeyance owing to their elemental struggle with raw nature in their workaday life, is exceedingly difficult. It demands much patience, keen observation and temperamental sympathy, as well as extreme tact, as it is essential not to alienate a little people who are instinctively of a very reserved and cautious disposition, especially in the presence of the white man intent on probing into their inner life. At the very outset it must be remembered that the primitive man does not reveal his inmost soul by word, look, or gesture. And even when he is inquiring into incidents seen with his physical eyes, the explorer often meets with invincible obstacles in the primitive man's instinctive reticence, as I learned from bitter experience during my expedition to Malaya. In my inquiries as to the attitude of the Bambuti towards religion I found that the negroes, from whom I really expected a great deal of help, disappointed me exceedingly. They smiled pityingly at my simplicity in thinking that the Bambuti followed any religious practices. " The Bambuti ! " they said, " why, they are just like the chimpanzees ! They too roam about the forest, and just live like wild beasts ! "

For all that, however, I frequently met negroes who were not quite so short-sighted, but had a fairly good idea of the genuine religious feeling of the pigmies, and who appreciated its worth. More than one elderly negro patron gave me some quite helpful information as to the attitude of the little people towards the spirit world and God.

I had already spent over a month among the Baf-waguda, earnestly but vainly seeking for any trace of religious observance. I had begun to develop semi-doubts as to whether the Bambuti believe at all in a supreme being—so much so that I recollect writing a letter in which I stated that I had, to judge by observation, discovered a people who had " no god."

And then I remembered that I had to spend a long time among the Semangs in India, making careful investigations before I saw even the faintest glimmerings of religious thought amongst them. Still I expected that the task would be easier among the Congo pigmies. They were not a silent and self-absorbed people like the Semangs, but, once they got over their initial timidity, they were an exuberant, garrulous and communicative little folk, passionate and fond of dancing. I had consequently expected that an emotional race of this type would soon exhibit evidence of their religious outlook.

Naturally I had expected to see definite fundamental differences between the religions of the Indian and the African pigmies. But I never expected to find myself apparently face to face with an attitude of blank negation. At length, however, fate put me on the right track, and I realized then once more that the explorer sometimes owes more to his lucky star than to his laborious researches.

L

From observing the daily round of their camp life, the Christian onlooker gets the impression that the Bambuti are actually a race devoid of any religious cult. This impression, an utterly fallacious one, is based on the fact that the Christian observer is wont to see all the demonstrations of religious feeling, whether in the form of congregational worship, prayerful reverential attitude, solitary meditation, or in any other obvious or external phase of worship, completely sundered from the activities of secular life.

These external demonstrations are either utterly lacking in the Bambuti religion, or, at least, the explorer sees no trace of them. The amulets and charms that the pigmies wear, have nothing to do with their religion, but are merely associated with their superstitious belief in witchcraft and magic which they have picked up from the negroes. But the religious invocations and ceremonials of the pigmies are of such an undemonstrative and unconventional form, that they would not be detected by an explorer, especially if he did not know the camp dialect. The reader will recollect that on a couple of occasions I casually heard such simple informal call to their god in the midst of the performance of their everyday tasks.

As I have already mentioned, the most obvious symbols of pigmy superstition are simple amulets of cord and fragments of wood, which are attached to the wrists and ankles of babies, to ensure that they will thrive. I noticed hunters also wearing similar bits of cord and wooden tokens, as well as rings made of snake-skin, which they never part with unless by mere accident.

I never succeeded in finding out how these amulets came to be adopted by the pigmies. Among the Babali negroes, the present patrons of the Bakango, the medicine-man, the " ischumu," as he is called, claims the right of making these magic charms. The Bakango also have a sort of ischumu, obviously patterned on the negro's.

In the ischumu's hands the magic fan is an object inspiring reverential awe—it is the symbol of his power. This fan could be more appropriately termed a broom, as it is just a bunch of twigs made of palm leaves tied together, on the pattern of the whisk that every negro carries to keep the flies off his face. The ischumu's magic fan is equally potent for good or evil, for prosperity or disaster at the mere whim of the man who wields it.

The Bambuti " ischumu " is equipped with a magic fan too, but it is just a miserable, scraggy imitation of the negro symbol. I once saw the magic fan wielded while I was among the Bafwaguda, as I have already mentioned.

I have already referred to the " pikipiki," which is common to both negroes and pigmies, as well as the magic rites and dances in connection with the quest of game, and especially the elephant dance.

Witchcraft, which one finds practised extensively among all the negro tribes in the Congo, is by no means unknown to the pigmies. Alianga gave as a pretext for his second marriage the plea that he had to leave his first wife because she was so frightfully disfigured with " buba " sores, which he attributed to witches' spells.

And then there is the Bafwaguda legend with a witch as its central figure. A Mombuti got married, so the story runs, and the young pair lived happily with the husband's mother. He made the old lady promise to accompany his wife everywhere and to cherish her carefully, so that no ill might befall her. And, apparently, the old lady did as her son requested. One day, however, when he went out to the negro village which was far away, the old lady pressed her daughter-in-law to accompany her into the forest, so that they might kill her own son with witchcraft spells. The young wife, of course, was horrified at the suggestion, and it was only when the old witch terrified her with threats of vengeance that she accompanied her. Many witches had collected in the forest to perform " Buloze " (witchcraft spells), but the young woman would take no part in the rites, and just looked on from a distance. When they returned home, the mother-in-law prepared a good meal, and laid it before the young woman, who refused, however, to touch it. Whereupon the old witch got furious and cursed her thus :—" May your mouth rot ! " And immediately the young woman fell ill, and lay sighing and moaning on the bed. When the son came home and heard his wife's lamentations, he demanded an explanation. But she evaded his questions and would not tell the truth. So he put a rope round the old woman's neck to strangle her. " Don't kill me ! " she cried in terror. And then she confessed about her evil incantations. When she had finished, the young man summoned the people in the camp, who piled up firewood round the hut, and set fire to it, burning the old woman, the young wife, and everything.

The Asunguda " ischumu " told me this story in jerky, incoherent sentences, and in a rambling strain which was absolutely baffling to one accustomed to the logical co-ordination of civilized speech.

He gravely expressed the view that it was a terrible crime for a mother to exercise witchcraft upon her own daughter. On the other hand, witchcraft was used to get rid of a malformed child. The witches cursed it until it died.

On the whole, the cult of magic which is so pronounced among the negroes, does not enter very much into the life of the pigmies. And indeed the negroes have a very poor opinion of pigmy magicians and sorcerers.

The worship of the dead, a very sacred cult among the Bantu negroes, which leaves its impress on their lives and their attitude towards the whole world, scarcely exists among the Bambuti. But they have a very definite impression about the human soul as an entity distinct from the body. They call it " Bukahema," and say that at death it departs from the body in the form of breath.

Many " Baketi " (spirits) surround a dying person, watching for the departure of the soul, with a view to pouncing on it at once, if it has been wicked, and casting it into the fire, which burns somewhere in the bowels of the earth. My informant was not quite sure whether it was only the " Bukahema " that was cast into the fire, or whether the body followed it. The souls of the good, he said, went straight to " Mungu " (god). " Mungu," he added, looked like a man, and all good Bambuti went to him when they died.

I was not a little surprised to hear this profession of faith from the lips of a pigmy. It was a definite refutation of the contention current among the negroes. I thought at first that the influence of the Mohammedan Wangwana might have coloured the religious outlook of the Bambuti, but I discovered that these pigmies never got in touch with any of the Wangwana.

When I asked the ischumu how he knew that thieves and murderers were cast into the fire, he looked puzzled, and stammered confusedly that he had been told so by his father who was also an " ischumu." And so I had to leave the matter at that.

Among the Bakango, he told me, the camp midwife, who is called the " woman's ischumu," digs the grave, while the ischumu himself, with the help of another pigmy, deposits the body in it. The dead man lies at full length on his back, with his face turned in the direction of his cradle, because the belief is that he will arise from his grave and go to the site of the camp where he was born. Sometimes the occupants of his cradle-camp see him coming and say to one another :—" Who is that ? " The apparition vanishes without saying a word. Days afterwards the news of his death comes to the camp, and they recollect the ghost that had passed among them, and say :—" Yes, it was he who appeared to us."

The ischumu places a poisonous extract, called " boko-boko," in the dead man's hand, saying as he does so :— " If you have died by poisoning, he shall also die who killed you."

The people standing around the grave, particularly the women, weep and lament for the dead man. And then the ischumu turns to them and says :—" Cease to weep, because he is gone to God."

The custom of placing everything that belongs to the dead man on the grave, so that he may lack nothing when he goes to Mungu, is also a feature of the negro burial ritual. I have already pointed out in earlier pages that this rite is not always performed at pigmy grave-sides, as they frequently keep the property of the dead as souvenirs.

The Bakango always assured me that they had no fear of the dead and of the grave, and yet I could never persuade a pigmy to point out a grave to me.

The Ngayu and Ituri pigmies bury their dead some-

times in accordance with negro custom. Frequently
they bury a dead man in his hut, which impels many of
them through superstitious dread to forsake the camp at
once. The Bandaka negroes, on the other hand, prefer
to bury their dead in their homes, which they do not
desert, however, on that account.

The Bakango mourn their dead until the next new
moon. During the entire period of mourning there is
neither singing nor dancing—a terrible ordeal, indeed,
for such a dance-loving little people.

In the foregoing pages I have frequently used the word
" Mungu," the name the Bakango give to the supreme
being. The Babali call the deity " Nokunzi." Among
the Wangwana we find the word Mungu and also among
the Babira negroes, who in all probability took the word
from them along with the rest of their language.

Here is a legend which has been handed down to the
Bambuti by the elders of their race :—

" In the beginning all people lived with Mungu, the
Babali as well as the Basua. One day Mungu sent them
all out to hunt swine. The Babali started out first, and
came back in the evening empty-handed. The Bambuti
then tried their luck, and killed a pig, which they ate on
the spot. When Mungu heard this he was so annoyed
that he banished them into the forest, where they live to
this day. The leader of the Bambuti whom Mungu
banished into the forest was called ' Mbera,' the ancestor
of all the pigmies. Although Mungu was very angry with
the pigmies, he was not cruel to them, and gave them
fruit trees from which they could eat to their heart's
content. These trees were the akbu, the akasi, the tobe,
the giezi and many others."

The young ischumu of the camp, who was my authority
for the above legend, informed me that Mungu created
all things. How he set about it, however, he regretted
that he had no information.

The Bakango idea of Mungu is rather cloudy. Sometimes he is represented as looking like a man ; sometimes he has rather a nebulous identity with the
Ambelema snake, which turns into a rainbow when it
climbs the sky. Many pigmies have insisted that Mungu

and the rainbow are the same. They have the same reverential fear regarding both. And here is a legend which gives the reason for their fear.

" Once long ago Mungu killed four Bambuti elders. They were returning home after a long tramp through the forest when darkness came down upon them suddenly, and they were compelled to spend the night in the open air. While they were lying down they were overwhelmed by a dreadful flood and drowned. Just as the flood was engulfing them the rainbow appeared in the sky and it was spitting fire from the point of its arc. Since then whenever the rainbow is seen, the pigmies crouch in their huts with their backs against the leafy walls, while they intone in terror without daring to look out :—' Toka Mungu, toka Mungu, sue toka ! ' (Go away, Mungu, go away, Mungu, depart !) The rainbow also likes to crawl along the tops of the giant trees, and that is why travellers fall ill and die when they are smitten by the big drops from the tree-tops after the heavy rain. And that too is the reason why the Bambuti hate to go out into the open after a rainstorm."

As I have already mentioned, the rainbow appears, in the pigmy mythology, to act in collusion with thunder. But I have never heard any Bakango contend that Mungu made thunder and lightning, although other pigmies are very definite on this point.

During a thunderstorm, the pigmies crouch very quietly inside their huts, even if the latter are swamped by the rain. It is only when the thunderstorm has passed that they start baling out the water from the interior of their huts.

During a thunderstorm they frequently pile a lot of leaves on all the fires throughout the camp to make a huge pall of smoke which rises towards the sky. When the spirit that has caused the thunder and lightning sees the smoke, he is appeased, and the storm blows past, the Bambuti assured me.

The view held by many of the Bambuti that lightning is a kind of he-goat that descends from heaven to earth with terrific noise, can be traced to negro mythology. Incidentally, the goat was first introduced to the pigmies by the negroes.

Before the hunter sets out in quest of game, he prays thus to Mungu : " Bapape gapai emi mama ! " (Father, give me game.) And the wild chorus of shouting, screaming and shrill pipe-calls in which the hunters indulge before dashing into the forest, is apparently also intended as a composite prayer for success in the hunt. Of course, according to our ways of thinking, it is rather unseemly to approach the deity for a favour by means of such an appalling din. But your simple-minded pigmy realizes that a great lord of all the beasts of the wilderness is above him in heaven, and he is just calling on him to bless his day's work.

I have already shown you how the pigmies also call god " father," when they go in quest of honey. As at first I had doubts as to whether the term " Bapa " (father) was really meant to apply to Mungu, I made inquiries on the point, and was assured by the ischumu and several pigmy elders that such was the case.

I never witnessed any formal ritualistic prayers, with the exception of the litany sung by the pigmy women as they marched through the forest. As a matter of fact there are no traditional formal prayers that are known to every pigmy. Your pigmy is in everything an independent individualist, and so far as he can, like a poet, he composes his song or his prayer to suit his emotion of the moment.

The ceremonial of the offering of the first-fruits, which I have seen everywhere among all the pigmies, is extremely interesting. And yet it is such an unconventional and casual ritual, that, had I not been told that such was the case, I would never have thought that it was intended to be a thank-offering to the Supreme Being. Take, for instance, the thank-offering after a successful hunt. They just cut a bit out of the heart of the slain animal and cast it into the woods.

Sometimes this thank-offering is made in a more reverential and solemn manner. A portion of the heart is laid on a clean leaf and placed in the wood with the ritualistic formula : " Munga dao a ie ! " (God, that is for thee.) It is not the hunter who performs this rite, but the eldest of the family-group, or his deputy, who also dismembers the carcase. But whether formally or informally carried out, this thank-offering must always be made. Otherwise there is a risk of never getting any more game.

A similar procedure obtains regarding the thank-offering for fruit. Nobody can taste of the fruit that he has gathered until Mungu gets his share. Mungu created the trees, and makes them yield fruit anew every year, therefore he is entitled to his share first. To us this ritual may seem rather gauche and silly, but it speaks well for the innate thoughtfulness and nobility of those simple primitive people.

On one occasion I came suddenly upon a number of young men who had just cut and cast into the wood a fragment from the heart of an animal they had killed. I asked them why they did this, but they could not offer any explanation. It was obvious that they had just mechanically followed a practice handed down from their ancestors, but had never learned what it symbolized. I met their fathers later on, who were fully acquainted with the portentousness of the ritual.

It is strange that no offerings are made to Munga from the roots and vegetables gathered by the women in the forest, nor from the bananas, which are supplied by the negroes. Perhaps the idea behind this fact is that those roots and vegetables grow from day to day throughout the whole year, and, therefore, belong to a different category to the fruits of the trees, of which there is only an annual harvest. Or perhaps they consider that thank-offerings should be given exclusively from the produce brought in by men. Of course, these are just surmises on my part.

There are apparent analogies between some of the thank-offerings of the pigmies and those of the negroes, but there is a fundamental difference between the two types of sacrifices. The negroes also put aside a portion of any game that they kill, but it is intended, as they state expressly, for their dead, and not for their God. And also when they are on the quest of honey, they invoke the aid, not of the diety, but of their dead.

I have already mentioned that I never succeeded either among the Bafwaguda or among the Bafwasende in getting a glimpse of the sacred utensils for the secret consecration of the youths. The negroes, too, were almost as secretive in this respect. That there is some connection between the consecration ceremony obtaining among the negroes and that of the Bakango there can be no doubt. In some cases they conduct the ceremonial in common, as I had occasion to observe. The rite of consecration of the youth of the Babali negroes, which is known under the name of " Mambela," has been adopted by the Bakango under the same title. And yet, on account of the fundamental difference between the two ceremonies, the consecration rite among the Bakango must be considered as quite a different ceremonial altogether from that of the negroes. The leader of the Mambela rites is called by the Babali, " Tata Ka Mambela," while to the Bakango their leader is known as " Ndiki," and his assistants as " Ischumu," or, more usually as " Kumu." With the " Mambela " rites the pigmies combine circumcision, which is quite unknown to the Babali. The boys, who are to be consecrated, live for a year in a remote part of the forest, to which the women have no access. Their fathers supply them with food. The Ndiki initiates the boys into the tribal customs, and he first teaches them about the " Maduali," the " whirring wood." The Ndiki introduces to them their ancestor ("Endekoru"), who is wrapped in a garment made of grass, and whose face is masked. The boys gaze at him from a distance with fear and dread. Their fear grows more intense as he sets the whirring wood in motion, to warn them not to dare to come any nearer. From certain hints I heard dropped I infer that the whirring sound of the Maduali symbolizes the pealing of thunder.

I have been told again and again that corporal punishment was a feature of the " Mambela," and I actually witnessed such an ordeal at a negro ceremonial. As the secret ceremonial of the initiation of youth is extremely important in its bearing upon the psychology of the pigmies, I felt all the more regret at not being able to witness it myself.

In virtue of his office the Ndiki is the leader of his clan ; he is one of the oldest members, if not the oldest. Owing to his initiation of the boys into the tribal customs he acquires great influence among them. The ischumu, or kumu, is his right-hand man, and he is, moreover, the medicine man of the camp, whom they call in to attend the sick, and who buries the dead.

The Bambuti believe in ghosts and fairies, but only in a very vague and hazy way. This I explain by the fact that the Bambuti wanders about a good deal by himself in the forest, and becomes so intimate and familiar with it that the creepy, lonely feeling that engenders the fear of ghosts very rarely unnerves him. But, as an old pigmy told me, sometimes when a man is going through the forest, a sudden fit of shivering, accompanied by depression and an inexplicable terror sweeps over him, and he knows then that a " Keti " (" the ghost ") has crossed his path. Whereupon he returns at once to the camp, and immediately lights a huge fire in order to frighten the phantom away.

I presume that the fire-dance that I saw was intended to protect the revellers from evil spirits. I regret, however, that I forgot to make inquiries on this point.

The details available about the religion of the Bakango are very slender and un-co-ordinated ; however, scrappy though they are, they are definite, and I found them very useful as a basis for following up my inquiries later among the Efé, among whom I succeeded in getting a deeper and clearer insight into the subject.

It was a difficult job, to be sure, to collect these fragmentary details I secured about the religion of the pigmies. Those primitive little people are not at all eager to present themselves in a favourable light to the explorer ; nor do they want to make themselves interesting to him. It is ingrained in them to be reticent about everything, and sometimes it is difficult to extract an answer to a question. I never met one of them who would voluntarily have discussed his spiritual attitude with me. I really think, at any rate, he would have been incompetent, even if willing, to do so. Thus the explorer must depend, in the case of people with the low-grade mentality of the pigmies, upon casual questions and observations in order to get an approximate idea of the trend of thought upon an abstract subject, as I have endeavoured to do.

CHAPTER VIII

THE AKĂ, THE NORTHERN BRANCH OF THE BAMBUTI

A FEW hours' trip by boat down-stream from
Avakubi, not far from the estuary of the Ngayu,
brings you to a track dating back to prehistoric
times, which runs northwards towards the highlands of
the Wabudu, the Balika and the Medje-Mangbetu.
There is a sameness about the landscape during the first
three days' journey along this ancient trail. The narrow
caravan track, faint and almost obliterated in parts,
winds along through the rank and teeming vegetation of
the forest, which in every respect, even including the
natives of the wayside villages, bears a striking resemblance to the Ituri Forest. The negroes for the most part
belong to the Babli and the Bandaka stocks, although
perhaps they are slightly more primitive and savage-
looking than their Ituri cousins ; but their strains are
obviously very strongly interblended—a fact that seems
to indicate that the mountain-path was used by the
Northern Sudanese tribes for inroads upon the Ituri
region.

One comes suddenly upon Babeyru settlements islanded
in Babali territory, and the Babali themselves in this
region, who live in fortified villages, are, so to speak,
" Babalised " Bandaka. Babeyru villages are clustered
around the landing-stage and the Ngayu ferry. They
are seen again further up on the other side of the mountain.
The Wabudu are their patrons there, and the Balika
on the Nepoko.

The big game of this district is exceedingly abundant
and aggressive, and is a terrible scourge to the negro
planters. In broad daylight one hears drums beating
to summon the villagers to drive off the elephants, which
play cruel havoc with the banana trees. Higher up

along the mountain slopes, there are small clearings occasionally in the forest. Everywhere around here the trail of wandering herds of buffaloes is in evidence, causing great anxiety throughout the caravan, as the negroes are only too familiar with the savage attacks of the big grey brutes. A bit further on a few wretched Babeyru villages are seen, whose inhabitants are in constant dread of incursions by elephants. The whole district is literally strewn with elephant dung, a fairly conclusive proof that there must be plenty of the pachyderms about.

My superstitious Babali bearer was also in dread of another peril associated with the neighbourhood. Pako's village, in which we spent the second night, was said to be the stronghold of the secret society of the " Anyota," or " Leopard men," who were wont to pounce upon women as they were working in the fields and to surprise men asleep at night and to mangle them with diabolical savagery by means of iron claws fastened to their hands. Afterwards they would carry their victims into the forest and eat them. There was a very strong suspicion that Pako himself was a member of this secret society. He was brought before the judge several times as a suspect, but it was impossible to convict him, as all the negroes, even those who abhorred it most, had an awful dread of the secret society, and nobody would dare to give information against it. A few days after we had left this dreadful village, we reached the Wabudu region just at the very moment that a white judge with a military escort was making inquiries about the society, which, during the previous fortnight, had perpetrated twenty-three murders under the very eyes of the official inquirers, so to speak. As may be imagined, there was a terrible panic in the neighbourhood at the audacity of the criminals. Some maintained—obviously in order to cloak the terrible atrocities, that it was a leopard that killed the victims, but the majority of the negroes fixed the guilt on the Anyota Society, and suspected certain individuals, whom they dared not, however, impeach openly. The circumstances under which the murders were carried out, pointed clearly to the fact that the Anyota Society had extended its hellish activities to this district too. Isolated

as they were among people of an alien tribe, my bearers
were in the terror of their lives, and when they found
that we had to spend the night in one of the most threatened villages, I had to secure huts for them in which
they promptly entrenched themselves. In fact, as a
measure of precaution I thought it advisable to barricade
the door of the rest hut. No mishap befell my caravan,
but I heard of a fresh murder in that very village the next
day.

I had toiled along painfully, however, into this danger-
ous locality, not in quest of sensational adventures—my
time was too valuable for such digressions—but to get
a glimpse at the pigmies, who lead their nomad existence
there under the ægis of the negroes.

In Mangbaro's village, not far from a Ngayu ford, I
got in touch with the Badeka pigmies, who call themselves Asua, but are known as Aká by the Babeyru.
That is the famous pigmy tribal name that Schweinfurth
made so well known in Europe. He met the Aká in the
extreme north on the Nele banks in Munza's village.
Since the Medje-Mangbetu and the Babeyru are racially
and linguistically allied it is no wonder that we encounter
the name Aká in such widely separated districts on the
Uele and Ituri.

Throughout the entire region the Aká, who roam alone
under the patronage of the Babeyru, have a distinct
language allied to the Medje tongue, while in the vicinity
of Nepoko we meet the Bakango again. In the two first
halting places we met only a few Bambuti, but when
we reached Lasa, a horde of pigmies, consisting of two
clans, met me. Lasa, a little Wabudu colony, is perched
on a hill, which is surrounded on three sides by rivers.
This makes it a natural fortress and a casual glance
suffices to show that it is an excellent site for a settlement.

My visitors were Kikango-speaking pigmies, who are
called by the Wabudu by the generic name of Bachwa.
I could measure, photograph and film them to my heart's
content. For hours at a stretch they kept up a non-stop
dance, interrupted by occasional thunderstorms and by
sleep.

These Bachwa sharpen their four top front teeth to a
needle point, like the Bakango on the Ituri, and the

women pierce holes in their upper lips and through their noses. The women are dressed after the Mabudu fashion. The Bakango women of the Ituri, like the Babali women, wear a short apron in front, and covering the buttocks a long strip of bast about four inches wide, which reaches below the knees, so that seen at a distance one would think they had tails. The Bachwa women of the Wabudu district, on the other hand, wear in front a narrow apron, some ten inches broad, while at the back a long gaudy tassel about eight inches long of woven liana strips, painted red or black and red, flaps like a tail on their hips. These tassels look coquettish, but as garments their value is negligible. However, even in the virgin forest fashion holds sway, and cares little for propriety, or impropriety, of attire. And to the dictates of fashion even the pigmy women must bow.

The Bambuti in this district call a dead man " Murunda." After the corpse has been washed, and some water poured into its mouth, it is buried in a crouch-ing position, but it is not bound up. No gifts, not even his own personal belongings, are placed on the man's grave. Five days after the burial they move to another camp.

In Lasa the weather played freakish pranks with us. On the second night a thunderstorm broke over our heads, and raged with true tropical frenzy for several hours. Next morning the sun shone brightly again, and our caravan resumed its march, only to be overtaken by another thunderstorm about half an hour after starting. As we were already drenched to the skin, it was imma-terial whether we turned back or went ahead. It was only when we reached the crest of the mountain, which lies between the Nepoko and Ituri that the sky was cleared once more. The descent down the mountain-side was much easier, but we kept slipping and sliding along the muddy path. When we reached the valley my servant had his work cut out to wash the clay out of my clothes. In appearance I was rather like a brick worker, as I had slipped and fallen full length several times.

On the other side of the mountain the ground sloped gently towards the Nepoko, one of the greatest tributaries of the Ituri River. The villages here were larger and more numerous. We were in the territory of the Wabudu, a new country with a different climate. On the opposite bank of the river there gleamed on a gently rising slope the buildings of the huge and prosperous mission of Bafwabaka. It lies just at the lip of a densely populated table-land, which I decided to traverse by motor in all directions during the next few weeks in order to study the natives. The plateau is covered with dense growth of ancient trees, and is hilly in parts. The forest is studded with numerous Balika and Wabudu villages, built in clearings, which seen from afar look like giant nests. Motor roads link up the villages in all directions. Towards the north the country merges gradually into the territory of the Medje, until suddenly the landscape opens out before you, and the broad stretch of steppes begins. And here comes the boundary of the domain of the pigmies, which approximately corresponds to the edge of the virgin forest.

I am indebted to the kindness of the late Father Debouge, a splendid man in every possible way, for the speed with which I finished my task in the Nepoko district. Not only did he put his own car at my disposal, but he accompanied me on several journeys, during which his knowledge of the land and of the people proved invaluable to me. In the course of only four weeks I was enabled to get into touch with the leading pigmy camps and to examine them thoroughly.

Although pigmies live quite close to Bafwabaka, they never see either the missionary or white men at all. This did not surprise me in the least, as I knew from my own experience that it takes a long time for the pigmy to get over his dread of white men, and to summon up enough courage and confidence to approach a European settlement.

Accompanied by a young missionary, who was very anxious to see a Bambuti settlement, I set out to visit the nearest camp of whose location I had received word. The track which had been pointed out as the Bambuti path, proved an unpleasant one, as, after leaving the nearest negro village, we had to wade across a morass and through water for half an hour. Our sudden appearance caused terrible confusion among the few women left in the camp, which numbered only ten huts. The men had just gone hunting with nets, but quickly returned to the camp in response to the cries of the women. They stared at us with just as perplexed an expression as those of their wives.

The miserable tiny camp impressed my companion, who observed everything with the greatest interest, and carefully examined the queer abodes and their even queerer owners. I soon discovered that here, too, the Kabango-speaking Bambuti lived, but that they called themselves Bachwa like their nearest neighbours. Never anywhere else did I see the reddish tinge of the hair of the Bambuti so pronounced as it was among some of the children of this group. Here, too, I saw the first and only case of leprosy among the Ituri pigmies.

Eventually I undertook to interpret my companion's desire to the pigmies, which was that they should have no fear of the white man, but should look on him as a friend and come to the mission. The young missionary felt himself drawn towards these wretched little nomads, and was most anxious to establish an alliance with them.

With kindling eyes they accepted our invitation, obviously tempted by our promise of gifts, and said that they would turn up the very next day at the mission. Once they had come, my young companion said, he thought that they would be induced to return.

The pigmies were as good as their word. Next morning a horde of scrubby Bambuti, men, women and children arrived at the gates. We were greatly surprised. It afforded me an excellent opportunity of taking measurements and of making records of their songs. They danced and were extremely happy, especially as I gave them plenty of tobacco, salt, beads and cloth so as to secure their confidence.

The young missionary addressed them and arranged that they should come regularly once a week to him. He assured them that they would not regret their promise. The little people parted from him on the most cordial terms—but they never appeared again! Great as was their longing for the splendid gifts he promised them— tobacco, salt, beads and cloth galore—their terror of the strange environments of the mission was even greater.

M

The Nepoko highlands are linked up with an extensive network of motor roads, which are kept in excellent condition, although now and again thunderstorms and floods wreck whole stretches of them. The road to Babonge was a splendid one for cars, and while passing along it I visited two Bambuti camps in which I met some pigmies who had assembled from far-distant camps. For a joke I took some of the Bambuti for a long run in the motor-car. It was their very first trip in such a vehicle, but they seemed neither very much scared nor very much impressed. It is a strange fact that our modern mechanical inventions which appeal to the white man's imagination and arouse his admiration, make no lasting impression on the pigmy. For a moment they gaze in speechless wonder at the strange device, but they very quickly become accustomed and absolutely indifferent to it. It is of no importance to them, because they feel that it has nothing to do with their way of living. But if you shew them any European invention that they can apply to their own end, it will arouse the keenest and most hilarious enthusiasm.

For instance, there had been a great craze for the mouth-organ in the Asunguda camp, as soon as one of the pigmies succeeded in playing one of the Bambuti dance tunes on it. I remember my astonishment when one evening, shortly after I had given Policy one of these instruments, I heard him playing native airs on it, while an admiring throng danced with frenzied delight around him. Although he had never laid eyes on it until then, he learned to play it right away.

Even the toy bugles I had brought for the children aroused tremendous enthusiasm among the Bambuti adults. The cinema and camera always left them cold, though I must mention that my electric torch struck terror into them, until at length one bolder spirit, at my invitation, approached it rather cautiously, and learned to turn the " Lightning " on and off by means of the switch.

But the gramophone always provided the greatest sensation, not when it rendered any foreign tunes, in which they took very little interest, but when it recorded their own voices and repeated them. Whenever I fixed up the apparatus for recording I always had a huge swarm of men, women and children around me. I remember that the first time that I got a group of them together to sing into the apparatus, some of them were listless while others looked terrified. But when the needle was reversed, and they heard the song they had just sung being repeated distinctly by the machine, there was a chorus of open-mouthed delight and amazement that momentarily drowned the record. How their eyes gleamed with glee while they kept hopping about in wild excitement! And then suddenly they became quiet again and listened intently, until one ultra-loud raucous voice, a few bars behind the others, blared out on the record, and was recognized and greeted with ironical cheers and convulsive laughter. If an explorer is anxious to get in close touch with the pigmies, and to break down the barriers of their ingrained reserve, I would advise him to have a gramophone and a recording apparatus among his equipment.

In the Babonge camp I met a smart Mubudu negro, who was going with his wife to visit his relatives who lived some distance off. Among his retinue was a pigmy youth, who walked behind his master, carrying a stool, and with a bundle on her back, presumably of provisions and cooking utensils, a pigmy woman trotted after the wife. Any patron of the pigmies can at will insist on some service from his vassals.

The Bambuti who lived in the neighbourhood, and whom, owing to the shortness of my stay in this region, I was unable to visit, declined my invitation to come and see me at the rest hut. They insisted that I should go to them and said that they would wait for me at the roadside. There was nothing for it but to do as they suggested.

Hardly had our car gone half a mile along the road leading from Babonge when the first pigmies emerged from the thicket. Without hesitation they clambered into the car, and accompanied us to a spot where the road swerved into the thicket. Suddenly we saw a very wretched dirty little camp consisting of only four huts. Even in a pigmy camp it is easy to gauge the standard of living by external appearances. If there are a good **many** huts, and if there are women in large numbers in a camp you will find that things are much more snug and comfortable than in a camp where there are only a few women, decrepit old men and dirty children. The latter was the case here. Two filthy little men, who not only by their stunted build, but also by their wild shaggy beards, reminded me of one of the goblins of fairy lore, I placed on my right and left respectively. Though I certainly am not of gigantic stature, these little old men passed under my outstretched arms without stooping, so tiny were they.

It was a cold rainy day, and the two little old men, as well as the rest of the pigmies, were crouching with their arms across their chests, and shivering with cold. One poor old fellow, who looked very ill, remained for some time slowly swinging a burning stick in front of his body to warm himself. After a while he toddled into his hut, and I saw him sucking some sort of medicine from a pot through a hollow reed. It was filthy looking stuff, apparently some root extract. It looked so beastly that I could not bring myself to dip my fingers in to see how it tasted, but if its flavour was half as bad as its smell it must have been truly appalling.

I never saw anything so pitifully filthy as that wretched little camp. Hens, the first I had seen in a pigmy camp, were running about scratching among the ashes and rubbish heaps, which were scattered all over the place. The huts were poor things in comparison with the comfortable beehive homes of the Bambuti. They were really mere wind-screens, consisting just of obliquely sloping roofs, with the front doors wide open, and both sides most inadequately protected against the weather with palm leaves. In short, it was such a miserable camp that it took me a long time to find some trifle to buy for my collection.

Meanwhile a considerable number of Bambuti had hurried from a neighbouring village, among whom I recognized two women, whom I had seen some days before in the camp on the Nepoko and in the Bafwabaka mission. It was apparent that these pigmies of Babonge and those of the Bafwabaka were allied, and belonged to the same stock.

We saw a large bright clean camp further on, below the one I have just described, almost on the very verge of the motor road. It was a camp that was unique in the variety of the architecture of its huts. On a vacant patch on the edge of the camp stood a ring of wind-screen huts. Then there were the conventional beehive huts and several little ones with gable-roofs after the style of the negroes, furnished with doors. I noticed that there was no plantation in the vicinity of this camp or of the forlorn-looking one I had visited previously.

The household utensils merely consisted of Balika pots, and mats that were worn by the women. The bedsteads were supported by upright forked sticks, which raised them about four inches from the ground. The hunters were all equipped with bows and arrows and wore beautifully woven Balika straw caps.

I noticed that the occupants of this camp had a different head formation from that of all the pigmies I had met previously. It was obvious that the back of the skull had been artificially elongated after the fashion of the Balika, who presumably have adopted the idea in conjunction with the Wabudu from the Mangbetu. This elongation of the rear of the head, which is effected in infancy by means of tight bandages, gives the bulky pigmy skull a more delicate contour, and softens the ruggedness of the facial expression.

The pigmy women in this region dress their hair very prettily in a series of coils encircling the entire head. Unfortunately they, too, mutilate their noses and upper lips like their sisters in the other parts of the Congo. They wear girdles of banana leaves round their hips.

Another trip with Father Debouge in his car brought me to the heart of the Medje territory and to the Majogu on the edge of the forest. I also visited the Bomakandi in the vicinity of Rungu. I was thus able, in the course of a few days, to discover the exact delimitation of the pigmy territory and the solidarity of the family groups in the northern tracts. In Medje, which is the headquarters of an administrator, I was extremely lucky, as during the course of my stay, I encountered four different hordes of Aká. I had now decided to give up measuring pigmy heads, as most of the little people

I encountered had adopted the vogue of the artificially elongated skull. The dark, almost black hue of many of the men was rather attractive, and they seemed, too, to be taller than their southern relations. Some of them, however, had the clayey brown skin and the characteristic Bambuti cast of features. This reversion to southern type was even more marked among the women, who also mutilate their noses, but not their upper lips. They imitate, and even improve upon the graceful Medje method of hairdressing. Their elongated heads, ringed round with rich serpentine coils, are really extraordinarily attractive.

The Medje influence on the Aká was manifested in many ways. On one occasion a young Aká chief visited me with his retinue, among whom there were some grey-headed men. The chief sat down with the airs of a pasha, his followers squatting on his right and left. Then a man with wooden rattles in his hands danced and capered before his master, while the women who sat in a circle around him clapped their hands and sang. These pigmies had obviously adopted negro ways in every respect, and I was rather surprised and disgusted with the entertainment that they had staged for my benefit. Such a performance would have been absolutely impossible among the natural, primitive, simple pigmies I had met previously. It was only too clear that negro culture had superseded that of the lowly little man of the forest. It would be unthinkable that a youth, scarcely twenty years of age, would have been tolerated as a chief among the Bambuti —and with such a vulgar retinue too. Still more unthinkable would it be that grey-headed men should attend a stripling.

The chief wore a gaudy straw cap, and I was fascinated by a voluminous multi-coloured apron. I soon came down to business with the young potentate, who unhesitatingly whipped off his apron and exchanged it for a bit of cloth and a girdle.

These Aká, as well as the Badike and a considerable portion of the Balika and Wabudu pigmies, speak Medje, which justifies the grouping of all of them under the heading of Aká.

The Baleu pigmies, whom I met almost eight months

later in the middle reaches of the Ituri, not far from Panga in the village of Mokope, should also be numbered among the Aká. Unfortunately I saw there pigmies, who live in the extreme west, under conditions very unfavourable for a detailed examination of their customs and standard of living. A terrific thunderstorm burst overhead just as a deputation from them called on me. I had only succeeded, before they left late at night, in establishing the fact that they belonged to the Aká, although they recognize the Wangelima, in whose territory they live, as their patrons, and are called Basungu by them. Their camp speech, which, like the Medje, has a large admixture of words from other languages, is very curious. The Supreme Being, whom they call "Nabagwá," is known among the other Aká by the title used among the Medje, while the Baleu use the term "Barumbie." They say that he causes the thunder by tramping on the sky. He is the creator of all things. They call him "Our Father." He existed from eternity, and he has no wife. All who die, both good and bad, go to him to his abode in the sky.

The thank-offerings given by the Bakango, to which we have already referred, are also customary among the Baleu, as well as the rest of the Aká.

They, like the other pigmies, have the greatest dread of the rainbow, which they call "Papae" ("Father"). He is the great snake that ascends from the water to the sky.

A few explanatory remarks about the Baká, as the Popoi call them, or the Basungu, as they are known to the Wangelima, obviously because they have no fixed abode, but lead a gipsy life, deserve place here. They are based upon the writings of Hutereau, who visited the pigmies of the upper Rubi reaches many years ago. These, and the Baleu whom I saw, unquestionably belong to a common stock. The Azande seemingly call them "Atikitiki," a name that previously I had never heard. According to Hutereau these Bambuti must have been very much affected by negro influence twenty years ago, which is not strange, inasmuch as they have pushed forward so extensively in the north-west. Incidentally we get a clue, in these investigations, to the wanderings of the negroes, which have involved great changes in all the races with which they came in contact, including the Bambuti.

The Balele negroes of these regions, like most of their forest brothers, intermarry with the Bambuti. They have to pay a good price for their wives to the pigmies, who demand fifty arrows, an axe and three knives per girl.

An outstanding case of the marriage of a pigmy to a Majogu negress, which Hetereau describes, is worth repeating here. Doto, an extraordinarily clever elephant hunter evolved into such an out-and-out capitalist, despite the socialistic community among whom he lived, that he had nine wives, who never lacked abundance of meat to eat. In the service of the negroes he hunted elephants, and piled up enormous wealth. Once, while he was hunting for the negro chief Maway, a negro maiden fell in love with him, and decided to thrown in her lot with him. Doto showed himself in no way niggardly towards his father-in-law, to whom he felt he could never show sufficient gratitude for his good fortune in securing a wife from a superior race. To please his new wife he even changed his manner of living, and employed negroes to build comfortable houses for him, and to lay out fields, which he presented to her. Unfortunately they fell out, after Itango (such was the wife's name) had borne him three sons and two daughters. Itango left him, and returned to her father. Doto, however, promptly called on his father-in-law, and demanded back his wife, for whom he had paid, but despite her father's orders that she should follow her husband, Itango refused to return with him, and accused him of having been meanly avaricious in his dealings with her and her relatives. The father did not believe this, as it was contrary to actual facts, and during the night he secured access for Doto to Itango's hut. In the morning the father found that Doto had vanished, while his daughter lay dead on the ground with an arrow through her throat. A short time afterwards Doto fell sick and died, and Itango's children returned to their grandfather.

A story which Hetereau tells about the Bambuti of the upper Rubi, shows how negroes and pigmies may form alliances, without, however, becoming incorporated with one another.

A negro, named Modinbongwe, a brother of a chief, Baruto, met a pigmy of the Bamunzi clan, and formed a blood-brotherhood bond with him. Both negroes and pigmies were glad to hear of the alliance. Now as Baruto was very keen to induce a horde of pigmies to settle close to his village, to keep him supplied with meat regularly, he sent Modinbongwe to act as intermediary. Modinbongwe went straight to Pimbi, the oldest man among the Bamunzi pigmies, and laid before him the chief's desire. Pimbi was not averse to the scheme, but he thought that precautionary steps should be taken first.

" Modinbongwe," he said to the negro, " I am well aware that you have formed the bond of blood-brotherhood with my brother Mazembe. That is excellent, but before I make any arrangement with Baruto, I want one of our boys and one of yours to be circumcised together."

As Baruto approved of the pigmy's prudent suggestion, a place and a day were fixed for the circumcision of the young pigmy and the young negro. When the blood of the two victims mingled the bond was sealed. The consequence entailed by this bond was that never at any future date should a pigmy of the Pimbi clan pursue and kill a negro of the Baruto tribe and vice versa, as such a murder committed between blood-brothers would involve a terrible vengeance.

And so the pigmies became the neighbours of the Baruto, hunted for them, and in return received the produce of their plantations. And once, when the pigmies went away on their wanderings for a long spell, Baruto and his negroes built huts for them and cleaned up their camp. When the pigmies returned they were greatly pleased to see how thoughtful the negroes had been about them during their absence. But the negroes knew well that this attention that they had shown them would not make the pigmies desist from their nomad ways. They were quite unable to give up their habits, and they came and went at their own sweet will. Once they remained away for a whole year at a stretch.

Another incident which is typical of the cruelty and

racial bitterness of which the pigmy is capable, is worth narrating. Hutereau vouches for its authenticity.

Bondo, a Mombuti of the Bamunzi clan, was the victim of an illusion once, when out hunting. He fancied that he saw an antelope through the bushes, and loosed an arrow, killing a dog belonging to Ai, Pimbi's brother. Bondo was ordered to pay compensation, which he did gladly, in order to escape vengeance. He sold his own sister to be the wife of a negro in return for a magnificent dog, with which he appeased Ai.

But bad luck continued to dog Bondo's footsteps. Later while he was out hunting he again saw what he thought was an antelope moving, fired, and hit Ai in the stomach, wounding him fatally. In sheer terror of the vengeance of the family group of Ai, Bondo fled into the forest. For years he wandered about, stopping now in one camp now in another, in order to put his pursuers off the scent. Eventually, as he felt in eternal fear of his life, he yielded to the advice of some negroes that he should accept service under a European. In this way they assured him he would elude the avengers for good and all. Bondo looked a different man after a negro friend had trimmed his hair and given him a piece of cloth to put around his loins. But though Bondo did his very best to adapt himself to his new environment, he failed. The very next day after he had taken up the job he hurled the loin-cloth from him, and cried in despair: " I am choking in your villages. I'm going back to my forest home ! "

So saying, he resumed his wanderings through the forest, until at length an invincible nostalgia for his own people swept over him. He ventured in reckless mood to enter the hunting territory of his own clan, with a view to finding out their attitude towards him. He sought shelter in Kalimba's camp. The latter, however, treated him very treacherously. Instead of showing him hospitality, he ordered him to be bound, and sent word to Pimbi, the brother of the slain Ai. Pimbi turned up at once, and led the captive to his own camp and bound him to a tree. Then he informed him that he would be the executioner himself, and that he was going to torture him to death. He first dug out the wretched man's eyes with an arrow, and then, standing some distance away, he shot arrow after arrow at him, until death ended his agony. Bamunzi, who was head of the clan, made no effort to prevent Pimbi's brutal act of vengeance, and indeed seemed to approve of it.

A few days later Bondo's sister heard of her brother's terrible fate and determined to avenge him. Had he been slain, as he slew Ai, she would have made no complaint, because in accordance with the code of the negroes in that district, his life was forfeit. But she could not forgive Pimbi and Bamunzi for their barbarity towards him. She made an insidious slow-working poison, told her husband that she was going to visit her family group, and left the camp. Soon she found an opportunity of putting the poison into Bamunzi's food, for she held him responsible for her brother's death, because he had not forbidden Pimbi to commit the crime. And as soon as she had satisfied herself that Bamunzi had eaten the poisoned food she disappeared from the neighbourhood and was never seen again.

This story is in the vein of the proverbial notorious barbarity of the negro code. Personally I have never heard of the incident from the pigmies. I am not venturing, however, to question the truth, especially as it is a story about those pigmies whose attitude has been very greatly affected by the negro outlook.

I shall just deal very briefly with the Bambuti attached to the Majogu negroes, whom I met with their chief, Magbada, who was more remarkable for his colossal physical dimensions and for his huge harem than for anything else. The Majogu actually live in the open country, and their pigmies, who are locally known as Basa, are steppe-dwellers, the only Ituri pigmies who live in a treeless country. I met only three groups of them, but I believe that they are fairly numerous in this district. The Basa have their own plantations, and their customs and ways are very like those of the negroes. In fact they seem to take special pride in apeing the black men, so that from the point of view of the study of the primitive culture of the pigmies they are hardly worth considering.

A story from the Majogu folk-lore, dealing with the genesis of the Bambuti, deserves repetition. Pwala, the ancestor of the Majogu, came down to earth from the skies. Feeling hungry, he was chewing a sugar-cane, which he had picked up, when a woman stepped up to him and started asking him a lot of questions. As he had never seen a woman before, inasmuch as he was the first man to walk on earth, Pwala concluded that, from the peculiar shape of her body, so very different from his cwn, that she must be diseased, and so he gave her medicine, which, however, produced no change in her. Just then God appeared, and after explaining to him the mysteries of creation, gave her to him as his wife. He called her Bogopemu.

The first fruit of the marriage was a Mombuti. The man hung the placenta on a tree, with the result that its branches forthwith burst forth into leaf and were laden with fruit.

The next two children were named Jogo and Begendwe.

The pigmy travelled through the wood and met a woman whom God sent him, and whom he took as his wife. The descendants are the Bambuti of to-day.

On another occasion he met another woman, whom he gave to Jogo, but their descendants are not Bambuti.

Later on a quarrel broke out between Jogo and Begendwe about eggs which their hens had laid, after which they parted in different directions. Pwala and his wife died a few years later.

A similar legend is current throughout the whole length and breadth of the forest belt. I heard it from the lips of the Balese, the Mamvu and the pigmies. A more detailed version of the legend states that the pigmies first taught the negroes how to make their livelihood. In yet another version they assume the rôle of initiating the negroes into the mysteries of the origin of life.

You would need to spend six months at a stretch imprisoned inside the leafy barriers of the virgin forest, to appreciate my feelings when the car, after topping an eminence, left the last giant trees behind, and suddenly emerged into the open country. Before us the open, undulating grassy steppe extended as far as the eye could see. As from our lofty point of view my eyes traversed the mighty expanse before me, I saw a few villages and plantations dotting the sun-kissed plain and the billowing grass lands. I looked backwards—there lay the black dark forest in its widespread gloomy immobility, under a grey pall of haze, on which the brooding sun beat down. A sea of trees without break, without salient feature on which the eye could repose. I was set free from the barriers of the primeval forest—I was once more in the bright sunshine—in the open spaces where the body and soul could breathe freely. This was my first emotion.

The Ford rattled along over hill and down dale in the gleaming sunshine. We began to feel the spirit of the African steppe when the sun beats down on it. There we were, two thousand feet above sea-level, where the air is more rarefied. On we went, further northwards, through the land of the Majogu, and on to Bomokandi, back again in the territory of the Medje—but there were no Bambuti there. We did not tarry long there. We had to get back to the forest, for the Bambuti dwell almost only in the shade of the trees.

CHAPTER IX

AMONG THE MAMVU-EFÉ

ANDUDU is perhaps the most delightful little spot I came across in all my wanderings through th Congo forest. It is an oasis in the wilderness, a sun-kissed clearing, snatched from the gloomy forest, where, instead of liana and moss-grown giant trees, oil palms and fruit trees flourish, and instead of orchids and marsh blooms, you have a wealth of fragrant flowers. How delightful after many months was this perfume from countless rose buds in which sparkling dew glistened every morning !

Andudu is some two thousand feet above sea-level, on the right bank of the upper reaches of the Nepoko. Its climate is, in consequence, mild ; even under the rays of the noonday sun it is endurable, but in the evening when the little village is fanned by the western breeze and flooded by the silvery moonlight it is a paradise. How often, since then, have I recalled the quiet moonlit evenings under the soughing oil palms with Father Debouge ! That wonderful boundless African calm ! There was not a soul near. The servants were squatting in front of their huts about a hundred yards away. The village lay nearly a mile and a half across the river in a sheltered valley. No sound of life came from it. A distant monotonous murmur, accompanied by the gentle whispering of the branches of the palm trees, as the soft wind disturbed their leaves, only intensified the solemn silence. This murmur came from the water of the Nepoko, about six hundred yards away, as it rolled downward to the sea, lulling nature into a soft repose.

But the exquisite Andudu, snatched from the gloom of the forest, is a desert, a fragrant " paradise lost," with the brand of the fall on its brow. The numerous warehouses that skirt this desert are empty, and their blank windows and doors stare spectrally amid the crumbling walls. Luxurious comfort and teeming life reigned here in days gone by. Now rats and snakes are the sole tenants of its ruined abodes.

On the top of the hill, surrounded by an extensive orchard, the resident magistrate's house once stood. You can see nothing now but its derelict ruins. During one of the numerous thunderstorms that so frequently burst over Andudu, it was destroyed by lightning. This sealed the fate of the village. The government offices were transferred further off towards the south-west ; the tradesmen and merchants and their black customers followed the officials.

Thus Andudu stands there desolate. Only the buds on the rose bush near a ruined warehouse, planted and tended in bygone days by soft feminine hands, recall poignantly happy times of yore. Another link with Andudu's former glory is the rest-house, still standing four square in its imposing contours ; a giant hut, spacious and comfortable, and far surpassing anything else of its type in the forest regions. On two occasions I was glad of the friendly shelter of this luxurious house. When I installed myself in it, I felt that I would give anything to stay there for at least a fortnight, but I could not do so, although I remained longer than I should have done in it.

It was a long, but not a difficult trip from Bafwabaka to Andudu. A few days after our return from Bafwakandi our Ford rattled once more along the road past Wamba to Gombari. We had travelled nearly one hundred and thirty miles towards the north-east, when at length we descended by a narrow track to the village of Aleku in the territory of the Mamvu. A motor lorry followed in our rear with all my luggage. I had planned to cross the forest regions of the Mamvu and the Balese as far as Irumu, intending to go from there past Beni to Ruanda, and then back past Beni-Pengi, in order to reach Avakubi. I wanted to search out pigmies in every possible place. And if I was to do this I realized that I must reckon on a further six months' travelling, for which I should need a more extensive equipment.

In Aleku I awaited bearers who had been appointed to
attend me through the cordial co-operation of the
resident magistrate at Gombari, as I wanted to travel
on foot to Andudu. And at this point I wish to express
my deep gratitude to the Belgian Colonial officials, from
the Colonial Ministry in Brussels to the humblest " agent
territorial." Everywhere I was received with the most
marked courtesy, and substantial help was given to me
in all my undertakings. Not only did they give me
financial assistance for my expedition, but also practical
help—all the district officials in the eastern and equatorial
province were instructed to come to my aid whenever
I applied to them. Were it not for this help, my freedom
of movement would have been very circumscribed indeed.
Just picture to yourself the obstacles a private individual
has to encounter to get a caravan of bearers together.
In most of the Congo districts it is almost impossible for
him to do so, as the negroes meet the white man with
passive resistance ; and it is in dealing with this passive
resistance that the Colonial officials are such a tremendous
help.

The Colonial authorities had absolutely no control
over the pigmies, and really I was not sorry for that.
I wanted to get into personal touch with these little
forest goblins myself and to win their confidence.
That I succeeded in so doing to a certain extent I have
already stated, and I have also already explained how
I succeeded in my efforts. I have shown that the Bambuti
will place their trust in the white man, and that they are
eager to do so, when they are convinced that he is kindly
disposed towards them and is prepared to help them in
any way possible. Accordingly I deliberately refrained
from anything calculated to make them distrustful or
from offending them, no matter whatever the provocation
might be, for I realized that anything of such a description
would imperil the success of my expedition. I found,
more than once, the need of prudence and restraint in
my dealings with them.

The practical help given me by the missionaries at
Stanley Falls and Lake Albert contributed immensely
to the success of my trip. In particular my thanks are
due to M. Grison, the Apostolic Vicar of Stanleyville,

who instructed his missionaries in Avakubi, Bafwabaka and Bungulu to help me in every way possible that was in their power. They all more than fulfilled his orders, and in the most magnanimous spirit. I was treated with equal cordiality by the Dominicans at Bunia. Not only did the missionaries show me the most warm-hearted hospitality whenever I visited their stations, but they also assisted me by their very sound advice, and often accompanied me on my shorter trips. Indeed any unprejudiced observer must take off his hat to these missionaries for their unremitting self-sacrifice in their work in the Congo, and explorers and globe-trotters who have partaken of their genial hospitality are unanimously loud in their praises.

In the afternoon our car arrived in Aleku, but there were no bearers in sight. We had waited a good while, when suddenly a motor-car came round the corner and two white men greeted me—a Colonial doctor of Russian birth, a merry, hilarious fellow-traveller, whom I had met on the Congo steamer, and with whom I had many a long argument on Colonial and home politics. His companion on this occasion was the resident magistrate himself, who had so often helped me in times of stress. He told me that the bearers would arrive presently. He had ordered them from the gang who were working a couple of miles away on a branch motor road. We jumped into the car, and away we went over the bumpy track to the spot where the road-makers were working. We had frequent stops in order to get fallen trees shifted out of the way, and on other occasions we had to fill up huge pot-holes. While I was selecting my bearers from the workers, the car returned to fetch more baggage, which was made fast with liana ropes and forwarded via the narrow track to Andudu. It took us from two to three hours to cover the road, which led alternately through abandoned plantation and gloomy forest, and was muddy and sticky after the rain. In the semi-darkness of the dense forest a little Bambuti caravan, bringing provisions to their camp, crossed our path. The women in terror rushed in all directions while the men, gripping their spears firmly and shivering with fright, huddled together by the road-side. They were the first Mamvu pigmies that I met.

N

The Efé, as I shall class them in future, is the name that they give themselves.

The station of Andudu lay on the opposite side of the little stream on a small hill to which a path led through a commodious village which belonged to retired native soldiers. It is the custom in the Congo for the pensioned native soldiers, both rank and file and non-commissioned officers, to have land allotted to them in the vicinity of the government station, where they settle and cultivate the land. They have some special privileges and manage to live fairly comfortably. Isolated from the community of the native villagers, they form a little colony of their own with definite rights. In times of trouble they are auxiliary forces to the government. The messenger, or, as he is officially termed, the courier, resplendent in tattered breeches, received us in the absence of the chief, and escorted us along the fairly broad road that led to the rest-house.

I learned through the missionaries, who visit this neighbourhood once a year, that a chief of the Mamvu, named Kerese, lived not far from Andudu, and that pigmies are to be found in his territory. My first anxiety was to get into touch with them.

In reply to a message that I sent to him, Kerese turned up in person to greet me on the next morning. His imposing retinue included Tebi, the only pigmy in the entire Congo area who had got a medal from the Government. The Colonial authorities had hoped by this gesture to get the pigmies under a federated control and thereby to bring them under their power. The efforts of the Belgians at establishing this control over the negroes have been eminently successful. But no satisfactory results could ever be obtained by adapting, or trying to adapt, such a method of procedure with the pigmies. Though the bright medal has been dangling for years around the neck of Tebi, the pigmies pay as little attention to him as to it, and continue to live as they did in the days of their grandfathers in the shade of the forest. They pay no heed to any propaganda about confederation and the overlordship of chiefs.

Kerese brought us presents, and we gave him gifts in return. Tebi, the medalled chief of all the Efé, riveted his eyes on me, the " Baba wa Bambuti."

A BASA PIGMY'S WIND-SCREEN
(*Page* 181)

EFÉ PIGMIES WITH ELEPHANT SPEARS
(*Page* 138)

TEBI, THE CHIEF WITH THE MEDAL, AND
HIS WIFE

(Page 194)

DRUM AND STRING MUSICAL INSTRUMENT OF
THE EFÉ CAMP AT NDUYE

(Page 201)

When the chief volunteered the information that, at a short distance from his village there was a pigmy settlement, I set out that same afternoon to pay him a return visit. The reception he gave me was a real African one. His hankering after European ways and manners was seen in many articles of his household equipment. When we were ushered into his presence, he was enthroned amid twenty wives, who giggled loudly as they huddled around him, sitting on stools. In the midst of the room, the Bambuti, whose singing we had heard long before we reached the place, were dancing. I was agreeably surprised to see such well nourished—I might almost say plump—little pigmies, hopping about in front of me. Moreover, their dances and songs were both in a new vein, and I was at once on the look-out for fresh impressions. My anticipations were not disappointed. I began to value this trip. Although in the main the Efé are patterned on the lines of all the Bambuti, they had sufficient original and unique features in their habits and outlook to justify a longer stay among them.

The camp, which lay in a " Tongo," or clearing, less than half an hour's journey from Kerese's " Boma," afforded very comfortable quarters. The water supply, however, was not very satisfactory. The path to the camp ran along a deep ravine, along which a rivulet bubbled. It was such a distance from the camp, that it was out of the question to use it for drinking purposes. Our water supply ran through a morass. Tracing its source to the roots of a giant tree, I set about draining the morass in the vicinity of the spring by constructing a timber bulwark. Eventually the spring ran clearly, and we had a plentiful supply both for drinking, washing, and for cooling baths. For the erection of huts Kerese placed some prisoners and two policemen at my disposal, and they set to work with a will. The Bambuti also displayed great zeal in clearing away the bushes, undergrowth and the brambles with jungle knives, so that in a few days an attractive sunny camping ground was laid out. Only a portion of the baggage was brought over from Andudu, the majority being left in the rest-house in charge of a pensioner.

Tebi was the chief of the Andeporu clan, who had

erected their leaf huts there. Scarcely had we settled down, when another clan joined us and built huts of a similar style. A bird's-eye view of the joint camps presented the appearance of an enormous figure eight. This shape was imperative in order to make full use of the clearing, as on both sides the gloomy forest stretched, which nobody would care to tackle. I counted twenty-eight huts, which were very neatly constructed with the exception of the last ones, which had been built in a great hurry. Apparently the negro system of building had affected the Efé architecture. It is true that their huts looked like the usual pigmy bee-hive structures, though perhaps some of them were somewhat taller. Their entrances were barricaded with a peculiar contraption made of saplings fixed with leaves, the effect of which was to form a little veranda. Its purpose appeared to be a protection of the interior against bad weather.

The entrance was between this windscreen and the wall, but only at one side. The better huts were neatly covered with phrynium leaves, but the last ones merely had layers of banana leaves, a very poor protection against a thunderstorm. The hasty manner in which these were made was shown by the fact that the owners did not consider it worth while even to get logs for their bedsteads, but were satisfied with banana leaves strewn on the ground. They had reckoned on a very short stay, which, however, lasted for fourteen days.

Kerese seemed to be a courteous and a broadminded man. He assisted me in many of my enterprises, and I was able to get food supplies for the camp from him.

I cannot speak too favourably of the pigmies in this camp. Possibly they were more reserved than the Bakango. Tebi himself gradually began to show some confidence in me, though occasionally he was rather unpleasant. They were not so obstreperous as the Bakango in begging for salt and tobacco, but there was always a great hubbub at the distribution of the food. There were also very marked divergencies of character to be noticed ; some were always loafing around my hut, while others kept a considerable distance away from it. I have a distinct recollection of a man whose chest was covered with a heavy coat of matted hair, and who was considered to be the best hunter in the camp. He was always squatting in front of his hut, and used to keep up a running conversation with his neighbours, but not even once did he come to my hut to beg for anything. However, like the others, he took all that was offered to him as a matter of course, without a word of thanks.

The Efé were not devoid of a certain courtesy and kindness of heart. They showed their gratitude for the kitchen refuse which my servants gave them by bringing them roasted ants and caterpillars. They even discussed the question of offering me these rare dainties with my servants. The latter, however, told them that I would not touch them, and ate the titbits that had been intended for me, with the greatest relish.

To judge by appearances the pigmies receive visits of strangers from strange camps with cold reserve. The women may welcome their own kin very cordially, but there is great reserve shown in greeting a stranger. The visitor sits down near the hut of a kinswoman, who naturally extends her hand in welcome. After that he sits alone until his arrival is known throughout the camp. Then after a little while odd members of the camp shake hands with him as they happen to pass, and then go on their way. The ceremonial of handshaking is performed by both parties placing their palms together simultaneously.

Meanwhile the hostess prepares a luncheon for her visitor, unless he has been invited to the general meal as is usually the case. Towards evening a crowd of men may possibly gather around the stranger to discuss news. If he is a good conversationalist, who can tell a story humorously, his audience will respond with genuine camaraderie, and there will be a feast of laughter with witty sallies. The pigmies always swarm round a wit, as they are a merry, laughter-loving folk.

I was once present at an entertainment of this type, when a jovial old fellow visited our camp as Tebi's guest. Peal after peal of laughter rang out from the eager throng of listeners, as he passed from story to story. The drollery of his yarns was enhanced by his very sedate, though pleasant demeanour, even when he was speaking of the most comic incidents. He was something of an actor, too, and illustrated a tale of an elephant hunt with vivid gestures that held his audience spellbound.

The life of the pigmies for the most part is a smooth and uneventful one. The primitive little Bambuti communities afford alike little scope for rivalries or bitter discord. Of course squabbles between hostile kindred groups are frequently cropping up. Serious disorders and enmity in the little cosmos of any given camps are, however, almost unheard of, despite the clashing of discordant temperaments among individual members, as my intensive study of the little people convinced me. Despite their instinctive reserve and disinclination to talk when first approached, I found that I was able to differentiate the many types of character that were to be found in the various groups.

Tebi seemed to me a taciturn, uncommunicative man when I first saw him sitting beside Kerese. His medal and his khaki tunic were the only interesting things about him. The timid expression with which he gazed at me on that occasion vanished later on when he got to know me better. Putting aside his tunic and his medal, he turned out in his feather-trimmed rush cap, with his bast apron round his loins or a bit of cloth that I gave him. In this attire he would sit in a creaking chair in front of his hut, chewing something or gazing dreamily into space. Frequently he would start a chat with his wife, who was always kept pretty busy in her hut. His was a childlike, simple and inquisitive nature. He had an idea that it was his duty to be always at my service, and consequently he always sat with his eyes fixed on my hut. I had only to call him, when the reply came promptly: " Besa " (" Here I am "). And then he would talk, although I could not understand a word of what he said. Next he would send for the interpreter, and ask him what I wanted. Whenever he called on me to inquire about anything he invariably brought the interpreter with him. The Efé, as I have mentioned before, do not know Kingwana.

He seemed to be vexed at the fact that he had no power over his pigmies befitting the status of a medalled chief, and was envious of the authority Kerese exercised over his negroes. He even took the opportunity of expressing himself on the matter once in the presence of his subjects, and complained that they did not come to him with their problems, as the negroes went to Kerese. They did not take the slightest notice of his protest, however.

On another occasion in a fit of pique he tied a red flag, made out of a piece of paper, to a pole and stuck it over his hut. Then he sat beneath it, in the panoply of his medal and khaki tunic and brooded over the limitations of his sovereign authority.

Sometimes Kerese used to send me bananas, which my servants hung over the door of my hut. Whenever Tebi's eyes fell on the tempting bunches, he would whine : " Muzungu, give me a banana." I always tossed him one, which he generally caught deftly with his hand, though sometimes it hit him on his naked chest. If, however, I remained deaf to his request he promptly got up, marched with solemn strides towards the bunch, broke off a couple, and strutted before me as he ate them. Then he strode back again with the same studied dignified gait, and squatted on his chair and laughed at me.

I found Tebi extremely useful for explaining to me many problems about his people. He had a vast fund of information on every topic. I shall deal later on with the details I got from him about the religion of the Efé.

He was very inquisitive, as well as a childlike type of man, and was very fond of shooting all kinds of questions at me. His mouth agape he would drink in my replies to random inquiries such as : " Muzungu, is your father still alive ? " or : " Muzungu, where is your village ? " Once when he saw me taking notes of his statements, he abruptly broke in with, " Muzungu, why are you writing that ? " And when I had explained to him to the best of my ability, he followed up with the worrying petulance of a child, by asking : " Muzungu, how do you write ? " This question left me speechless. I vainly tried to suppress a smile. Tebi looked at me reproachfully with his large, mournful, dark eyes. I believe he thought that I was pulling his leg.

His wife was a good-humoured, fat and pleasant-looking woman. They had no children. Tebi, in confidence, explained that her barrenness was due to the fact that a negro had bewitched her.

The custom of filing the teeth to a point is not general among the Efé. Circumcision has only recently begun to be adopted by them, as a result of negro influence.

They very rarely pierce their upper lips, and the customs of piercing the nose and tattooing the body are completely unknown. On the other hand they pierce their ears in the usual way, and insert little bits of wood.

I could get anything that I wanted from the Efé in exchange for glass beads, and they revelled like children in the gaudy colours of those baubles. Women and girls often sat stringing them very tastefully for hours at a stretch. Even Tebi did not disdain to wear a string occasionally.

Like all the Bambuti, the Efé love dancing. To the accompaniment of the rolling of the drums, " bones," rattles and singing, they keep twisting and turning in sinuous mazes for hours on end without shewing a trace of fatigue. Incidentally, I never saw Tebi joining in the dance. Presumably he thought it beneath his dignity to do so.

Their tunes and their dances, both of which are very rhythmical, resemble in many ways those of the Bakango. One striking difference was that the music intermittently would stop, and the dancers would stand stock still, staring up at the sky, while their heads, necks and eyes would work convulsively, as though they had been struck with epilepsy. Then suddenly the dance would start again. I presume that these contortions had a symbolic signification as the dances were called chimpanzee dances, elephant dances, etcetera. They showed how the various beasts reacted to stalking and attack.

A chimpanzee dance which I saw in another Efé camp, demanded considerable histrionic ability on the part of the performers. Only men and boys take part in it. They proceed through the entire camp with slow serpentine movements, their faces working in weird grimaces. The eldest of the group, armed with bow and arrow, represents the hunter, who lurks behind a bush or a tree, and takes aim at the revellers. Off goes the arrow, while the dancers scatter, roll about the ground, grin and roar. The drama is rehearsed again and again to the accompaniment of the thunder of the drums.

THE " PALIENGBE " GAME
(Page 201)

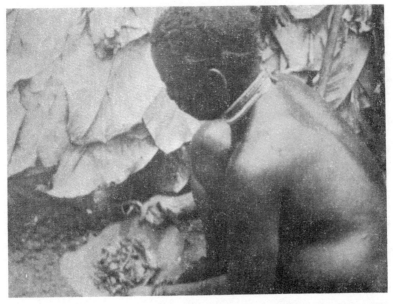

" HIS WIFE CAME ALONG PRESENTLY TO DRESS THE CATERPILLARS"
(Page 203)

AN EFÉ HUT IN UNDETSE VILLAGE
The annexe is used as a bedroom for the children.

EVEN BABIES JOIN IN THE DANCE

Paliengbe is a game in which men and women take part. First a bunch of bananas is hung from a pole in the middle of the camp. On one side the men stand, armed with little bows, but instead of arrows they use little bits of stick. Their task is to defend the bunch of bananas against the onslaught of the women, who are armed with cudgels and have their heads protected against the men's arrows with upturned baskets. With deafening hand-clapping and singing the phalanx of women charges the ranks of men. The latter loose off a shower of arrows. Some of the women get scared, but most of them drive man after man with their cudgels in panic-stricken flight into the thicket. The men rally again, and there is another fusillade of arrows, which drives the women back. An auxiliary force of women comes on the scene, however, just as the men have shot their last ammunition away. The game ends in the headlong flight of the men, and the women celebrate their victory with peals of derisive laughter and triumphal singing.

It is strange that the Bambuti have no folk songs apart from their dance melodies. I never heard anything in this line except abortive efforts at marching songs. Possibly the explanation is that the pigmy specializes in rhythm and not in melody, with the result that every song is primarily a dance tune. Hence their passion for drums and bones.

The Efé have a peculiar type of drum, really a cross between a drum and a bass-viol. A piece of bark is placed over a cavity hollowed out in the earth and held firmly in position by upright blocks of wood. This is the drum that is beaten with a cudgel. Through a hole in the centre of the bark a piece of rattan string is introduced, and tied at one end of a horizontal stick on the inner surface of the drum, while the other end is attached firmly to the branch of a tree. Then the player twangs the string and pounds the drum to the accompaniment of the strains of the singers.

The menu of the Andeporu is superior to that of the Bakango, probably owing to the generosity of Kerese, who is more liberal than most negroes with his supplies of bananas. Moreover, the Efé eat practically anything that comes their way, and do not even turn their noses up at carrion. On one occasion a pigmy had come upon the carcase of a semi-putrid ant-eater, and his comrades were just about to bring it into the camp when I stopped them. The most coveted dainties among the Efé were ants and caterpillars. The flying periods among the ants are in April and September, and are gala days for the pigmies. The camps are then deserted, the family groups scatter, and each family seeks its own ant-hill which is somewhere in the forest and is regarded as private property. As it is extremely important not to miss the ants as they fly out, the huts are often deserted for several days in advance, so as to be in time, for by missing a night the entire booty might be missed.

The ants build their nests under the ground, and in the process push it up into big hillocks, which look like humps on the surface of the ground. Tebi's ant-hill was about half an hour's walk from the camp, and one morning when he was going out to visit his property, armed with a jungle-knife, I went with him.

Tebi led the way, and slashed at the overhanging liana, to cut a path for both of us. We travelled very slowly, as my leader was peering in all directions. There was not a tree in his path that he did not scrutinize very closely. I was just wondering what he was looking for, when suddenly he halted and began to slash at the shrubbery all around with his knife. I was rather puzzled at his manœuvres. Reading the question in my eyes, he made a silent gesture, and pointed his knife towards a crooked tree, whose trunk seemed to be covered with moss. On closer inspection I realized that it was thickly coated with caterpillars. By cutting away the shrubbery Tebi had marked his discovery as his own property, as he was obviously not in a position at the moment to collect the countless caterpillars. He would return later for that purpose. Tebi had, so to speak, branded the caterpillars as his, and nobody would contest his find with him or steal it from him. So we proceeded ahead, and found the ant-hill a little distance away on a gloomy steep declivity. Tebi immediately set about cutting a thin segment out of the hill, so that the ants' tunnels were partially exposed. In every aperture he stuck a tiny fragment of wood, in order to observe the effect on the ants. It seems that by this device the pigmies can discover the flying periods of the ants, for the nearer their burrowing approaches to the surface, the more imminent is the flight. Therefore about this season the pigmies go out every day to make observations. They measure the depth of the tunnels which are ever being pushed towards the surface perpendicularly.

On this occasion Tebi timed the flight for the following night, as ants only fly by twilight or at night.

When a flight is so near, a tiny windscreen is erected at the foot of the ant-hill and is occupied by the family. Then the entire hill is covered with a thatch of leaves ; if possible wild palm branches are used, and a deep trench is dug round its base. A fire is lit in the hut, and chips of pinewood are piled up near the hill. At the approach of dusk the flight starts. The ant-hill hums with a murmuring and a rustling sound. With wings outstretched the insects soar into the air, but strike against the leafy thatch and fall to the ground. Meanwhile the fire near the trench flares up, and the insects crawl towards the light, only to fall into the hole that the pigmies have made just in front of the fire. The wife is squatting close by, and she shovels the fat insects with both hands into a basket and covers them with leaves. The booty is divided into portions, packed up in leaves and sent to the camp, where the feast begins.

Ants are prepared in various ways by the pigmies. Sometimes they eat them alive, after picking off their wings. They prefer to roast them wings and all, when they cram them into their mouths, until the fat trickles down from the corners. Another method of preparing them is to pick off their wings, pound them with salt in little wooden mortars and then boil them. This is considered a particularly dainty dish.

Hardly had they returned to the camp, when Tebi and his wife, who fetched a basket, started off afresh to gather the caterpillars. Incidentally it should be noted that the only edible caterpillars are medium-sized greenish and hairy ones. They did not take long to collect their booty and to carry it home.

Tebi's wife then set about cooking them. She placed

glowing coals in a vessel, spread a handful of caterpillars on them, and started to shake and turn the
contents. Then she picked out the roasted caterpillars,
and spread them on leaves, whereupon Tebi and a guest
whom he had invited tucked into the banquet.

A simple but less appetising way of eating these larvæ
is to catch them by the heads between two fingers of one
hand, squeeze them out of their skins with the fore-
finger and thumb of the other hand, right into the mouth
of the consumer.

Other pigmies go to the length of boiling the roasted
caterpillars over again, and using them with the boiled
ants as an entrée at the usual evening meal.

If an Efé has men as guests, he eats with them while
his wife has her meal alone. Otherwise husband and
wife dip their fingers into the same pot and eat together.

The Efé prefer ants, caterpillars and snakes to game.
A probably correct inference, suggested by this prefer-
ence, is that these primitive creatures subsisted entirely
on such grubs and insects before they became acquainted
with hunting weapons.

The Andeporu have, definitely of late years, not been
skilful enough hunters to subsist on such game as they
killed. Tebi told me that they used to hunt elephants
when they lived near Aleku, where those animals abound.
He also mentioned individuals among his people who
used to hunt elephants in former times, which seemed
credible enough to me as I had no difficulty in securing
hunting spears.

Tebi contended that there was no use to-day in hunting elephants for a reason which he explained in grave
detail to me. When the Andeporu left Aleku to attach
themselves to Kerese—whether they were bribed by him
or not he could not say—the rest of the Efé of Aleku
were jealous and furious about it, and practised pikipiki
magic, so that their renegade brothers might never again
slay elephants. And their spell was effective, for never
afterwards did the Andeporu attempt to kill elephants.
However, I suggested to Tebi that a more likely explanation was the fact that all the elephants have been chased
away from the vicinity of Kerese's village.

The hunting-net is also unknown to these pigmies—at

any rate they never use it nowadays, but they are keen bowmen. Their wooden arrows are not poisoned, but to make them more serviceable in the quest of small game, they harden the tips with fire. Their iron arrows which are furnished with enormous barbs, are made by the negroes, who sell them, mostly in exchange for game, to the pigmies.

I am inclined to doubt the assertion of these pigmies that they occasionally hunt buffaloes with spears, for I never saw any buffalo-horns anywhere while I was among them.

The successful hunter announces his return by blowing his hunting-whistle and with shouts of joy, but if a wild hog has been killed, all the hunters return silently until they are close to the camp, when they whistle and scream and raise a terrific din to which the women in the camp respond with equal zest. And after that they have a sumptuous meal, followed by a very hilarious dance.

In this camp and a neighbouring one, I noticed that these Efé have very few children, a circumstance that seemed all the more peculiar as all the other pigmies I met were very prolific. Apparently this is due to the negroes' influence, as both the Mamvu and their cousins, the Balese negroes, singularly enough, complain of the great dearth of children. The fact that it is only the pigmies attached to the Mamvu that have so few children, while the opposite obtained among the Balese, is a clear proof of the effect of closer association with the negroes.

The explanation which the negroes and the pigmies themselves generally give for this ominous phenomenon among the races affected, is merely the outcome of Congo superstition. They say that the sterility of the women is attributable to themselves, as they invoke the aid of the pikipiki. The power to break the spell of the pikipiki is alleged to lie with the mothers-in-law alone. The latter make capital out of this idea, by acting in collusion with their daughters in order to extract repeated relays of presents from the husbands, who long for children more than anything else in the world.

The Mamvu negroes rarely marry pigmy women, apparently, but the Balese negroes are very keen on such alliances, as they say that Bambuti brides are always fruitful, while the women of their own race are barren. "Every Bambuti woman, even when she is old, can still bear children," said a Balese negro to me, "but our women, even in their youth, cannot produce even one child."

The pigmies have a very definite solution for their mother-in-law problems. Mothers-in-law and sons-in-law have absolutely no transactions with one another— they never even talk to one another. The same thing happens in a lesser degree in the case of father-in-law and daughter-in-law. I remember a young couple in the Asunguda camp who built their hut near that of the husband's parents. The young wife, who frequently used to sit in front of her hut, erected a fence of phrynium leaves so as to cut off the view of the abode of her parents-in-law.

There is no ritualistic ceremony in connection with a marriage among the Efé, just as is the case with the other Bambuti. Sometimes there are cases of elopement when the young man is too poor to give compensation for his bride. The decision rests with her. She can stay with her lover if she chooses, and perhaps some form of indemnification may be given to her people, as I have already mentioned.

It is the custom among the negroes of the forest regions that on the wedding-day, the bride's family group and especially the bride's mother, demand many presents from the bridegroom. The bride is escorted to the bridegroom's village, and the procession moves very slowly, taking several days to do the journey frequently. Again and again the bridal procession pitches camp, and invariably the bridegroom is informed of the rate of progress. At definite stages a hint is conveyed to him that the procession is unable or unwilling to go any further. Every time this happens the poor fellow takes the hint, and more and more gifts are dispatched, until at length the pre-matrimonial blackmailing game is finished. The pigmies too have adopted this system when a marriage with a negro is contemplated. The relatives accompany the bride-to-be on a slow-motion procession, camping frequently on the way, at their own sweet will, in order to extract presents from the prospec-

IN THE EFÉ CAMP AT NDUYE

EFÉ WOMEN PLAITING SLEEPING-MATS OF PHRYNIUM LEAVES

PIGMY GIRLS STRINGING GLASS BEADS
(*Page* 200)

PLAYING " PIKIPIKI " FLUTES
(*Page* 205)

tive groom. The negro, however, is not always in festive
mood or generous humour on his wedding-day. He often
just sends a friend ahead to abduct the girl for him, or
maybe he will pounce on her himself, pick her up and
carry her off to his village. The cheated pigmies pursue
him with taunts and insults to the negro village, but they
are very lucky if they get a few bananas as compensation
for the outrage inflicted on them.

The pigmies always take care to carry a good supply
of game on a bridal procession, so that at a moment's
notice, provided ample presents from the groom are forthcoming, they can stage a magnificent wedding feast.

Some quaint ceremonies among the Efé in connection
with childbirth are worth recording. When a woman
feels that her time has come, her husband summons the
aid of the other women among whom is the camp midwife. Some drops of the juice of the mpempe fruit,
mixed with various medicinal leaves which have been
reduced to ashes, are poured into the mouth of the new-
born babe, and some of it is also put into the water in
which it is washed. The umbilical cord is severed with
an arrow in such a way that a little piece is left adhering
to the navel and is sprinkled with ashes. After a while
it drops off, whereupon the mother wraps it in a sachet
made of leaves, and hangs it round the infant's neck.
The pigmies believe that this makes the child grow.
When the child has grown up, the fragment of umbilical
cord is buried in the forest in the vicinity of a river or a
pool. The portion of the cord that has been severed with
an arrow is buried either in or near the hut, and the
placenta is interred in the forest.

After her delivery the mother takes a three days' rest,
after which she starts about the daily tasks again, and
whatever work she undertakes, no matter how strenuous,
she always carries her infant in her shoulder-sash.

I have never seen twins in an Efé family myself, but
the latter told me that dual births do occur, although
the children die very soon. I could not ascertain whether
they were killed for some superstitious reason, or whether
they allowed the poor little things to die through a
fatalistic belief that they were doomed to death in any
case.

Taking all in all, I have lived for many happy days in the camp of the Andeporu, and have seen and learned many strange things. Even the very weather was in my favour. The sun was shining brightly most of the time, and I only remember one hurricane which suddenly burst upon us. It uprooted the banana trees and levelled many of the primitive pigmy houses to the ground. As the little people stayed a good deal in the camp, I had many opportunities of watching their daily routine and seeing their simple pleasures. There was an eternal sameness about the lives of the old people. I still have in mind a very old grey-haired little woman—1 do not recollect to what family group she actually belonged—who lived under a roof that was full of holes, but remained stoically crouching in a corner even during torrential rain. The women of the camp brought the poor old thing food every day. She worried about nothing else.

There was also a little old man with an ashen face, ringed round with a bushy, greyish yellow beard. He usually sat alone in front of the fire, and kept looking straight ahead of him with an infantile stare. I never remember having exchanged one word with him. I frequently spoke to him, but his sole reply was a galvanic grin. The only thing he ever did was to poke the fire, and, when he was tired, he lay down beside it and fell asleep.

The younger Efé women and the girls paid great attention to their appearances. They were always ready to barter anything for little hand-mirrors. Although like all pigmies, the Efé simply will not wash themselves, their women occasionally rub their faces and bodies with a black oil, made by melting kernels of the oil palm in a pot over the fire.

My departure synchronized with the period of the ant harvest. Apart from Tebi and his wife, just a few old people remained in the camp. As the pigmies intended to stay away for rather a long spell, I had to hunt for bearers in the negro village. A motley assortment of large and small men were rounded up to carry my baggage to Andudu. Thence I was to travel to the land of the Balese, as soon as Kerese had got together the necessary number of bearers.

And so once more I rested in beautiful Andudu and waited with African stoicism for the bearers. Almost every day I had visitors. Hordes of pigmies from the outlying regions came to me with little gifts. Among one of the batches that swarmed round my veranda, I noticed a young mother with a charming little baby. When I inquired about its father, somebody in the crowd of scrubby youths replied quickly : " It has no father. We are all its father ! " The merry look of the young woman showed that her unmarried condition did not worry her very much.

Kerese fixed a date on which the promised bearers were to turn up in Andudu ; but they never appeared at all. Again and again I sent messengers to him, but they always came back with fresh promises. Once it was to the effect that Kerese's messengers were already in the villages, rounding up the missing men. Another time I was told that the chief had also come to the aid of a lady, alleged by one to be an English woman, and by another to be an American, whom the bearers had deserted in the heart of the forest. All I could do was to grin and bear it.

At last Kerese himself came along to hunt up the men for me. And as soon as the first eleven of them appeared I set off with the absolute minimum of baggage, leaving the rest behind in charge of my hunter and a policeman. It was the only possible solution to the difficulty.

CHAPTER X

AMONG THE EFÉ ATTACHED TO THE BALESE

MY purpose was to cut diagonally through the Balese forest in a south-easterly direction. Among the thickets hosts of Bambuti roam in quest of antelope, wild pig, chimpanzees, elephants and okapi.

The pigmies in this region are definitely the most racially pure and the most primitive that I have met. So much so that they give one the impression that they have, at some former period, been independent of the negroes. Moreover, they have preserved their language and their culture better than the other pigmies. Of the negro tribes, which, through repeated racial inroads, were driven towards the forest, some settled in a southerly direction near the Ituri and even beyond it, while others, who travelled on a more easterly route towards the upper reaches of the Ituri, seem to have been held up at the Epulu and the Ngayu, so that the Efé remained unmolested by them. Later incursions were more successful, and negroes from the north and east invaded their forest regions. Their numbers cannot have been very great, however, as they did not gain nearly the same mastery over the pigmies as did their cousins in the more westerly tracts of the forest. And this led to an evolution in Efé culture of a different type from that which we have already observed among the Bambuti and the Aká.

In the second part of my journey from Nduyu I had my choice of striking the more frequented Kilo-Irumu route, or of travelling in a more southerly direction towards Mombasa on the Epulu. I decided on the latter course, as I believed that I should thus meet more pigmies. I was wrong in my conjecture, as for four days at a stretch we went through an almost depopulated region.

The Nepoko River, whose rippling musical murmuring I recollected so pleasantly at Andudu, here showed itself in a more angry mood. Its swirling waters which thundered along between muddy banks held forth no invitation for a cooling dip. It was spanned by a long rickety wooden bridge, which could only be crossed at one's imminent peril by springing from one creaking log to another. It seems that for years no attempt had been made at renovating it. Apparently the reason was that, since the alteration of the district boundaries, the traffic across it had been very slender. While the Gombari district was extended to the Mamvu, the Balese, who live on the left bank of the Nepoko, are almost all under the control of Mombasa.

On the caravan path from the Nepoko to the Epulu and across the Nduye, lie many villages of the Balese, a negro tribe which is closest to the Mamvu racially and linguistically. The Balese are divided into many sub-sections, among them the Dese, the Masa and the Karo. The genuine Balese themselves dwell on both sides of the Ituri in the vicinity of Irumu. The rivers passing through the Balese territory are the Nepoko, the Nduye, the Ngayu and the Upper Ituri.

The distance travelled during this journey was something over one hundred and thirty miles. It took me nearly six weeks, as I stayed for a fair time in the various camps. My longest halts were at Tongepete and on the Nduye. At least one horde of pigmies was attached to every negro village, but I could not devote my attention to them all, as my bearers were hired from time to time to cover definite stretches of ground. But the Bambuti never failed to turn up in every village, so that at least I was able to get an impressionist glance at them as I passed on my way.

We had just put in two hours' steady going after crossing the Nepoko bridge when we came upon a group of pigmies who seemed to be in the process of striking camp, as the women were laden with heavy burdens. These Bambuti, however, could not have heard of my visit to the Congo at all, for scarcely had they seen me when they vanished into the gloom of the forest like shadows.

Our first halt was in Orokoto. The little negro village,

with a snug rest-house facing the clean street, held out the promise of a comfortable night's rest. The bearers settled down and started to prepare their food. While I was arranging with the negroes for a visit to the nearest pigmy camp, two young men, bathed in sweat, came running up to me with my post. After that I had neither eyes nor ears for anything save the news from home. I read letter after letter eagerly, and, as answers to many of them were urgently needed, I sat up until a long time after midnight writing feverishly by candle-light, so as to have my mail ready by morning for the same runners who had brought me the letters. These simple, swift-footed couriers work in relays, carrying the mail from village to village, for several hundred miles until after many days they reach the post office at Wamba.

The path which we struck next morning and which traversed a dreadful desert, skirted the little villages of Madangba, Abemon, Mbau and Undetse. The last-named provided an agreeable surprise for us with its pleasant position on a hill devoid of trees, in contrast to the other villages which were buried in the twilight shadows of the rank luxuriant forest.

Abemon met me as I was passing through his village, and invited me to stay there for a while, as he also had pigmies who wished to meet me. I suggested that they might meet me at Undetse, which I had intended as my next halt. But Abemon shook his head, saying : " Undetse's chief is my enemy. We have no dealings with one another." I shrugged my shoulders and passed on. But in spite of Abemon's attitude a deputation of his pigmies waited on me a few days later.

In accordance with custom each village changes its name on the accession of a new chief. Undetse is an exception to this rule, as it still bears the name of the late chief—a precedent that Europeans would welcome other Congo villages to follow, as it would not entail a perpetual changing of names in maps and indexes.

On my arrival the chief immediately placed one of his huts at my disposal, but I preferred the open club hut to the windowless clay structures of the natives, not only because it was more roomy, but also as it was brighter and more airy.

Hardly had I settled down comfortably, when the bargaining about bearers had to be gone into once more. I knew I could count no longer on Kerese's promise that he would forward the baggage I had left behind. Undetse, on the other hand, could supply four bearers at most, while I needed at least thirty. However, before I had all my baggage, it was quite useless to continue my journey. Some way out of the dilemma must be found. The only thing was to bribe the bearers who had accompanied me so far, with a promise of double pay if they would return and fetch my other baggage from Andudu. At the last moment, however, a smart gang of men turned up and said they had been sent by Kerese. At once I dispatched them ahead with a portion of my equipment so that at least I would be certain of avoiding a repetition of the same trouble, when I resumed my journey.

Close to the negro village, in a valley, there was an abandoned and weed-covered pigmy settlement, which the next morning pulsated with the sounds of renewed life. The Bambuti whose camp was deep in the forest had taken a notion to settle down close to me, and consequently rebuilt the former camp. Men and women cleared the ground with jungle knives, removing the weeds and thatching the huts with fresh mangongu. In a few hours the camp looked shipshape, and the Bambuti were already dancing to the beat of the drum when I appeared among them. They were not a bit afraid of me ; in fact, their expressive eyes lit up with a warm smile of welcome. I was amazed as I realized how a large pigmy camp with over one hundred inhabitants had sprung up before my eyes apparently out of the ground within the space of a few hours. Spiral columns of smoke were ascending from many fires, and while tobacco pipes were passed round, a busy exchange of pigmy souvenirs for beads and cloths was in full swing in a few minutes.

Two emaciated and obviously consumptive women crouched dejectedly in front of their huts. I also saw some decrepit aged folk, too, but the majority of the people in the camp were hale and vigorous, and there were children galore.

Beside a fire in front of his hut a pigmy was hammering an iron spear head into shape—the first and only pigmy smith that I met in all my wanderings. He had learned the trade from the negroes in the village and then set up for himself.

More and more pigmies, singly and in families, drifted into the camp to greet me. A young fellow who did not belong to the camp, entered my hut, and, after crouching before me with an uneasy look in his eyes, suddenly flung himself flat on his face, simultaneously striking the ground as hard as he could with his right arm. Then he got up, wheeled round and disappeared without saying a word. It was the first time I was greeted in this quaint fashion. Another man welcomed me by removing his straw hat, and hissing at me, while he placed his hand on his brow. This apparently was the usual form of greeting in this district.

In the course of traversing the Balese forest, I was surprised to observe that, the more I proceeded southward, the more striking was the resemblance between the negroes and the Bambuti. There can be no doubt that in these regions the races are very much mixed—a fact admitted by the negroes themselves. I frequently heard the inhabitants of one village assert that all the people in the neighbouring one were Bambuti. Of course this was an exaggeration, but it showed the recognition of the fact that the more southward one went the more obvious were the evidences of a mixed strain. In one village you heard negroes boasting that they had married pigmy women through choice, while in the next they said that there was no use in marrying Bambuti girls as they would be bound to run away as soon as the gipsy strain in them lured them off to their own folk into the forest.

It is not so long since the negroes and pigmies were engaged in open warfare with one another. The little men put up a stout fight against the invasion of the forest regions by the blacks. Moreover, the pigmies plundered the banana plantations whenever the negroes refused to give them what they considered a fair share of the fruit, with the result that on this score alone many fierce encounters took place between the two races. If a negro was killed in such an engagement, all the pigmies vanished for a long spell until forced by hunger they would return. When they did come back the first thing they did was to offer the negroes a pigmy girl by way of compensation, in order to deprecate the vengeance. Whereupon they were permitted to settle down in peace in the vicinity of the village. And that was how the Efé generally came to be parasites on the negroes.

The first accounts I heard about the fights between the forest negroes and the pigmies were given me by some grey-haired pigmies who had fought against the Mangbeli (Mangbetu) of Gombari and had successfully repelled them. They explained to me how the pigmy and negro methods of warfare differed. The pigmies never advanced to battle in formal ranks, but crept up stealthily under cover of the forest towards their enemies, at whom they discharged a volley of silent insidious arrows, and then retired noiselessly, leaving no trace of their whereabouts.

It seems that the pigmies formerly acted as guides to the negroes, when the latter went to the River Nduye in quest of fish, and in the process came into conflict with their own stock. The inevitable result was that the Efé and their patrons made common cause against all their enemies, be they negro or pigmy—a tendency which strongly prevails even at the present day.

Symptomatic of the merging of the two races in this territory is the tendency of negro and pigmy to share one another's pastimes. The pigmies as well as the black men took part in the funeral dances which I witnessed in Undetse.

Probably a leading factor in the interblending of the two races was the fact that the negroes who had trekked into the forest, came without any women at all, and helped themselves to the wives and daughters of the pigmies.

There is a legend to the effect that Etogba, the first Mulese negro who penetrated into the forest of the Bambuti, built a village with their help, and then invited them to settle down with him in it. They refused, however, because in accordance with their hereditary customs they preferred to roam the forests.

And here is another legend which points out how the negroes brought the sturdy pigmies under their control, more through trickery than straightforward fighting. A negro whose house was built among crags wrought great harm among the Bambuti by his magic dances. An old hag who lived with the negro lured a pigmy, who was passing by their plantation, into a trap. " A wild beast is laying waste our field," she said, " I beg you to kill it. Grunt like a pig, and it will appear at once, when you can kill it." The pigmy did as she told him, grunted, and waited in readiness for the boar. The grunting brought the negro on the scene, dancing his magic dance and jangling his bells. The pigmy took aim, but his bow-string snapped, as the woman had previously cut it half through. The negro then killed the pigmy and all the other Bambuti, whereupon the woman returned to the field and brought home the bodies and ate them.

The chief was now the only survivor of all the Bambuti. Later on the old hag beguiled him, too, to go into the plantation to kill the wild pig that she said was doing such terrible damage to the banana trees. When he reached the plantation he saw the great damage that had been done, but also observed that the whole field was covered with blood. He sent the old woman home, and tested his bow, whereupon the string snapped. Immediately he suspected treachery, but taking a spare string, which he had secreted about him, he fixed it to his bow. Then he started to grunt, whereupon the negro appeared and began to dance. The pigmy took aim and hit him in the chest. The negro ran back staggering, and soon collapsed among the rocks, dead. The pigmy chief then cut off the arm of the negro and fled into the forest, where all the Bambuti women were waiting for him, and he went away with them until they came to a great stretch of water and waded through it.

I have tried as far as possible to reproduce in my translation the quaint, primitive phrasing of the pigmy who told me this legend.

After I had waited patiently for several days all my baggage arrived from Andudu, and I was prepared to take up the trail for Tongepete.

As the chief of Undetse could not give me all the bearers that I needed I appealed to the pigmies for help, and was successful. A huge number enlisted on my promise of payment with bales of cloth. The more pigmy bearers I could hire the better for me, as I knew that the carrying capacity of the little fellows was very limited, and that a negro could easily do the work of two pigmies. They lacked the black man's physical strength as well as his training in carrying burdens.

The start of my march through the forest, in company with this mighty caravan of pigmies, was quite hilarious. At first they tackled the job with the greatest zest, and to the accompaniment of songs and wild cheering they vanished into the thicket with such speed that I had the greatest difficulty in keeping up with them. Very soon, however, they began to show signs of languor and exhaustion, and again and again batches of them, oozing perspiration from every pore, sat down on the ground, exhausted, beside their loads.

The " capita," or leader, a shrewd little fellow, the blacksmith I mentioned before, had his work cut out in urging his listless crew ahead. In his capacity as leader he carried very little himself. In fact, with the exception of some wild cat skins, which I had collected for friends at home and which he attached apron-wise to his girdle, he had nothing but his spear.

The first to give up was an old man, who staggered along under a thirty-four pound bag of salt. An hour had hardly elapsed after we left Undetse when he quietly dropped his bundle on the ground, muttered something to the man behind him about having to return to the camp, and forthwith vanished among the trees. When I arrived at the scene a good while had elapsed without his showing up again. His comrades shouted his name again and again, but got no reply save the echoes of the forest. The pigmy had deserted us, and the bag of salt lay abandoned on the wayside. A thirty-four pound bag of salt is a small fortune in the Balese forest, and not to be thrown away lightly. When at length the blacksmith came up and saw what his kinsman had done, his rage was only equalled by his embarrassment, and he relieved his feelings in a torrent of incoherent words. As the nearest village was not far off I hoped to be able to find a bearer there, and meanwhile left my hunter in charge of the salt.

Angode was a little village with a rickety rest-hut. The inhabitants had a sinister reputation as furtive cannibals, so my cook told me. As far as possible all travellers avoided this village. Only the day before our arrival a Mungwana and his wife had been obliged to spend the night in its gloomy and musty rest-hut. In the middle of the night the husband was aroused by a strange noise, and discovered that an attempt was being made to burst open the door which he had barricaded. Peering out he saw knives gleaming in the darkness, and knew at once what was afoot. Seizing his spear, he shouted as loud as he could, whereupon the attackers took to their heels. The man remained awake, still gripping his spear, until dawn, when he and his wife fled from the place with all possible speed.

Personally I found the natives of the place a very surly and unfriendly lot. I asked the chief to send a bearer to fetch the bag of salt, but he started making excuses. The only way to deal with the sullen brute was to try the effect of bullying him, which I did. The result was that, with as bad grace as possible, he sent for a man and ordered him to go and fetch the salt. The man, however, taking his cue from his master's tone, protested volubly and menacingly. Whereupon I caught him by the back of the neck and literally rushed him at a trot out of the village. The effect was magical. In less than no time he was back with the bag of salt, and without a protest he followed the Bambuti when we resumed our march.

After leaving the sinister village, our path, which was up hill and down dale, became more and more rugged, and put a terrible strain on the poor little pigmies. They were absolutely exhausted when at length we reached the negro village of Awasa, which nestled in a neat little valley.

The villagers supplied me with bananas and two pots of banana beer in exchange for salt, and my tired bearers settled down to what they regarded as a banquet. How their faces beamed as they squatted round the beer pots. After they had emptied the two pots they were in such excellent spirits that, when I ventured to increase their burdens on our taking the road again, they made no protest. Mainly these were curios that the negroes had pressed on me.

In Tongepete village, where a young man welcomed me in lieu of the chief, who was away, I discovered that I was quite near a Bambuti camp, which struck me as being appallingly badly situated. To make matters worse it had been visited by a thunderstorm just before our arrival, and the ground was a maze of rivulets and mud. The pigmies were all crouching together in their huts, staring blankly at the dripping trees. I had intended spending a week in Tongepete, but I realized that it would be suicide to take up my abode in such surroundings. The camp, literally, was pitched in a thicket, and encircled a tiny marshy valley. Rarely did I turn back so promptly on a Bambuti camp. However, some of the pigmies escorted me to the village, and as we walked, I suggested that they should shift their camp as near as possible to the rest-hut in Tongepete, where I had taken up my quarters. With great alacrity they decided to follow my advice. I must admit that the presence of the deputy chief, who cordially supported my suggestion, probably influenced them to a certain extent in their decision.

The very next morning I was greeted with the pleasing news that the Bambuti had pitched their camp as near as possible to my hut. The spot they selected was dry, and the huts were built in a circle in the shadow of some giant trees in such a way that in the centre there was ample open space. Family group after family group joined the camp, and very soon it was quite an imposing affair.

The camp was so close to my hut that I could hear the pigmies talking. Consequently there was no need to build a new hut for me, and I merely got my pigmy friends to erect a shelter of phrynium leaves for me, in the shade of which I usually stayed during the daytime.

In the middle of the camp they had left a small tree standing, to which the drum was tied, and in whose shade I could look on at the dance. But on the following day the Bambuti were in a regular frenzy of rage, for a downpour during the night had swamped the ground in such a way that puddles formed in the low-lying spots. But that did not deter the Bambuti. Soon both young and old were dancing in a ring round the tree wading up to their ankles in the mud.

In this camp I saw a type of dwelling that I had never met before. A group, consisting of several families, occupied the same abode, which was really a gigantic windscreen, with the front entirely open. All the other families had, as usual, their own private huts.

The garb of the men was just the same as that described in the early pages of this book, but the women's dress aped the fashion of the Balese women. A haughty young woman, who wore a rush-cap at a saucy angle on her woolly head, caused quite a good deal of amusement. It is a headgear that looks picturesque on men, but rather grotesque on women.

The forest around Tongepete swarmed with game. It abounds with chimpanzees, which thrust themselves on the notice of visitors by their wild screams, although they never venture outside the cover of the thickets.

In order to test the dexterity in marksmanship of the pigmies, I suggested that they should have a chimpanzee hunt, and promised a generous reward if they had a good bag. A few minutes later, it was about nine in the morning, a troop of young men and boys started with bows and arrows. Near midday the news was already in the camp that a female chimpanzee had been hit with three arrows, but that it was impossible to get at her, as she had crawled with her baby into the top of a tree. I was asked to send a rifle to kill the animal. My hunter set out for the spot and brought down the animal with a direct hit. When the mother's body hurtled to the ground the baby was uninjured and clung to a branch. With anxious looks it peered down from its dizzy height, undecided as to what to do. As it showed no signs of coming down, a youth climbed up the tree to fetch it. The baby chimpanzee, divining his purpose, scrambled down to the ground, and threw itself on its dead mother's body, to which it clung convulsively. It took some force to unloose its grip.

The hunters arrived at my hut yelling, singing and dancing. I never saw pigmies create such a shindy before, and I eagerly seized the opportunity of filming it. What the gist of their song was I could not make out, but it must have been something very lively, as they kept hopping and leaping around all the time, while a young lad held the frightened-looking baby chimpanzee over his head with both hands and dandled it to and fro. Its mother, bound with liana coils, lay on the ground.

BUBI
(*Page 221*)

SMEARING THE FACE WITH ASHES

AN EFÉ ELDER

AN EFÉ MAID ENJOYING ROASTED BANANAS

Presently we tethered Bubi, as I named the pretty baby, to a cord. He refused to touch the milk placed before him, and remained huddled up, as he gazed mournfully on the ground, and whined as if his little heart would break : " Hu, hu, hu." Then he would stop his lamentations for a moment to rub his nose with his left paw, and start to howl again. Bubi knew instinctively that he had lost his mother. As he still stubbornly refused to touch the milk, I dipped his face into it a couple of times. He liked the taste of it, and started to lap it up of his own accord. When he finished his milk I peeled a banana, and put it into his little hand. He tackled this promptly with great gusto.

I gave the mother-chimpanzee to the pigmies to eat, but asked them, if possible, not to break the bones when dividing the meat. They promised to go very carefully about the job, but hardly was I out of sight, when they split the breast bone in two, to facilitate the division of the spoil. I was rather annoyed, as I was anxious to secure a complete chimpanzee skeleton for research purposes.

As Bubi still kept whining after he had been two days tethered, I felt so sorry for the poor little beggar that I unloosed him. He was now quite free to return to the forest, but he preferred to stay in the camp. He took a particular liking to my hunter, who often took him in his arms, but he dogged me like a retriever. Sometimes I held him by the hand and took him for a walk. On such occasions he would hop along in upright position, using his left forepaw as a sort of walking-stick. Again I would take him by both hands and make him dance, to his intense amusement. In short, Bubi was a source of entertainment to all the camp.

I got a box placed on the veranda of my hut as a bed for Bubi. As soon as it was dusk he clambered into it, huddled himself up with his face to the wall and fell asleep. A lighted match or a candle terrified him dreadfully ; whenever he saw either he would wail pitifully, and stare at it open-mouthed ; then he would look at me with anguish in his eyes. And then I would stroke his head, and he would drop off to sleep peacefully.

Bubi was an early riser. At peep of day he climbed

out of his little house, crept quietly to my bed, opened
the mosquito-curtains with both hands and kept calling :
" Ho, ho, ho," until I awoke. Then he laid his head on
my bed to be stroked. He stayed with me until I got up,
when the servants gave him milk, after which he foraged
around the kitchen, where there was always something
to steal. If I took him into the pigmy camp with me,
the children played with him and made him dance. If
grown-ups, however, tried to get him to dance he always
bit them.

I had been very anxious for a long time to secure a
pigmy's skeleton for research purposes. The more I got
to understand the mentality of the pigmies, however, the
more I realized that only by strategy could I succeed in
my objective. Of course, if I had not cared for the
consequences there would have been no difficulty at all.
All I had to do was to dig up any Bambuti grave I came
across. Such a thoughtless act would have brought an
abrupt ending to my expedition. Not that the pigmies
would have had recourse to violence, but their respect
for me and their affection would have turned to loathing,
and owing to the uncanny speed and silence with which
news is disseminated in the forest, my position would
have been untenable in every single pigmy camp in the
Congo. Thus I carefully avoided doing anything that
might jeopardize my good name among them.

I was determined, for all that, to get a pigmy skeleton,
by hook or by crook. At length I hit upon what I thought
was an artful device while I was in Tongepete. I learned
of the site of several pigmy graves, both from the little
men themselves and from the negroes. There were two
in the middle of the village, and two more not far from
the camp. I was only concerned with the two in the
village, as they had recently been made. To let people
see me disinterring the bodies was, of course, unthinkable ; consequently I let two influential negroes into my
scheme, which was to have a hut for my servants built
over these graves, and subsequently, under the cover of
night, to unearth the remains. They cordially fell in
with my plan, and placed a gang of young negroes at my
disposal. These immediately set about collecting the
building materials, while I myself got busy measuring

the site for the hut. No sooner, however, had the pigmies seen me at work, than their suspicions were aroused. Now one pigmy, now another, would come into the village, look hard at me and go away without uttering a word. Next morning, just as we were about to start the building operations, one of the negroes whom I had taken into my confidence came to me as spokesman for the Bambuti. The pigmies did not think it right, he said, that I should build huts right over their graves, seeing that there was plenty of clear ground available. They threatened to go away, he added, if I did not abandon my project.

There was nothing to do but to give up both the idea of building the hut and the hope of obtaining the coveted skeleton for the present. I consoled myself with the hope that a more favourable opportunity might occur in some other camp in the future. Alas! I was doomed to return home without one.

On this occasion I learned that the pigmies will not allow the negroes to make plantations over the graves of their people. They consider it as desecration. And they show no mercy to the desecrater. At the very first opportunity he is doomed to die pierced by a shower of sure and silent arrows.

A few days later I discovered to my amazement that the Bambuti had all trekked away together with the exception of one old man, who was just clearing out himself. When I overtook him, he tried to dodge me at first, and when he was cornered, he told me that the others had scattered about the forest in quest of ants. Of course this was a mere evasion on the old fellow's part. Shortly afterwards I was informed by the negroes that the pigmies had decamped for good. It turned out that I was the innocent cause of their sudden flight, and this is how it all happened.

The news had reached the camp that a young Mombuti, who along with some others had been hired by a negro to take part in a hunt, had died. Friends of the dead youth were already on their way to him to bury his corpse in his native forest land. Now I was anxious to see a Bambuti burial, and so I waited for a long time, but in vain, for the arrival of the funeral procession. When eventually I saw nobody appearing, it occurred to me that perhaps my presence was not desired, and that they would have the burial in secret. Consequently I wandered down all the secret Bambuti paths in the vicinity to see if I could overtake the procession anywhere. While thus engaged I suddenly met a pigmy woman, who, as soon as she caught sight of me, dived into the undergrowth. I followed her, with the result that she ran back to the camp in a panic. Whereupon all the pigmies cleared off as quickly as they could.

Under the circumstances I decided to move on, and to try my luck elsewhere. It so happened that some days previously I had sent a messenger to Mombasa to ask the local administrator to provide me with bearers as I desired to resume my travelling. And it turned out that very opportunely, shortly after I discovered that the pigmies had deserted me, four military policemen arrived in the village with a letter for me from the administrator, in which he said the police had been instructed by him to round up bearers for me with all possible speed. He added that he had followed the reports on my expedition with great interest, and that he hoped to meet me in Mbula, whither he was going with his wife and child.

Imagine my surprise when on the following day, when the bearers, who were to carry my baggage to Mbula, were dribbling in from the neighbouring villages, my truant pigmies returned and reoccupied the camp. They started dancing gaily as if nothing untoward had happened. They greeted me cordially, but it never occurred to them to apologize for the abrupt and unceremonious way in which they deserted me the day before. For my part I was very glad that they had come back before I left the village, and I took very good care to make no reference to the misunderstanding that had arisen between us.

Mbula, which is nearly three thousand feet above sealevel, is important owing to its central position, and that is presumably why the seat of administration has been transferred from Andudu. Like Undetse, Mbulu is named not after its present chief but after his predecessor, who was shot dead some years ago by one of his policemen, whose wife he had seduced. The chief's

CHAMUNONGE'S MANSION
(*Page 225*)

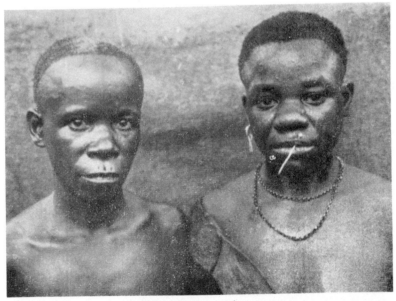

TYPICAL NDUYE EFÉ WOMEN

HEMP IS SMOKED IN BAMBOO PIPES

(*Page* 229)

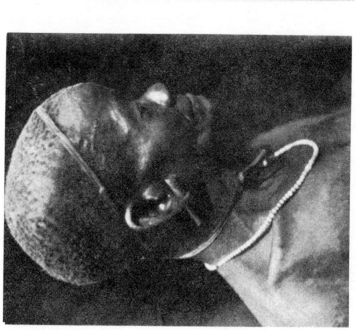

AN EFÉ WOMAN WITH ROLLED LEAVES IN HER
PIERCED EARS

family group speedily avenged his death. Two women enveigled the assassin into their toils, bound him, and beat him to death with cudgels. Mbula's brother is the present chief of the village.

I spent two days in Mbulu in the pleasant company of the administrator, M. Giedt, and his family, with whom I travelled to Nduye. Mbula was valueless from the point of view of my research work, as no pigmies lived anywhere nearby, although in the nearest village to it, through which we passed on our journey, a great number of pigmies greeted me with festive dances.

On the banks of the Nduye, a tributary of the Epulu, is the home of Chamunonge, the most powerful of all the Balese chiefs. He is a protégé of the Colonial authorities, who have conferred on him numerous honours and tokens of their favour.

Chamunonge, who is a very intelligent type of negro, proudly showed me his red-brick residence—or rather his residences. He has two magnificent one-storied houses side by side—one for himself and the other for his eight wives. He proudly led me through room after room, every one stuffed with dust-stained European furniture and all kinds of useless and ugly junk.

I persuaded the local pigmies, who came to greet me, to leave the camp which was pitched near a little river, and to come nearer to Chamunonge's village, where there was a huge open space, from which the negroes had previously expelled them, because they were afraid that the little fellows might make too free with the plantations.

Over fifty huts grew out of the ground, so to speak, overnight, in the shadow of mighty giant trees. Some were enthroned on ant-hills, while others were propped against the trunks of the forest trees. The general impression one got was a series of family group huts clustered together. My roomy hut and that for my servants, both built by village negroes with the help of the pigmies, stood in the foreground, facing the river, so that the Bambuti huts ringed them in a semicircle.

This was the big camp of the clan of the Bataa or Bataka, as the negroes called them. A portion of the clan lived formerly in another village. It was Chamunonge, who had arranged to bring these Efé from another

P

territory into his village, because the number of normally resident Bambuti had been too small for the great elephant hunts which were his chief source of revenue. The Bataka had a great reputation as expert and agile elephant-hunters.

Bubi whom I had brought along with me, as a companion to the caravan, took up his abode in the Nduye camp on the veranda of my hut. At first he was always sent on ahead in his box, but as he kept playing the most extraordinary tricks on the bearers, I had to devise some means of putting a stop to his capers. So we used to tie him fast on the top of one of the loads, and from that point of vantage he could survey the whole line of bearers, whom he kept amused with his droll pranks. I had only to shout Bubi to evoke an immediate responsive scream. Whenever he caught hold of an overhanging branch he clung to it firmly and wriggled and squealed, until the bearers allowed him to swing to and fro for a little while. His most cordial and sociable moments were those when he had a banana in his little fist, and grunted contentedly as he chewed it. We all had a little peace on those occasions.

If you showed Bubi his milk, but did not give it to him, he would fly into a terrible rage. His screams were ear-splitting ; he dragged at people's clothes, and rolled on the ground like a naughty boy, in short, kicked up an appalling row, until he got his milk. He quickly learned to hold the cup to his mouth with his own hand and to drink out of it. Often, in his hurry he raised it so greedily that he spilled the entire contents. Then when he found that the pot was empty, and realized the damage that he had done, he stared with a woebegone face into the empty vessel and grunted in a shamefaced way. He was in perpetual terror that somebody would take the pot from him. He was frequently given the stick when he became too fierce or unruly. But even here his resourcefulness was shown. He would hold his milk-pot firmly with his hands, while he gripped the stick with his feet. He knew what it was for quite well, as he often got a taste of it.

One day I thought we had lost him, as he was nowhere to be seen, and he made no reply to our repeated calls, a most unusual thing for him. We searched everywhere, and poked into every hiding-place, but in vain. I glanced casually at my bed, and saw Bubi lying full length on it. I was very annoyed and shouted at him, but to no purpose. Then I seized him by the nape of the neck, and gave him a good thrashing. As he ran away screaming in a terrible rage, he nursed his hind-quarters. In a few minutes he was back in my bed again. He even tried it a third time, but he got such a beating then that I think he never forgot it. Ever since that time he harboured a certain pique against me, but he never went near my bed again.

In the pigmy camp he had his sleeping-quarters on the veranda of my hut, where a hammock made of cloth was rigged up for him. Bubi held strictly to the orders of the day. No sooner was his hammock unslung at the approach of dusk than he clambered into his box. In the morning he considered it his job to wake us all up.

Again and again I took him with me into the dim forest, and left him suddenly and disappeared behind a tree. From there I could observe his movements and his genuinely terrified expression. He would try to hobble after me, but he was too slow, and soon he lost sight of me. Then he would stand quite alone, overwhelmed with fear and he would begin to tremble and wail pitifully : "Hu, hu, hu," until I suddenly showed myself again. The minute he saw me, he rushed towards me, leaped into my arms and shouted in an ecstasy of delight : "Ho, ho, ho," while his little heart pounded madly.

Bubi foraged a lot on his own account among the Bambuti huts, and stole to his heart's content. The other pigmies looked at him hungrily—they would love to see him roasting. The children, on the other hand, played pranks with him, but kept out of his way when he was unescorted, as he had a real gift for biting, if they teased him.

Such was Bubi, my little friend in the wild African forest.

The pigmies in the big camp were extremely friendly to me and had great confidence in me, so that I suspected that Chamunonge had put in a good word for me. Day by day I wandered again and again through the vast camp, and peered into all the huts, on the look-out for anything unusual. If perchance I came upon anything that I did not understand I immediately sent for the interpreter. I always had tobacco or cigarettes in my pockets, and for this reason at any rate the pigmies were always glad to see me.

One curious characteristic about the pigmies in this district was that some of them splashed water on their faces in the mornings and even washed their mouths. Of course they never gave themselves a real scrub.

The elders controlled the internal affairs of the camp, as successors of a certain Mirisumbi, who was dead, but of whom everybody still spoke with awe as an outstanding personality. Chamunonge had also appointed a sort of " Sultan " in the camp. The fellow was actually merely a nominal chief, and only acted as a liaison officer for Chamunonge and conveyed the latter's commands to his own people. He was eaten with ambition to attain a similar status in the camp as Chamunonge held among the negroes. Apropos of which I will tell of a little incident typical of his lofty aspirations.

One night after darkness had swept down over the forest with that eerie swiftness characteristic of the tropics, and the shadows of the pigmies crouched round the fires cut fantastic shapes, I sat in my arm-chair on my veranda and gazed into the gloom. The chief's hut, perched on an ant-hill, was a bare five feet away from mine. As I did not even move, he apparently thought me asleep, and it struck him that it was a favourable opportunity for addressing his people. His sonorous voice reverberated through the whole camp, but of course I was unable to follow a single word of the voluminous discourse. Suddenly the idea struck me to play a joke at his expense. I fetched my gramophone very quietly and took it to a spot near the orator and succeeded in recording all that he said. When he had finished silence brooded over the camp, broken only by the crackling of the fires and the fitful, subdued and drowsy hum of conversation.

Next morning I sent for the pigmies and their chief, and trotted out the gramophone. They stared goggle-eyed when they heard the instrument reproduce faithfully every word of the harangue of the previous night.

The gist of his speech was soon interpreted to me. He began by adjuring his people to keep very quiet in the camp as their " Muzungu " was already asleep, and must not on any account be disturbed. The rest of his oration was devoted to a fervent appeal to them to come to him with all the problems and disputes, as the negroes went to Chamunonge and he would solve their difficulties fairly and impartially.

Perhaps this pigmy had a notion, like so many others, that I would or could confirm him in his office as "Sultan." As he was a sensible and peace-loving man I invited him to take part in our discussions, and he probably thought that this would help to strengthen his position.

The chief arranged to have a considerable number of his people measured by me, and in fact was the first himself to take his place in the line. And very many difficulties that cropped up between me and the pigmies were always settled by him amicably. One morning, when there was a little commotion because I clipped and kept some specimens of hair from the heads of some of the pigmies, his intervention was most opportune. It seems that one pigmy who was a great exponent of negro superstition disseminated the rumour that I would use the specimens of hair to cast magic spells on all the camp and make them ill. The chief and one of the elders ridiculed this idea and asserted that I was a good man, whom nobody need fear. However, I took the hint and thought it advisable to cease collecting specimens of the woolly locks. One result of the intervention of the two old men on my behalf was that both men and boys swarmed up to be measured and I distributed gifts galore, mainly the much-coveted mouth-organs and pipes, in order to put everybody in the best humour.

While rummaging through the huts I collected a great many valuable curios, including a Bange pipe, used for hemp-smoking. The owner of the pipe was rather reluctant to part with it, although I gave him a handsome gift in return. " It gives you power to kill elephants," he said, as he filled it for a final smoke. The pipe is a cunningly made contrivance of bamboo, containing a water chamber through which the hemp or tobacco-smoke passes before it is inhaled by the user.

An ingenious primitive method devised by the Bambuti for extracting the stimulating juice of the kola nut, which Schweinfurth many years ago considered so refreshing, and which grows wild in the forest, is worth describing. As a rule the pigmies carry it about with them in bags when they are travelling and chew it when ever they feel inclined. When they are in camp they prepare a decoction by first pounding the nuts to a pulp and adding water. In order to filter the kola water they cut a hole in the phrynium leaf into which they insert the bushy tail of an antelope or a buffalo ; they then pour the stuff over it, with the result that the fluid trickles clear into a pot placed underneath.

As the pigmies as a rule detest cannibalism, the candid admission made to me by some of the elders of the Bataa that their grandparents, and even some of the parents, were very fond of human flesh, is rather significant. Though the old fellows assured me that they themselves had never been addicted to cannibalism, a look that passed between them during the conversation made me inclined to believe they were lying.

During a fortnight's stay in the Nduye camp I had a very good opportunity of acquiring a considerable amount of information about the pigmies, as I found the older men very willing to place at my disposal all the experiences of a lifetime. Unfortunately my ignorance of the Efé language hampered me very much, although with the help of the negroes I succeeded in compiling a synopsis of its grammar and a glossary.

The numerical system of a people is undoubtedly a test of their primitiveness. The pigmies frequently count in accordance with the negro system and sometimes get as far as number ten. Tribes which come less under negro influence can only reckon up to three, while the most primitive among them know no number beyond two. In Tebi's camp the numerical table never reached beyond five ; in Tongepete, no pigmy, no matter how hard he tried, could discharge five arrows one after the other and then state how many he had shot. The Efé have two numbers, i.e. " itene " for " one," and " egbe " for " two." " Egbe " apparently sometimes carries the significance of " many." The usual method of reckoning

IN THE EFÉ CAMP AT NDUYE. THE HUTS OF THE AUTHOR
AND HIS SERVANTS
(*Page* 225)

THE MAKING OF THE DELICIOUS KOLAWATER
(*Page* 230)

A GROUP OF PIGMIES

AN EFÉ MAN'S SIESTA IN AN ARMCHAIR MADE OF BAMBOO ROOTS

among the pigmies is to take the objects to be counted in their hands, one by one, laying them down again, saying as they do so: "This there—and this there—and this there."

Others again count by placing—say an arrow on the ground and another beside it, saying :

"Lai ane, lai oa." "This there by that there."

Then they lay another pair of arrows side by side with the same words, and so on. But at the finish the enumerator will know just at little as he did at the beginning about the number of arrows he has laid down.

One man whom I observed closely said each time that he laid down an arrow : "Ladi dere, ladi dere." "Thus it is, thus it is." This poor fellow really thought that he had invented a marvellous numerical system.

The words "lai ane, lai oa," just mentioned convey the same idea as "egbe." This idea of duality or multiplicity is the only one that exists in the minds of the Efé, while the conception of a higher number seems to be unknown to them.

If anyone kills a wild animal he usually takes one of its hind legs back to the village, places it in front of the prospective negro buyer, saying : "two arrows." The negro immediately sees that this is the price that the pigmy wants for the carcase, and if he does not seal the bargain the little hunter looks for another customer.

The arithmetical problems that I set to a cheery old pigmy in the village of Nduye camp, caused peals of laughter among the listening negroes. The old fellow counted a number of arrows that I handed to him in pairs, saying each time that he took a pair "egbe." Eventually he had a very long row of arrows placed side by side in pairs, but could not tell how many he had.

And now I played a little joke on him. I took four of his own arrows, which he could easily recognize, and four belonging to another man, and placed them together. He immediately picked out his own arrows, just four and no more. Again I put the arrows together, removed two from the lot when he was not looking, and then asked him to pick out his own. My old friend counted again "egbe, egbe." "Have you them all ? " I said, when he had finished. He looked first at me, then at the rows of arrows, and said at length :

" No, there are some missing."   " How many ? " I enquired.

" Two," he replied.   Whereupon the negroes burst out laughing, which perplexed the old man very much.   He insisted, however, that " some " were missing.   When I told him to search for his own arrows among the pile he picked out three.   It was obvious that one of his own was not there.   He was certain that two were missing, one of his own and one from the other man's lot.   Whereupon I produced the two that I had hidden behind my back.

Now, as it is absolutely clear that the old man had no higher conception of numbers than two, I think that there can be only one explanation of his solution of the arithmetical puzzle that I set him.   Though, like all the Efé, he could only count up to two, he had a very clear mental picture of the actual number of the arrows. This imprinted itself so quickly and so clearly in his mind's eye that he immediately detected what was missing, because the picture he looked on showed a gap. The Efé keep the picture, but not the number of things imprinted on their memory.

In reckoning five the old man's method was to put down three arrows first, and then the other two, whereas in the case of the higher uneven numbers he generally started with two.

The greatest problem for the explorer in pigmy land is and always will be the language question.   I am not surprised that most of my predecessors could not get beyond a very scrappy glossary.   On account of my longer residence among the little men I succeeded in getting an outline of their grammar of the series of languages and dialects, but I am far from satisfied with the results of my labours in this direction.

As I mentioned before, every pigmy community understands and speaks fairly well the tongue of its particular patrons.   But it must be remembered that this " trading language " is not the " camp language " of the Bambuti in every case.   The " camp language " is that which they use when they are by themselves.   If a genuine primitive pigmy language does exist it must be one of the many " camp languages."

The whole problem is more complicated than it would appear at a casual glance, and all the pigmies, even the Efé, are polyglot. Some tribes speak five different tongues, as I have personally noted ; most, however, speak just two or three. While the number of " trading languages " among the Bambuti corresponds to the number of negro tribes in the Ituri Forest, they have just three " camp languages "—Kibira, Medje and Efé.

Efé, the tongue of the eastern pigmies, and also that of the Mamvu and Balese negroes, who are few in numbers compared with the pigmies themselves, deserves particular notice. Now, as the Efé are all monolingual, it seems extremely probable that Efé is an aboriginal pigmy language, which was adopted by the negroes who invaded the eastern regions of the Congo Forest, i.e. the Mamvu, the Balese and the Bambuba.

It is true that Efé shows many points of affinity with the tongues of the eastern tribes—the Logo, the Bari and the Lendu—but its vocabulary is so varied and extensive that it must have a considerable number of borrowed words. Not only is it probable that Efé is an aboriginal pigmy language, but it seems a very reasonable inference, if we sum up all the available evidence on the point, that it was the language spoken formerly by all the Ituri pigmies before the negro tribes made incursions into the Congo Forest.

CHAPTER XI

MAN'S PLACE IN THE COSMOS ACCORDING TO THE EFÉ

I SHALL now try to reproduce the Efé conception of man's place in the cosmos, as revealed to me in my talks with Tebi and my old friend in the Nduye camp. I also picked up a lot of illuminating views on the subject from various other sources.

I have already mentioned Tebi's penchant for shooting all sorts of random questions at me. " Muzungu, what kind of job has your father ? " was the strange query that he put one morning. " He is dead, Tebi," I replied. Whereupon Tebi bowed his head, and remained silent for some time. Then he gave a whimsical smile, and, his eyes sparkling, he set me a regular *questionnaire* about my views on death and the immortality of the soul. After a while the conversation turned to the funeral rites of the Efé, whereupon Tebi's wife, who was working inside the hut, shouted to us that she did not want to listen any more to such depressing chatter, and, if we did not talk about something else, she would go off into the village. Tebi did not take the slightest notice of her interruption.

When I met him again I decided that it was my turn to ply him with questions. I had heard that he was fond of airing his agnostic opinions in the camp, and so I asked him what were his views on the hereafter. Pushing a banana into his mouth as he spoke, he assured me somewhat abruptly : " Death ends everything, because you never see a dead man again."

I saw that he wanted to dismiss the subject with this curt reply, but I was determined to keep him to it.

" Death is but a sleep, Tebi," I suggested.

" The sleeper will eat, when you awaken him, but the dead man will never eat again," came his quick retort, " He will never rise again."

" How do you explain dreams, Tebi ? "

" Dreams ? Oh ! They are just rubbish—nonsense," he retorted in a blasé tone.

I saw that Tebi was not in a communicative mood on the theme at the moment, and our discourse came to an end.

The next day Tebi called to see me on his own initiative. He trailed his creaking arm-chair behind him, spat out a chunk of kola-nut that he had been chewing, and fixing me with burning eyes, said :

" Muzungu, listen to me now."

Whereupon, without waiting to be invited he sat down, while I picked up my note-book and pencil.

Tebi began his disjointed sentences, his eyes all the time fixed on me rigidly.

" Last night I dreamt about my brother who is dead long time, a very long time. I can still see him clearly before me. He wore a loin-apron made of cloth. He said to me : ' Where is your drinking water ? I want a drink,' and I answered him : ' No, I want you to give me some of your drinking water.' But he insisted, and I gave him some of mine. He looked at it for a long time, and then pushed it away from him, saying reproachfully, ' Do you drink such dirty water ? You should not do it.' Just then I awoke. During the whole night after that I kept thinking of my brother. Muzungu, what did that mean ? "

As I made no reply, Tebi started afresh :

" A good while ago I dreamt about my brother too. I said to him : ' How is it, brother, that you are such a long time dead, and yet are standing before me ? ' ' No,' replied my brother, ' I am with you ! ' Muzungu, what did that mean ? "

I still refrained from replying purposely, but answered him with another question, which I hoped would lead to further voluntary unburdenings on his part. From previous conversations with him I knew that the Efé call the pulsation of the heart " What makes the tukutuku in the breast," or, as Tebi put it, " That whereby the living man differs from the dead." Further I knew that they call the soul " Borupi," and the breath " Ekeu."

I asked him what were the views of the older people about the Borupi.

" They say that the Borupi goes to Tore above, in the sky, but what it is like up there I know not. The Borupi is small, so very small that at the death of a man, the " Akirao " (flies) take it away from the mouth and fly with it up to Tore above. Things are good up there and they are bad down here. Lightning also takes a man's soul away and carries it up there."

In the course of our conversation Tebi told me the following legend :

" Long ago, at the beginning, the earth was up there where heaven is now, and heaven was down here. The Efé were hungry, and therefore they appealed about their plight to Tore, whereupon the earth with all its food supplies fell down below, to the position it is now, and heaven then went up in its place. The Borupi goes up there ; all the Borupis are gathered together there. Now, I'm not saying that all this is true, or that it is false. I'm just telling you what the old people think."

Tebi laid particular stress on the last few words, looking at me apologetically, as though to deprecate all responsibility for the authenticity of his tale.

From personal observations I can vouch for the fact, that on the death of a camp member, all the people assemble to mourn him with clamorous lamentation. The women, following the negro custom, smear their faces with white clay as a sign of mourning.

The body lies, in state, in the hut of a brother. Long ago they used to let a body lie in state for about a fortnight, by which time it was semi-decomposed, whereupon they all deserted the camp, leaving the corpse unburied. In some cases they carried the body to the forest and placed it against a tree in a sitting position, and left it to the mercy of the reptiles and beasts of prey.

Nowadays the pigmies dig graves, after the negro fashion, with knives, and place the body in a sort of alcove excavated at the side of the grave about a foot and a half below the surface. Before burial, the body is washed, rubbed with oil and wrapped in phrynium leaves. It is then deposited with its head to the south-east. This position is imperative, as otherwise many more men will die. The grave is covered first of all with pieces of wood, on top of which earth is shovelled, care being taken that none of it comes into contact with the corpse. Some place on the grave the personal belongings of the dead man, and sometimes the weapons are left there. Two days after the burial they abandon the camp, as they contend that the ground is unhealthy, and that disease will break out if they stay. The mourning concludes with a thorough washing of all utensils and everything else in the camp, except themselves. It is stated that the relatives of the dead man visit his grave periodically in order to keep it free from weeds. I should imagine that they do so just for the first few weeks, to judge by the graves in Tongpete, which looked very neglected.

It is quite obvious that many negro usages have crept into these pigmy funeral rites. A typical instance is the custom of striking the mother after the death of her son, and of the wife after the death of her husband, the suggestion implied being that they were, respectively, to blame for the bereavement. Long ago the negroes used to kill the women, whereas nowadays they strike them with the " ndundu," a bullet-shaped lump of iron, which is usually given as a portion of the marriage dowry.

When we met again for a chat, Tebi told me that Tore, the great spirit to whom the souls of all dead men went, was also called Muri-muri. He was only the size of a pigmy, and frequently wandered in the depths of the forest. He always killed anyone who encountered him. At night time he was wont to squat in tree-tops or to swing on liana creepers, and utter a hooting cry: " E, e, e ! "

It struck me, as Tebi was telling me about this Muri-muri's nocturnal prowlings in the forest, that the owl's cry suggested this particular myth. However, I made no comment, and he went on.

When Muri-muri's hooting cry was heard at night in the vicinity of a camp, all the pigmies remained absolutely silent, the children were hurried off to bed and all fires were kindled to a blaze. Muri-muri's cry was a warning that somebody was going to die in the camp soon. It was also a foreboding of an outbreak of sickness. But Muri-muri was not exclusively a harbinger of woe. His wail was sometimes a hint that the next day would be a lucky one for the hunters.

In the beginning men were evil, and committed all sorts of crimes, in punishment of which Muri-muri threatened them with death. He also laid down a code of instructions as to what they should do and what they should refrain from doing.

Tebi told me the legend about the origin of death. In the beginning men did not die at all. In those days Muri-muri gave a pot to a toad, ordering him to be careful not to break it, as death was shut up in it. If the pot got broken, he pointed out, all men were doomed to die. The toad went on his way, and met a frog who offered to carry the pot for him. The toad hesitated to do so at first, but as the pot was very heavy, he eventually handed it over to the frog, warning him to be very careful with it. The frog hopped away with the pot, but let it fall. It broke into fragments, and death escaped from it. And that is how men came to die first.

Tebi told me that the hunters, before they go into the forest, sing hymns to Muri-muri and invoke his aid, so that they may get a good bag, because he is the lord of all things.

The more one proceeds southwards, the more definite are the concepts formed by the Efé about the Supreme Being. The most significant of these is the view of the Nduye pigmies. In Tongepete there was a fundamental difference of belief from that held by the Mamvu-Efé. In the eyes of the Tongepete pigmies Muri-muri and Tore are different beings. Tore they regard as the Supreme Being, of whose physical appearance nobody has any idea. He lives in heaven and from his abode there he can see all men. Tore is malevolent, because he sends fatal illnesses by night to men. Muri-muri, on the other hand, is a strange mysterious creature of the forest, being mainly composed of a head, resting on the base of a pyramidal thorn.

When I heard this legend it occurred to me again that the silhouette of the owl, seen dimly by night, suggested this concept of Muri-muri's contours.

Owing to negro influence it seems that among the Mamvu-Efé, Tore and Muri-muri, two totally different spirits, have been fused into one. The Balese negroes to the south of Irumu visualize Tore as the Devil.

In the camp of the Bataa on the Nduye I questioned the chief and his brother, both of whom were in the middle forties, about their creed regarding the attributes of Tore. They shook their heads deprecatingly, and said that they were far too young to speak with any authority on the subject, and they sent for the oldest man in the camp, who, incidentally, was a great friend of mine. He brought with him the second oldest inhabitant to corroborate his statements. These two shrivelled elders were the guarantors for the following scrappy oddments of pigmy theology.

Muri-muri, they told me, is also called Tore-Boichu. He is small of stature and is covered with hair. Tore, on the other hand, is tall and handsome, but is also hairy from head to foot. When he walks through the forest you can hear his footsteps.

A fragment from the heart of the animal slain by the hunters is cast into the woods for Tore. As an explanation of the fact that this rite is not universally practised at the present day, the elders assured me that Tore was only too well aware how poor the Efé were, and how they had to share the produce of the hunt with the negroes. Accordingly he voluntarily renounced his own share of the booty. Parcels of ants and caterpillars wrapped in leaves must always be placed in a hollow tree for Tore. Before this is done the banquet must on no account be started.

Tore is occasionally invoked thus, when the pigmies go into the forest in quest of game :

" Tore, lao ! Mune odue ete ! " (" Tore, thou ! Give me food.")

Tore always gets his share of the fruit harvest first. For instance, they always open the bombi fruit, of which both men and chimpanzee are equally fond, or the gum-tree fruit, and place them on the ground as food for Tore, intoning the while :

" Tore, lekeni manue ! " (" Tore, take and eat.")

My question about the rite connected with the quest of honey caused extraordinary enthusiasm among the old people, as it aroused memories of delicious banquets in their minds. They said that first of all honeycombs had to be cast about in all directions. Nobody would dare to eat the honey before the rite was fully carried out. Tore, they contended, had made everything grow and flourish, and therefore was entitled to a share of everything. Nobody would dare to refuse him his share, as otherwise he might stop the growth of everything.

When I asked them who created everything around them, they shook their heads uncomprehendingly. Only when I asked them what was the actual reason for offering fruits to Tore, did the gist of my questions dawn on their consciousness. The elder of the two jumped to his feet and said :

" It all belongs to Tore. Tore made everything. Tore eroba ogbae. Tore eroba Pucopuco. Tore namosi." (" Tore made the trees. Tore made the pigmies' ancestor. Tore sees us.")

" He hears every word," chimed in the other old man. " He sees when any man is doing wrong, and punishes the evil-doer through magic, because it is Tore himself who made magic."

They told me that Tore used lightning to kill men. If anyone throws food away carelessly, lightning will kill either him or one of his relatives.

Tore makes men die, and takes them to himself by removing their hearts and souls from their bodies. Sometimes they speak of the dead man as Tore, because Tore has taken him away.

About retribution after death the elders of Nduye knew nothing. They only knew that all the dead went to Tore. The first man was Pucopuco and was a brother of Befe, who was sprung from a rock. The resplendently beautiful Mato was the wife of both of them, and from them all the pigmies came. The pigmies stole fire from Oruogbu, a personage famous in legend, who fell asleep near the blazing fire he was tending. Thereupon the pigmies surprised him and ran away with the fire.

In the Nduye camp the legend about the stealing of fire from the chimpanzee village, which I have already given, was told to me once more. Among many other legends that I heard, was the following about lightning, of which the Efé contend that they have no fear.

While on an elephant hunt the Efé went astray, and reaching a lofty mountain, they followed a path which led to the village of the Lightning. As there was nobody to be seen there to whom they could speak, they squatted on the ground and remained absolutely still. At last the Lightning appeared, saw the strangers who had squatted in his village, and came down on them with a terrific crash. When a moment later he looked around him the Efé were still squatting on the ground as calmly as before.

" I'll teach you ! " growled the Lightning, and darted down among them a second time. But the pigmies did not stir, whereupon the Lightning was rather astonished. Just then his daughter came up to him and said :

" Look father, the pigmies have spears, just like those that hunters of elephants carry."

When questioned on this point, the pigmies admitted that they were elephant hunters, whereupon the Lightning immediately changed his attitude to them, because an elephant had been laying waste his plantation for a long time. He begged the pigmies to kill the elephant, and promised them princely rewards for their services.

Next morning the pigmies set out in quest of the elephant. As soon as he came in sight, an old pigmy whispered to his son :

" Go you, give him the first blow ! "

The young man drew his spear, and drove it through the elephant's knee-joint. The giant brute roared with pain, and collapsed a few yards further on.

Thereupon there was great jubilation in the Lightning's village. He gave the little pigmies princely gifts, and conducted them in safety to the earth, where they were fortunate enough to reach their own camp. And from that date there has been friendship between the Efé and the Lightning. They are no longer afraid of him. He may flash and peal all around them, but he will not harm them, for he is their friend.

I can personally testify that the Efé are quite convinced of the truth of this story. While my hut was under the open sky, as I had all the giant trees around cut down before settling there, the pigmies had their huts actually leaning against the trunks of these mammoths of the forest. Lightning actually did strike a tree which was growing at the base of a huge ant-hill on which the chief had built his hut, and wrenched off a huge branch, which came crashing to the ground. Of course I did not fail to draw the attention of the pigmies to the great risks they ran owing to the lofty trees, but it had no effect on them. The chief answered with a smile :

" You see now how lightning may give us just a fright, but it kills none of us."

Yet these pigmies flee before a storm into the camp, just like all other pigmies. Of course, though they may not, as they say, fear lightning and thunder, perhaps they are afraid of falling trees and branches. I have personally seen the pigmies in the Nduye camp running helter-skelter on one memorable occasion, and jotted notes about it in my diary. The thunder rumbled for a long time in the distance, before the storm broke with all its fury, twisting and bending the trees in all directions. Here and there a woman with a bundle of firewood or food darted through the darkening camp into her hut. Anxiously alert, the pigmies huddled under the leafy thatch of the trees with the heaviest foliage, their backs close against the trunks, so that any down-hurtling branches might fall clear of them.

A woman shouted from her hut :

" My man has not come back yet," and darted out first to her neighbour, and then all around the camp, calling out again and again at the top of her voice and in the teeth of the gale and thunder :

"Opukekwe. Opukekwe!" Apparently the poor devil was far away from the camp, as she got no reply.

The leaves fell rustling to the ground, the first rain-drops pattered heavily on the thatch of the huts, and soon the rain came down in torrents, while the gale screamed and the thunder pealed. An ominous groaning and creaking sound from one of the giant trees brought the whole camp running out. They all fixed their eyes, full of tense anxiety, on the top of the forest colossus. They screamed and called to one another, and moved as far out of its range as they could, while the storm twisted and cracked the trunk of the tree.

" It cannot stand the strain. It is too slender," piped an old man, looking backward fearfully as with the others he made for the huts, for the rain was now penetrating the dense tree-tops. Then all of a sudden a blinding flash lit up the camp. A huge tree split in two. I was numb with fright.   The chief who was standing under the ill-fated tree shuddered and looked dazed, but he soon got over the shock.   The lightning had done him no harm !

For a long time after, the lightning continued to flash, and the thunder rumbled, but the might of the storm was broken.   In huge rivulets the surface water raced to the nearby river, which had swollen to a raging torrent that nobody would venture to cross.   And just then a man shivering and dripping wet came into the camp.   It was Opukekwe, whom the thunderstorm overtook on his way home, so that he had to run for dear life amid the tempest and rain through the forest.

A missionary witnessed a thunderstorm ceremony in a camp on the forest's verge near Kilo.   The rain came down in sheets, mixed with hail-stones, trees creaked and groaned, and many of them had been torn up by the roots. The pigmies were under a spell of terror.   The gale was at its worst when the oldest man in the camp stepped out of his hut, and first threw leaves upwards in the teeth of the wind.   After that he sprinkled ashes on a leaf, and smearing himself with some of it, threw the rest of it up into the air.   Was this an exorcism, or was it a prayer to God, whom the pigmies in that region called Kalitinda ? The negroes in the caravan said that the old man was calling on God to lull the storm.   The significance of such ritualistic ceremonies which one blunders upon, off and on, is not always obvious, and only too often their meaning is very confused and nebulous.

I am not in a position to say whether the Efé attribute to Tore the precepts which regulate their community life and safeguard their customs and moral code.   Adultery is regarded as a crime, and has been, in the past, the cause of bloodshed, when the outraged man killed his rival, en-tailing bitter feuds between the clans or family groups.

A thief is flogged, after the stolen property has been recovered from him.

Acts of violence by children towards their parents are regarded as heinous crimes.   Shortly before my arrival in the Nduye camp, a youth who had raised his hand against his father, had to flee with his family as his outraged father threatened to shoot him.

Sexual relationship between members of the same clan

is strictly prohibited, while there is no restriction in the case of unmarried couples of different clans.

There is a moral obligation to share one's food with one's comrades. Big game is divided among all the members of the clan, but small game is just apportioned among the family groups. But I have been told that there are also Efé who prefer to eat alone and in secrecy the honey that they find and the game that they kill.

Sick people and old members of a clan are never left to fend entirely for themselves. Somebody always looks after them, and thus they never lack the bare necessities of life. A humanitarian attitude is adopted even towards members of strange clans, who may be found ill by the wayside. They are invariably brought into the camp and nursed back to health.

I stayed for fourteen days in the Nduye camp. Bright and pleasant days they were too. Apart from Chamunonge, who visited me off and on, the negroes left me severely alone, so that I could devote myself altogether to the pigmies who treated me magnificently.

When the time came for my departure, I had no difficulties in getting the pigmies to shift my baggage out of the forest. I had to wait in Chamunonge's village despite myself, as the chief had left suddenly on a journey to Irumu, and nobody had taken the trouble to round up bearers for me. However, during the three days that I was forced to spend in the rest-house, I had further visits from pigmies, and seized the opportunity of studying the customs of the Balese negroes.

The whole forest region is honeycombed with secret societies, some of which have originated from outside sources and have a dual purpose. Especially, I have in mind the " Mbeli " or " Nebeli Society," an innner circle of which is known as the " Imami " or " Mani." It has recently penetrated to the very heart of the forest, as far as Chamunonge, where I learned some details about it. The society only admits initiated members to its meetings, and they are all sworn to give no information to strangers. At their gatherings in the depths of the forest wild orgies are carried out. Every Nebeli man must have a Nebeli woman, who is not his own wife, at these reunions. At the meeting places the very best household equipment is provided, and they all make themselves as comfortable as possible for a feast intended to last for several days on end. A second aim of the society is organized resistance to European encroachment.

Negroes in Nduye, of course not members of the society, maintained that there are Bambuti in its ranks. The latter deny this absolutely. In the Nepoko region a Mombuti is said to have been murdered by members of the society because he happened, by accident, to blunder into one of their meetings, and consequently had to be put out of the way. Just as was the case with the leopard men, the society tried to deflect suspicion on to the Bambuti, with the result that a pigmy was arrested on suspicion. It is a fact that the Bambuti keep aloof from all the secret organizations of this type. The only secret societies that appeal to them are those connected with religion and the initiation of the youths.

The Nduye Bambuti never came into touch with the Wangwana, not even in those days when the latter strove to bring the Mangbetu-Medje into subjection. Their incursions were in a north-westerly direction from Nduye along the Ngayu. The negroes appear to have withdrawn across the Epulu where their position was safer. Old negroes often told me of sinister bygone days during our long moonlight chats. No village was secure from its neighbouring village, and cannibalism was the order of the day. Prisoners were always eaten. Imagine the feelings of the poor victim, who looked on while his murderers apportioned in advance the joints from his body, and put distinguishing marks on them so that when the poor wretch was killed and dismembered, there should be no squabbling about dainty bits. The Bambuti in those times were in constant terror of being eaten by the negroes.

These orgies have almost been stamped out by the white man, a boon which the negroes greatly appreciate, although in other respects I have heard them make bitter complaints of European intervention.

As the time of Chamunonge's return was uncertain, I took the reins of government into my own hands, at least as far as the rounding-up of bearers was concerned. Chamunonge was a modern, progressive type of man, who was thinking of buying a car, and consequently was having a motor road built to Mombasa by forced labour. I sent for the overseer of the gang of one hundred workers and picked out the quota of men that I needed. The poor devils were only too glad to exchange their hard jobs with pick and spade without remuneration for the comparatively easy task I was giving them for good pay.

The pigmies were performing a farewell dance in my honour in front of Chamunonge's houses, when I heard a wail of lamentation from an annexe of the building. An old woman had just died. Immediately the dance stopped and the pigmies fled.

The new road sweeps with a gentle upward slope from Nduye, and swerves towards the east at the negro village. I found in the next village that there was a death there too. The men were squatting in mournful silence in the club-hut, in front of which a newly-dug grave yawned. Women, whose faces were smeared with clay, were performing funeral dances. They seemed to have been at it all night, for their faces looked tired and tense. A great wave of mortality seemed to have visited the whole region. We saw mourning and funerals in most of the villages through which we passed. It was a pleasant change to witness a native wedding in Muto Embe.

I finally camped in Boro. During the previous few days I had been indisposed and weary. My long tramp, which caused me to sweat heavily, banished the fever which was creeping on me, and eventually I felt better and could eat again.

One the east side of Boro the road branches off towards Irumu. It was a better surface than the other, along which, in my ignorance of the geography of the locality, I had travelled to Mombasa. After a six hours' march through mud and morass, in the dim twilight of the forests, my caravan arrived in Ambutsi. This brand-new settlement had a very good rest-hut, but was wretchedly poor, for plantations yielded no return so far. My bearers, aware of the state of affairs, had brought bananas as well as the baggage, to save themselves from dying of hunger on the way. But that was hardly a substantial enough diet for them, so I asked the chief for a hen for myself and some sweet potatoes for my bearers. The bearded negro made a long speech, declaring that he himself was on the verge of starvation. He had nothing to give and would give nothing. Neither my bearers nor I believed him. They drew my attention to a fine sweet potato field with a manioc patch facing it. Accordingly I repeated my demand, but after a few hours of futile waiting, my patience was exhausted, and I gave the inhospitable negro a box on the ear. I may add that for this I rendered myself liable by Congo law to a seven hundred franc fine, or, in default, ten days' imprisonment. When a man is tired, sick and hungry, however, and is responsible for the maintenance of his thirty bearers, the last thing he thinks of is the law. The negro took to his heels as he saw that I meant business. Then I gave the men orders to get the food for themselves from the plantation ; I was, of course, prepared to pay for it. From the huts came a volley of abuse. The women were going as fast as they could in the direction of the fields, with baskets on their backs. Half an hour later a pile of sweet potatoes and a hen lay at my feet. Ambutsi had given the hen. To reward him for this and to compensate him for the box on the ear, I gave him a piece of cloth.

A troop of Bambuti waited on me, the last I was to meet on the southward march to Mombasa. All the other hordes who previously had lived in these regions, seemed to have emigrated, as it was almost depopulated. The Government had established little settlements on the wayside and forced people to live in them so as to maintain the road. The group that I met were Efé, but they seemed to be more civilized than their northern cousins, if clothes are an indication on this point. The influence of Mombasa was evident.

The two days' tramp seemed to have quite freed me of my disposition. In the evening I lay for hours in the best of spirits in my arm-chair in front of my hut and gazed at the glorious sky.

The next day's march was likewise through dense forest land devoid of any trace of human habitation, but the road was shorter and easier for travelling than the previous day's route. Korungo was a tiny Balese settlement built on a river of the same name. Rice-growing is the staple industry here. As no pigmies live in this region, I devoted my time to my bearers some of whom were Bambuti half-breeds, as was obvious from the colour of their skin and the shape of their faces. In general the Balese is stocky and badly proportioned. You rarely see the tall slim black figures of the north ; the southern negroes are, for the most part, thickset.

A peculiar ailment of the teeth, "Undese," is very prevalent in this district both among the negroes and the Bambuti. Chamunonge himself was a victim of it while I was there. The teeth of the victims become sometimes extremely yellow in tint and sometimes the colour of frosted glass, and the gums swell so abnormally that they dilate and fill the mouth in such a way as to give it the appearance of being stuffed with food. I have never heard that there is any pain in connection with this malady.

For hours the caravan waited in Korungo's village, as one of the bearers, who had complained of weakness for days, was missing. Messengers who were sent out to look for him, at last brought him into the camp in the evening in a state of collapse. I diagnosed fever at once, and decided that he must have caught a chill on the first day as we marched in the rain. As I presumed it was an ordinary fever I treated him accordingly during the following night, and as a precautionary measure had him wrapped in blankets. The next day we sent him back, after providing him with food, so that he might keep going until his friends and relatives met him in a couple of days to take him home. We were only one day's march from Mombasa. The fate of that poor man wrings my heart to this day. If I had any idea that he was suffering from pneumonia I should have sent him to Mombasa. The poor devil died on the following day in a strange land, and his friends who came to meet him could only bury him.

A negro village keeps guard on the ferry over the Epulu. To the different tribes which converge here the river owes its various names : Epulu, Efulu and Ihulu. About an hour's journey from it is Mombasa, whose site is charming, but whose buildings are rather unpleasant. I was cordially received by the administrator. I decided to wait a while in Mombasa. The post had been dogging my heels from Batwabaka, and I was waiting for two parcels containing provisions from Avakubi for my journey to Ruanda, where I wanted to study the Batwa, to make a film and to visit my good friend, Father Schumacher. Meanwhile I could have a quick look at the Senegal gold-mines, and I had a chance of seeing the local Babira and Bambuti. The latter are industrious and skilful hunters, who spend their whole time in the forest with their nets, and provide the white man and their workers in the gold mines with game. This secures them a comfortable existence which makes for their independence and self-reliance in their dealings with the negroes. The chief of the group was a stubborn sly young fellow, tremedously self-conscious. Aping the negroes, he ordered his underlings to carry him about in a sedan-chair, when he felt in extra-aggressive humour.

CHAPTER XII

BETWEEN LAKE ALBERT AND THE ITURI

IN Mombasa a new phase of my expedition began. It was then October. Great was my perplexity when my cook and hunter, two intelligent and reliable married men, announced that they were weary of the loneliness of the forest, and wanted to get back to their families. Moreover, they said that they were afraid to travel any further, as we had just come to the region of Beni, the centre of sleepy sickness, while further south the place swarmed with the dreaded " Kumputu " tick, which caused intermittent fever and blindness and other terrible ailments that often ended fatally. As I had neither the power nor the inclination to force anyone to take part in perilous undertakings, we parted in peace. My personal servant went with them, and I sent Bubi the chimpanzee too, as it was impossible to take him with me in my wanderings up and down the forest. I gave instructions for him to await my return in Avakubi. For the first time since I entered the Congo I was without servants, and it was rather unpleasant at the beginning. As I had, up to that time, always found a way out of my difficulties, I trusted to my lucky stars once again.

From Mombasa I started on a series of journeys of exploration in all directions. Within the space of three months I not only visited the pigmies on the edge of the forest at Kilo and Irumu, but also those from Beni, facing the mountain of Ruwenzori. I wandered in the lava-stream areas of the Kivu volcano, where the Batwa and the gorillas are found in a territory protected by the Government. I tramped all through the majestic mountain land of Ruanda as far as the residence of the newly dethroned king, Musinga. My fourth month I devoted to crossing the Ituri Forest once more, from Beni to

Avakubi. These great journeys through the heart of the African forest where once Emin Pascha, Stuhlman and Stanley toiled painfully onward, are quite a simple matter these days owing to the excellent motor roads. It is an easy and safe undertaking to go exploring the Congo forest. Even the man who is studying pigmy life is more comfortably situated than those early pioneers of the last century, as the motor roads run right through the forest on both sides of which the pigmies occasionally appear.

Another thing that has made it more simple to get in touch with negroes and pigmies in the neighbourhood of Lake Albert and Semliki is the lavish hospitality of the missions of Kilo, Bunia and Bungulu. I personally found the knowledge that the missionaries had acquired about the land and the people, was exceedingly useful to me.

A census has been made by Monseigneur Matthyson in Bunia of the pigmy clans along the Irumu–Mombasa route. In that region he reckoned that there were forty-one clans with one thousand two hundred and four adult men, who recognized twenty-one Babira chiefs as patrons. Along the region from Ndirapanda to Nduye there were thirteen clans with three hundred and twelve adult men and thirteen Balese patrons. If one considers that most of the men are married, and calculates two children to every family, this gives the number as about six thousand Bambuti in the triangular territory comprised by the area I have mentioned together with a portion of the district through which I travelled on my trek from Nduye to Mombasa. That is a relative good population for nomads who are scattered over a wide domain.

At Christmas I was working in the neighbourhood of Kilo and Benia. The racial position around Lake Albert is extraordinarily complicated, and the solution to many a linguistic and anthropological riddle can be solved in that region. Far away in a remote part of the forest are the Balese, while further south are the Bambuda and a portion of the forest Banande. In the midst of the latter there is a settlement of the Banyari of Kilo and another of the Banyari of Geti. Right between these two tribes is a region belonging to the Babira of the steppes, who are allied to the Wabudu, living in the extreme north-west.

All the forest tribes are patrons of the Bambuti ; so, too, are the Wamba arid the Watalinge who live in a district south-west of the slopes of Ruwenzori.   In the steppes between Lake Albert and the forest, dwell the Allur and the Logo, whose immediate neighbours are the Balendu of Kilo.   South of the last-named are the Bahema, who again border on the Babira of the steppes, but who have no dealings with them.   On the confines of the latter are the Balendu of Geti, whose territory touches on that of the Banyoro.   These tribes have no pigmies allied to them. The Bambuti do not live in open country.   They are, however, acquainted with the pigmies, and have coined special names for them.   The Balendu call the pigmies " Pe," obvious synonyms with Efé, while the Balese calle them Afe, and the Balendu call them Aue.   The Bahema know both the Bambuti and the Bambuba as Awamba.

In a negro village in the vicinity of Kilo I met a civilized pigmy in breeches and a pith helmet.   The ragged old fellow created a great impression in the village, and smoked cigarette after cigarette, while he kept the local loafers in roars of laughter with his humorous back-chat.

The language of the pigmies who live around Kilo is Efé—they also speak the language of the Banyari, and belong, like all the other pigmies as far as Ruwenzori, to the Efé tribe.   As far as I know there are no Landu-speaking Bambuti.

In company with Father Van Roy I undertook a ten days' circular tour through the Balendu–Banyaru–Balese region.   After crossing Geti-Fataki and Mboga we reached the forest, and penetrated the Banyari village of which Chabi is chief.   There we took up our quarters, and we had an opportunity of getting acquainted with various groups of Bambuti.   At first the Banyari put difficulties in our way and insisted that the pigmies were no longer with them ; we might, however, they said, meet some in the neighbouring village, which was inhabited by Banande.   We retraced our steps to Seremani, as the village was named, and as we approached had the pleasure of hearing dance-songs that recalled the Bambuti to us. Before we reached the village, a courier overtook us with

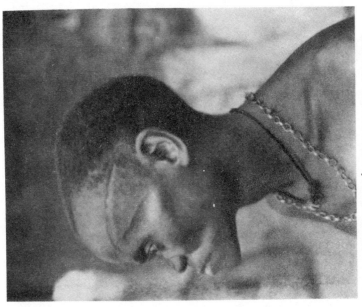

A LANYARI EFÉ FROM CHABI'S VILLAGE

(Face 256)

AN EFE FROM THE KIO TERRITORY

(Page 256)

OLD PIGMIES FROM THE BABIRA FOREST

PIGMIES DANCE TO A NEGRO DRUM. A BANYARI
EFÉ GROUP
(Page 252)

the joyful news that Chabi's Bambuti had turned up in great fettle and were waiting for us.

The Pan-flute dance that I had so often seen was firing a crowd of men and women to a frenzy. They were decked in green, and were dancing in a ring under the shade of a tree with such zest, that the dust was eddying around their heels. Our sudden emergence from the thicket was like a bomb hurled among them, but they soon got over it and the dance began again.

After staying for a while we hurried back, to greet the pigmies of our camp who were marching up in goodly numbers. While my companion distributed salt, I took some measurements and photographs, and made a few language tests, as a result of which I felt satisfied that the pigmies here spoke Efé. We were very much astonished at the extraordinary agility of the oldest man of the crowd. Despite the fact that he was past ninety, and was nearly blind, he stepped out firmly without the aid of a stick along the big stretch from the camp to the village. He told me that he was the father of twenty children, by one wife, and that fifteen of them were still alive. Some of his sons, who were among the crowd present, were already elderly men. The delight of the old fellow, when I wrapped a huge piece of brightly coloured cloth around his body, was touching. He fairly trembled with excitement.

After a brief rest we turned up late in the evening at the Bambuti dances in the illage, where the pigmies leaped and waltzed around the camp-fire, but withdrew after a while as we expected a surprise in return for the presents that we had given. It seemed that we were doomed to wait in vain. I had already retired to rest, and was dozing off when a persistent tooting sound from the direction of the forest aroused me to full consciousness. The eerie notes rang out like a warning bugle through the stillness of the night. I was on the veranda in a jiffy and peered out into the dark. The village was absolutely still. Not a fire was flickering, but here and there a torch was moving in the direction of the forest. We listened— not in vain this time. The forest resounded with loud tootings, followed by a shrill, unearthly community singing. The eerie strains came ever nearer to our house, until at last an infernal din broke out on the open space in front of us. With the lamp in my hand I stepped out into the open air to see the show from the best point of vantage. About twenty men, negroes and pigmies, moving in symphony one behind the other, were dancing in a circle with utter abandon. The pigmies were the musicians and they blew on three pot-shaped wind instruments of different sizes. The biggest pot they called the mother and the little ones the children. The music produced was such as a boy makes when blowing into a shell. The big pot was full of water. The performer evoked the melody by blowing through a short reed, which set the water in motion. The crowd sang and danced in a circle around the musicians, who squatted on the ground. Some of the singers produced a droning syncopated effect by pressing their nostrils with their fingers. The composite result was an uncanny jangling fantasia rather terrifying to one hearing it for the first time.

The pigmies played and danced for me for over an hour, and promising to renew their ear-splitting din in the forest by daylight, vanished, still playing among the giant trees, which long re-echoed their weird strains in muffled tones.

We started in the morning with a number of pigmies, who, according to their promise, were to repeat the performance in the forest. Our path led to the pigmy camp, a good two hours' march. As we went on, a slightly bent reed, about six feet long, was taken out of a spot in the undergrowth, where it had been hidden. It was a wooden trumpet, known as the " Asaragba," and was carried by a youth on his shoulder, while another walking behind blew into it at measured intervals. The forest reverberated the strains again and again. The eerie, inevitable tooting accompanied us along our journey through various little negro villages. When we approached a village, the improvised trumpet blared more blatantly, and young lads from our retinue dashed ahead to announce us. It was extraordinary to see how on our approach women and children, who happened to be engaged in field work, dropped their knives and baskets, and rushed back to the village, where they crawled into their huts and barricaded their doors. In one village a rather inquisitive woman ventured to look round after us, with the result that the procession surrounded her, threatened her and scolded her, and only released her when she gave a hen in compensation for her curiosity. I was informed that in former times such inquisitive women were thrashed and had to pay big fines, sometimes amounting to two goats. When we approached the pigmy camp, the trumpet was hidden somewhere in the thicket. The musicians branched off by a different route from the others in the procession, with whom we stayed. In the distance we still heard for a while the notes of the trumpet, and then suddenly there was complete silence. We never saw the trumpet again.

I had been anxious to secure pictures of the dancers and of the quaint musical instruments, but I failed to do so. It was obvious that the pigmies had suddenly become estranged, taciturn and aloof. Their negro patron was responsible for this. At first he had made obsequious advances to us, as he expected generous presents, which I should have given him after he had, so to speak, delivered the goods. As he had been given nothing on account, it seems that he became rather distrustful, and aroused the suspicions of the pigmies too.

There was nothing particularly striking about the camp itself. I saw negroes who came to buy wooden arrows that had been steeped in a poisonous extract from a species of liana.

I observed that while the pigmies in this district prefer the usual " head for head " system of marriage, they are willing to give a bride in exchange for a dog, five spears and twenty iron-headed arrows.

In the next Balese village, named Kalimoholo, I attained my wish to get an insight into the ritual of the initiation of the youths, which I knew was carried out throughout the entire region. A couple of hours after our return from the forest I entered the club-hut where many men had assembled, and after all the children and women had been chased out, I made a brief speech in which I pretended that I knew all about the secret ceremonies, and gave details which seemed to bear out my assertion. They all looked perplexed and gazed open-mouthed at one another. Then, following up my pretended familiarity with the ritual, I asked to see the

" Abitiri," i.e. the masters of the ceremonial. When I uttered these words, all present stared at me, at first, in blank astonishment, and then jumped to their feet laughing hysterically, and, as I thought, looking extremely silly. Then they all shook hands with one another, and I knew that the ice was broken.

The Abitiri were summoned, and I asked them to allow me to witness the ceremonies. They agreed to do so, and a very friendly conversation ended with an agreement as to the presents that were to be given to them in return for the revelations that they were willing to make.

Equipped with my camera I was escorted to a desolate patch of shrubbery outside the village, which was surrounded with rank " matete " grass. A narrow path led to a sort of windscreen, which was called the " Panda " (initiation hut). By its side were several of the pot instruments, which I have already described, and which I now learned were called " Pengi." In the matete grass a wooden trumpet was concealed. The two Abitiri, the elders of the village, soon appeared, wearing skin caps. Their faces were painted and they waved green branches. In the distance I heard the now familiar bleating of the " Asaragba " trumpet, which came nearer and nearer to the panda, where we were standing. In the intervals could be heard the rhythm of the pot instrument. Young men ran ahead of the procession and drove the women and children into the huts. When they arrived at the panda, the Abitiri danced, waving their green branches as they did so, while the musicians played. No Bambuti were present on this occasion, but I was assured that the ritual hailed from them originally.

The pigmies in this region, as well as the negroes, are circumcised, and many of them are members of the men's secret society. Panda is known as the " village of the men's secret society," while Leku is called the " village of circumcision." They also call Panda and Leku the villages of Tore and Londi respectively. The Balese call God, Londi ; occasionally, too, but very rarely they call him, Tore ; generally Tore is synonymous with the Devil among them. Here we found, as is the custom with many other nations, that the deity of the subject people is condemned to play the rôle of devil for their conquerors.

"MY ATTENDANT DISTRIBUTED SALT"

(*Page* 253)

PIGMY WOMEN IN CHABI'S VILLAGE CARRYING THEIR CHILDREN
IN SASHES

A FLUTE DANCE OF EFÉ AND BANANDE TRIBESMEN IN SEREMANI VILLAGE

(Page 253)

The name Tore is also used as a comprehensive term for all the instruments and vessels, including the whirring wood (Pahudjuhudju) used in connection with the secret initiation of youth. The boys who are to be initiated are called " Ade." The boys, in speaking to either of the Abitiri, address them as " Hudju " (grandfather). It is Tore, they say, that gave the sacred instruments and vessels to their ancestors. Any transgression of the rule that neither women nor the uninitiated can see these instruments or witness the initiation rites is severely punished.

The whirring wood symbolizes the voice of Tore. It is used as well to terrify refractory women. If a wife is sullen or quarrelsome with her husband, but especially if she bites him, the ominous sound of the whirring wood is heard at night-time near her hut. She knows then that she must expiate her crime. She sets off into the forest with all speed, and goes to her own clan the next morning and begs for a gift, which she offers as atonement to her husband.

Although women are absolutely excluded from the initiation ceremonies, there is a Tore dance in which both sexes take part. The women wave their arms about at these dances and the men swing green branches.

My trip to the Kilo–Irumu Bambuti had not been included originally in the scheme of my journey through the Congo, owing to my lack of information about local conditions. I had no idea that there were so many clans of pigmies, and clans with such original traits, too, in the districts on the forest's verge. But the primary cause of this digression from the route that I had mapped out, was an unpretentious-looking pamphlet of ten pages, which a friend had given to me in Landu asking me for information about the language in which it was written.

The compiler, a negro missionary, named Apollo, claimed that it was a first reading book in the " Lumbuti " language. I could also glean that it dealt with the pigmies of Central Africa. Beyond this, I was completely in the dark.

The little pamphlet had lain for months among my papers before I got the key to its contents. There was no doubt that it was written in an Efé dialect, but the

R

question was which dialect ? It was during my Ruanda trip that I heard by mere accident of a negro missionary, named Apollo, and a few questions about him made me believe that he was probably the man I was looking for. I was told that he was a Uganda negro, who some years before had crossed over to the Belgian territory, and conducted the Mboga mission.

I was extremely anxious to meet the man, and travelled from Bunia via Geti to Mboga. There I got a lot of information about Apollo, and was even directed to the neighbourhood where I would be most likely to meet him. A few days later I stood before his clay hut in a negro village, where some of his flock were building a chapel. I was greatly disappointed when I could not find Apollo. Some of the negroes maintained that he was at home, but his wife, who just then came out of her hut, said that he had set out for the forest that morning, and would be away for several days. I cannot say whether Apollo was at home and did not want to see me, although I could see no reason why he should refuse to do so. Although a chat would have been useful, I was able to get the gist of his pamphlet without his help, as I got into touch with the very pigmies in whose language it was written. After I had made some changes in his translation of it, for he had several serious errors, the reading of the Lord's Prayer runs thus, in the Efé dialect of Mboga-Irumu :

Amu afu hocha halu tida, na hitu habula fua, oka nibai habula fua, osani nibai habula fua halu tida bai hène. Eti anu amubai amuhanu obala, au au amubaie, amuahenue ode amue ahesimagu ledeai, nagitsu amue idere anue nedo uda eda.

As so far, with the exception of Apollo's little pamphlet, nothing has been printed in any pigmy language or dialect, and as no European scholars have so far paid any attention to the subject, it occurred to me that my readers ought to be interested in this specimen of the speech of the little men of the Congo.

Just off the motor-road from Irumu to Beni, which has recently been extended to Ruanda, in the territory of the Bambula, there are large numbers of pigmies. I spent a whole day among those attached to the village of Mwera.

Mwera himself, a Munande chief, had under his control the Banande and Bambula as well as a considerable number of pigmies.

The pigmies are called Awasomba by the Banande, but they are known among themselves as Bapakombe or Wamba as well as Bambuti. They speak both Efé and Kibira. Incidentally it seems that the word Bambuti belongs to the Kibira tongue and is probably derived from " gbutiu " (little). I noticed that the Mwera pigmies hang little bundles of food-stuffs from the branches of trees, after the negro fashion, to protect themselves from reptiles and rats.

The Mwera Bambuti lived almost on the fringe of the plateau which slopes down to the Semliki. From the other bank of that stream rises the mighty bulk of Ruwenzori, with its peak capped with eternal snow and ice. Very rarely are its colossal jagged summits visible, although I was lucky enough on several occasions to feast my eyes on the majestic outlines when they were silhouetted against a cloudless sky. The euphonious name Ruwenzori is a rather happy mutilation of its title in the vernacular, and so is that of the stream that washes its base, the " Semliki."

CHAPTER XIII

ACROSS THE FOREST OF THE BABIRA-BAMBUTI

I STILL had to cut through the huge forest region on the left bank of the Ituri, to visit the Bambuti on the Lenda. Actually a month was not a sufficiently long period to study very carefully the pigmies along the Beni-Okaiko-Avakubi route. In fact through lack of time I had to give up the idea of visiting the south-westerly tracts towards Makala.

The forest track, dating back to the days of the slave traffic, when it was crowded with caravans, is overgrown with rank vegetation to-day. This is due to the constantly changing arrangements by the Government regarding settlements and district boundaries. Such eternally shifting arrangements entail the making of new tracks, very much to the disadvantage of the stationary negro villages. I heard numerous complaints on this score. It is the business of the inhabitants of the villages to keep the paths in order and to construct new ones. Many inconveniences and hardships are incurred when new roads are being made, as they involve the building of new villages and the laying-out of new plantations. The old ones cannot be looked after, as they are too far away from the new settlements, with the result that very soon they are overgrown with matete grass and brambles and bushes, and are laid waste by wild beasts. We were constantly coming upon such " Matongas," as they are called, upon our journeys. The caravans were so buried in matete grass that the heads of the bearers were hidden, and we stumbled over fallen tree-trunks, and frequently were drenched to the skin in a few minutes by the chilly morning dew.

I was glad that among the bearers who were awaiting me at Bungulu there were some pigmy half-breeds with whose aid it was much easier to win the confidence of the true pigmies.

Almost the entire region which we traversed from Beni to Avakubi is inhabited by Babira negroes who differ very little in their speech from the Bambuti themselves.

The greater number of my bearers belonged to the forest Banande from the villages which we traversed in the first few days. The Banande, a sturdy, agricultural people, penetrated slowly into the forest and drove back the Babira to the north-east, just as they forced the Bambuba towards the north-west, deeper and deeper into the forest. The forest itself gave way before the axes ; they culti- vated it piece by piece, and made extensive tillage and pasturage lands, while the Babira and the other forest negroes merely made clearings, which were overgrown again after a while. It seems likely, as some missionaries maintain, that the deforested heights east of Semliki are due to the agricultural activities of the Banande.

Marabu, a little negro village, was our first halting place. No rest-hut being available, I stayed for the night in the club hut, as I was obliged to do repeatedly during this trip. The natives complained that they suffered terribly from the damage done to their plantations by elephants at night time. Certain steps had been considered for dealing with these nocturnal raids, but nothing was done. As my hunter had left me at Mombasa, I did not take the trouble to secure one in his place, and I also got rid of my guns, as I do not care for hunting myself, and it was absolutely unnecessary for my personal protection against attacks in any part of the Congo territory.

In Kinombe's village on the river Tabir, where most of the bearers were within easy reach of their homes, the pigmies assembled from the outlying camps. Although they live under the sway of the Banande, they speak their tongue very poorly. This seems a clear indication that until a comparatively short time ago the Babira were their patrons, and that they were hurled back by the invading Banande, while the Bambuti held their ground. As we reached the village in the forenoon, I had several hours available for making inquiries about the Bambuti. I was present here at a celebration of a secret initiation cere- mony. It was essentially like that obtaining among the

Efé with a slight difference in some accessory details. It was a half-breed, the fruit of a Mubira and a Bambuti mother, who administered the rites. As he himself had been through the school, he was well acquainted with the ritual. When we discussed the subject at Kinombe, for which purpose I brought some other pigmies to the hut, nobody was inclined to speak at first. I could get absolutely no information from any of them until the half-breed spoke to them pretty bluntly, and pointed out that I was no mere stranger, and that, besides, I knew all about the mysteries already and was unlikely to betray my knowledge to the women. The older men then seemed more at ease and conversed in an undertone for some time. I learned that a long wooden trumpet and the whirring wood, but not the pot instruments of the Banyari Efé, were used in connection with the rites.

Every clan has its own " Lusomba," as they call the trumpet here, and each clan has a separate name for it. It was clear that the trumpet was a symbol—not merely a musical instrument. Every clan has its own specially sacred species of animal, which no man dare kill, and which is called by a special name. Likewise every Lusomba has its special name. The Basomba—the plural of Lusomba—are considered as the genii of the clans. Women must on no account see them ; if they do they will become barren. The Lusomba trumpet typifies the sacred animal species of the clan ; it is the symbol of the totem animal.

The intimate connection between the secret rites of initiation and the totemism cult, which is so widespread among the pigmies, is clearly evident here. Totemism is not so clearly defined in its details among the pigmies as among many other peoples, but its essential features are present.

" If anyone among us kills the poru, we all get fever and sit shivering by the fire," said Tebi to me once. Now the poru is the totem animal of the Andeporu clan. Again the prohibition of marriage between people who worship the same totem is very widespread, though by no means universally recognized. I have already referred to the fact that many pigmies recognize marriages contracted by parties of different family groups, but not of different clans.

There are almost as many pigmies under the patronage of the Babira as under the Balese. Apparently, too, they are better fed, as they are of more sturdy build, and, as I discovered by measurements, somewhat taller. Moreover, their skin is slightly browner. Perhaps one might rightly attribute their higher standard of comfort to the fact that they have been living for a long time in mutual interdependence with the negroes. There can be no doubt that the association of the Babira and the Bambuti is extremely close. If one examines, carefully, the distribution of races in the Congo, one cannot help inferring that the Babira must have been the first negro invaders, and consequently the first to come into close contact with the pigmies living in the forest. And that is how they have given their language and many features of their civilization to the pigmies. On the other hand there has been a great influx of pigmy blood among the Babira.

Many Babira villages have sound commercial reasons for keeping on good terms with the pigmies. It is no exaggeration to say that it is mainly through the successful elephant hunting of the Bambuti that many Babira villages have attained such a standard of prosperity that they need not work at all themselves, and can devote their time to wild carousals. Never did I see anywhere else in the Congo such indications of negro prosperity as among the forest Babira. The much prized and costly ivory goes through their hands, and the profit from it is theirs alone, without their having to do anything towards the acquiring of it. The Mombuti takes the ivory to his patron's village, after he has killed the elephant. The negro keeps piling it up, until a dealer buys the whole lot for a good price. He has not even the trouble of bringing his ivory to the market. The Babira frequently trap elephants themselves, but the main providers are the pigmies.

During my journey a rumour, disturbing to both pigmies and to negroes, was circulated through the district that the Colonial Government had issued a decree forbidding elephant-hunting. It made the marrow boil in the bones of the Babira, and the Bambuti were furious about it. If such a decree were passed, I think it would be most unjust as far as the Bambuti were concerned, as they are the aboriginal owners of the forest, and hunting for them is their means of livelihood.   Moreover, it would be far more fitting to debar Europeans, who kill elephants by dozens with Mauser rifles, from their so-called sport than to put such restrictions on the Bambuti, who do not kill for the mere pleasure of killing, as their civilized brothers do, but merely to secure a livelihood.   Moreover, the Bambuti, with their spears, could never appreciably reduce the elephant population of the Congo, whereas a few sporting Europeans would not take long to destroy whole herds with their rifles.   Should such an order be put into force, financial considerations are at the back of it, as is so often the case when Europeans interfere with the hereditary and national rights of the natives.   The white hunter pays sporting dues—a handsome figure for every elephant killed.   The pigmy, on the other hand, pays nothing.   Therefore his hunting is unproductive in the eyes of the Colonial treasury, and must be stopped.   Consequently one can understand the rage of the pigmies when they heard the rumour.   The problem might be far more efficiently dealt with by the pigmies themselves delivering the ivory to the authorities, instead of to the negroes—in return for payment, of course.   I tried to discuss the solution of the difficulty with a crowd of Bambuti near Sabani, who questioned me in rather agitated tones about the decree.   I said that it really only affected the negroes, and hastened to add that they should not be so stupid as to hand over the ivory to the black men, but that they should sell it themselves.   My advice was given in dead earnest, but I was just talking to the wind.   They knew, and I knew, that it could not be carried out until another middleman, instead of the negro, could be found to negotiate between the pigmy and the purchaser.   The pigmies themselves have not the slightest idea about the way to handle ivory.   Sometimes you come across little ivory mallets for stripping the bark off trees.   They never use it for any other purpose—not even to make trinkets for personal adornment.

From Tabir the path led through forest and stretches of deserted plantations to the banks of the Luhulu, into which the Tabir flows.   Crossing the Luhulu at a spot where it divides into two branches, which enclose an

MUSICAL INSTRUMENTS FOR THE SECRET CEREMONIALS OF THE
EFÉ TRIBE

(*Page* 254)

A PIGMY CAMP NEAR SABANI'S VILLAGE

(*Page* 268)

A PRIMITIVE DARBY AND JOAN
(Page 267)

A SUSPENSION BRIDGE OF LIANA CORDS
OVER THE LUHULU
(Page 265)

island, was the most romantic experience. From the tops of the giant trees which shed an eternal twilight over the water, hang hundreds of liana cables, which have been cleverly interwoven and support a frail gangway of sticks in such a way as to form two huge suspension bridges, on which you can cross quite comfortably by using your arms, i.e. if you don't get too dizzy in the process. Some bearers from the steppes, who had never seen such bridges, were terror-stricken as they looked at the water foaming far below them, from their swaying perches. They laid down their burdens, and crouched shuddering beside them until some with stouter hearts brought both them and their baggage across safely.

One sees many such bridges in this district, but the one over the Luhulu is the largest and the best kept. Its architect deserves both praise and admiration. For this reason I was very astonished when my bearers insisted that the Bambuti had built the bridge. This may be so in the sense that the pigmies, who are clever climbers, did the work, but the Babira must have been the supervisors and inventors of the scheme. At any rate the pigmy has scarcely any need of bridges of this type for his own purposes, as the territorial boundaries of each clan usually run level with the river bank.

As these suspension bridges often rise to dizzy heights, they could only have been built by good climbers. The liana coils that hang from the huge trees on either bank are skilfully spliced to form the suspension cables, and round sticks, cleverly interwoven with these cables, form the gangways. Such a bridge must, of necessity, be bow-shaped, as in the case of broad rivers, even the longest lianas are too short to make a level pathway possible. The curve of the bridges spanning small rivers is slight ; the broader the stream, the steeper the bridge.

In every negro village we met groups of Bambuti. I cannot say whether they turned up voluntarily, or if their black patrons ordered them to appear. Frequently they could not be stopped from accompanying our caravan for some distance when we resumed our journey.

The landscape rivalled the forests of Nduye and Ngayu in wild romantic charm. The Biena River thunders down a dark ravine, through which in the course of centuries it has grooved the solid rock with a deep narrow channel some two hundred yards long. At the bottom of this the water roars and foams. After every heavy rainstorm the channel overflows, and the swirling river races through the ravine, in whose abysses many a traveller has met his fate. Such an uncanny reputation has it, that the negroes have erected " ghost huts " on its banks—tiny structures of twigs, roofed with banana or phrynium leaves. In front of these little huts, bananas are left by travellers as offerings for the souls of those who have perished there, in order to permit them to continue their journey peacefully and in safety. You meet similar ghost huts in every Babira village. I never saw any in the pigmy camps, though it may be true, as the Babira say, that the Bambuti, too, occasionally do build such houses.

If a Babira pigmy has no luck at the hunt, he chops off the head of a hen, and watches the carcase as it twitches in its dying convulsions. He then cooks and eats it, and scatters its liver around, at the same time calling on the dead to assist him in the quest of game. This ritual they have certainly learned from the Babira negroes, who have recourse to it when in dire straits. The Babira-Bambuti have occasionally hens in their camps.

Every day the bearers begged me to give them a full day's rest, but they always went ahead again voluntarily, when we reached negro villages, as they were invariably too uncomfortable to invite us to stay long. Either there was inadequate housing or the food was lacking—sometimes both. We had to wait until we got to Kissenge's village with its fine plantations before taking our very much-needed rest. I only met this shrewd chief on the evening before we resumed our journey, which I regretted all the more, as I got quite a lot of useful information from him during my brief conversation. Before he turned up they tried, by all means possible, to persuade me that there were no pigmies attached to the village. Finally, they condescended to call in the outlying pigmies, who greeted me with the customary dancing.

The men squatted beside the huts and played and sang, while the women danced, every muscle of their bodies seeming to twitch in rhythm to the time. Even their faces kept time with these expressive movements to the beat of the barbaric melody. The leader of the women, a merry-looking, toothless granny, danced so gracefully and joined in the syncopated singing with such zest and in such perfect time, that she attracted the admiration of everybody, including myself. When I inquired about her husband, the oldest of the men stepped forward, a grey-headed little fellow with a massive head and wearing an okapi girdle, and, standing beside his wife, put his arm tenderly around her. A primeval Darby and Joan! A living refutation of those dogmatic theorists, who assert that tenderness and sentiment are foreign to the nature of the " dawn man."

At Kissenge's village, which was on the confines of the districts of Beni and Mombasa, our path virtually ceased to exist. On resuming their march my bearers travelled for hours through wastes of matete grass, which practically hid both them and their burdens from my view. We gave a sigh of relief when once more we entered the forest, and felt beneath our feet its soft mossy track instead of the rankly luxuriant tongo which kept tripping us up with its maze of brambles, liana and long coarse grass. The murmur of running water showed that we were close to a river. Following the direction indicated by the sound we soon reached its banks, where we rested for a short while before crossing. Then we waded into the stream which was shallow at first and, as it got deeper, was spanned by a frail bridge of tree-trunks, which we crossed with eerie dread that at any moment we might be precipitated into the raging torrent beneath.

A long day's march brought us into the heart of the Babira Forest. In the afternoon we approached the village of Masaburi or Sabani. About half a mile from the village we met two creatures swathed in gaudy cotton clothes, who were apparently waiting for somebody. Whether the news of the arrival of our caravan had been reported in advance by some means or other I cannot say. The features of the elder man proclaimed him a Mombuti. I was in doubts about the younger one, a sturdy fellow. I presumed that he was the village chief, as he announced himself as " Sultan." Soon I saw that I was mistaken, and that he was only a Bambuti Sultan.

Although facial contours might easily mislead one in a region where there are so many half-breeds, his behaviour very quickly proclaimed him a crabbed, secretive Mombuti, compared with whom the negro is relatively a more plastic and bright fellow. Sabani, the chief, met me at the entrance to the village.

I stayed for several days in Sabani, dismissed my bearers, who had been carrying my baggage for a full week, and sat about looking for the pigmies. Sabani, the son of Musaburi, had taken over the reins of government in the village, following legal proceedings, which had been taken against his old father for cloaking and abetting illegal elephant-hunting by a European. Musaburi told me many a tale of horror about the Wangwana slave-dealers. He maintained that the tradition among the Babira of that district, about an attack by the Efé on the Mawambi in the Babira Forest, which they carried out triumphantly as far as Biena, was founded on fact. It seems that the Efé, led by a resourceful and bellicose hero, a Napoleon of the pigmies, overran the entire forest. At Kokonyangi they invaded the Babira fastnesses, forcing the negroes to flee to Biena, where the great pigmy offensive was held up. The strange thing about the tradition is that the negroes still shudder as they give details of the war, while the pigmies seem to have forgotten about it completely.

One of Sabani's camps lay about a quarter of a mile away on a gentle rise, close to the caravan track. The huts were so overgrown with creepers and parasitic plants of all kinds that one could hardly guess what their architectural scheme was, a proof that it was a permanent camp and had been occupied for years. All the inhabitants were crack elephant-hunters, and therefore they were greatly prized and very well looked after by the negroes of Sabani's village. Not only were they well fed, but they were well clothed, like the two men whom we met as we were approaching the negro village. I could see clearly that Sabani was very anxious to keep the youthful pigmy on his side. He gratified every wish, and had him always loafing around his hut, where he could get plenty of food and beer at any hour. The pigmy chief wallowed in indolence and luxury, but saw that his

A QUIET DOMESTIC PICTURE

THE BABIRA-BAMBUTI, SETTING A HUNTING-NET
(*Page 269*)

THE BAG—AN ANTELOPE IS EXTRICATED FROM THE NET
AND TIED UP
(*Page 270*)

little subjects kept busy hunting elephants, and trapping antelopes and wild pigs in nets.

One morning, accompanied by a negro, I set out with the whole pack of pigmy hunters. Their nets hanging round their necks, their spears in their hands, they walked leisurely along the forest track, while the women carrying their babies, and with troupes of children in the rear, made a terrific din as they formed the rearguard. When we got deep into the forest the women squatted on the ground, while the nets were spread by the men. Young lads hooked the upper part of the nets to bushes, and the ends were made fast among protruding roots of trees. Then the women moved off accompanied by some men. After a while they returned extended in semicircular formation towards the nets, yelling and screaming as they did so, in order to drive any animals in front of them towards the huntsmen who were on the alert with spears poised for the blow. Hunting dogs, with wooden bells round their necks, darted to and fro sniffing the ground. At length an antelope started towards the net, but scenting danger, turned tail and broke back through the ranks of beaters.

Taking their initial bad luck stoically, the men unhooked the nets from their fastenings, and slung them around their necks once more. Then they crammed tobacco into their pipes made of phrynium leaves, lit up, and emitted thick clouds of smoke from their mouths and nostrils. Meanwhile the women kindled fires and the children romped merrily around.

The pipe is a simple extemporized one, made by wrapping three or four bits of fibre in a phrynium leaf in such a way that one end is broader than the other. Then the smoker bends the leaf at the broader end. The next process is to wrap twine round the pipe, after which the bits of fibre are extracted, one by one, and the job is completed. A little tobacco is rammed into the broader end of the pipe, and all that is needed is a bit of burning stick with which to light up.

After the pipes had been passed from mouth to mouth and finally tossed away, the pigmies moved about half a mile further on, and once more spread their nets. Again the forest rang to the shrill screams of the beaters and the yells of the children. Silently the hunters crouched behind their nets and waited. They were doomed to disappointment again. Two further attempts were equally unsuccessful. In the afternoon, however, they killed a considerable number of antelopes.

Every day these Bambuti supplied me with antelopes that they had just killed, for which I paid them with cloth, beads, salt or tobacco.

These Bambuti know how to use fire whirls, and I frequently saw them playing on negro musical instruments.

During the next four days there were very few pigmies in the camp. They were busily engaged executing orders given them by the negroes. The boys and young men together with some negroes were rounded up to work on the new caravan road linking Mombasa and Beni, and were rarely seen about the camp.

At the other end of the village, a little way off the main path, I saw a wretched camp consisting of five huts, which literally swarmed with children. They kept running to and fro, and even with the help of the adults I failed in my attempt to sort them out into their different families.

There were two newly-born babes in the camp, one of whom was only four days old. The young mother, who had wrapped it in swaddling clothes made of fresh phrynium leaves, cuddled it to her in her arms, and gazed upon its tiny wizened face with eyes aglow with happiness and love. The other women of the camp smiled with delight, as they swarmed in a circle around the little mother, who squatted on the ground listening proudly to the compliments paid to her infant.

In the very same camp as I saw this beautiful picture, I also gazed into the eyes of pain—the eyes of a mortally sick old man, who sat on the ground, with his back against two stakes, which had been placed cross-wise and driven into the ground. His face was distorted with agony, but not a sound passed his tightly-compressed lips. Even when I asked him about his symptoms with a view to trying to assuage his pain, he refused to speak. There he sat by himself, all alone, utterly oblivious of what was going on around him. The inhabitants of the camp sitting

CASTING THEIR NETS ON THE GROUND, THE MEN MADE PIPES
OF PHRYNIUM LEAVES
(*Page* 269)

BABIRA-BAMBUTI MEN WITH ARTIFICIALLY POINTED TEETH

A NEW-BORN MOMBUTI BABE SWATHED IN
PHRYNIUM LEAVES

(Page 270)

FATHER AND SON, FAMOUS BASUA ELEPHANT
HUNTERS, FROM PUMBA'S VILLAGE

in front of their huts, seemed utterly indifferent to the poor old man's agony. It is possible that they were inclined to be reserved owing to my presence. The sick man would definitely never have been abandoned by his own family group, and presumably these two sticks placed cross-wise were the very utmost that they could contrive in the way of an invalid chair. Sights such as this bring home to one the crude primitiveness of pigmy culture.

The trouble about bearers started afresh in Sabani's village. Even Moke, my cook, expressed a desire to return home with the Banande bearers, as he had a horror of probing any further into the boundless forest. A dispute, which he had with some of the bearers, however, frustrated his scheme, and he was afraid to venture alone on a seven days' tramp through the forest.

With the very best intentions Sabani did not seem to be in a position to supply the necessary number of bearers. Many Babira stalwarts sat idly in front of their huts, but not one made a move to obey his chief's order. Nobody was very keen on earning a few francs. Many of the negroes were richer than I was. Eventually I decided to set out with some of the Bambuti and Babira, and left the bulk of my luggage behind in Sabina's village. As I had done already on a few occasions, I tried the experiment, once more, of moving from village to village, with as little baggage as possible, being confident that the rest would follow in due course. The negroes are afraid of having to accept the responsibility for loss of baggage, and consequently are only too anxious to forward any stuff left behind as soon as they can. When I reached Paiso's village I picked my bearers almost exclusively from the pigmies.

The religion of the frontier Banande has reacted appreciably on that of the Babira, and has also coloured the pigmy conception of God. They call him Muema. His home is in the forest, and they never fail to give him thank-offerings of game, fruit and honey.

The further one travels from Beni towards the Ituri, the more one finds the name Kalisia applied to the deity, instead of Muema. The Babira assured me that Kalisia was exclusively used by the Bambuti. From Kalisia I was told all good things come. He is gracious towards

the Bambuti, while the Babira dread him. He stands
by the hunter when he is on the trail of game, inspires
him regarding the proper place and time to seek his prey
—in a word he drives animals across his path. Standing
behind the pigmy, as Horus of yore stood behind Pharaoh,
he bends his bow and inspires his aim, so that he may not
miss either elephant, buffalo or wild pig. Kalisia always
gives him a hint, too, about days which are likely to be
unlucky for hunting. On such days the pigmy squats by
the fire or loafs round the camp.

Near the camp in a gable-roofed hut are placed the
sacrificial offerings for Kalisia. Against this structure
the pigmy props his spear at night, and appeals to the
deity to give him luck in the morning's hunt. And as he
steps confidently through the forest on the following day,
if he feels something brush against his shoulder he knows
that Kalisia is telling him to be on the alert, as there is
splendid game right ahead of him.

Before lying down at night the pigmy puts an arrow
under his head. If he dreams that he will kill an animal,
it is a hint from Kalisia which he follows up without
demur the next day, as he knows that he will return with
a good bag.

Kalisia is the guide of the wayfaring Bambuti. He
walks ahead of them and points out the road. He tells
the elders in their dreams where to pitch camp, and when
to abandon the old one.

For four successive days we marched for very long
stretches at a time until we reached the Ituri, opposite
Pengi.   Plodding through the scorched and desolate
plantations under a burning sun was most exhausting
work. Moreover, in every village I had little tiffs with
the chiefs, who really found it extremely difficult to secure
the requisite number of bearers for me. Pigmies generally
came to my rescue at the last moment.

At Kapamba I saw a little settlement of Bambuti
elephant hunters, who had little gable-roofed huts after
the style of the Babira dwellings.

Among the Babira–Bambuti I found the results of
my researches among the Efé, and the Aká in general,
were confirmed. Although in accordance with the Babira
custom, marriage by purchases prevails among many of

them, the " head for head " system is the traditional and the most preferred one. If one of the women who marries under this system, has several children, while the other one has either none or only one, her family group must give the family group of the prolific woman either a present or a young girl. The Babira are very fond of getting pigmy wives, in return for which they are glad to give iron-ware, while on the birth of the first child they give two goats. If a woman proves barren, a portion of the dowry is returned to the negro. Marriage outside the clan is approved by the Bambuti of this district. Unmarried young men are forbidden to have liaisons within their own clan. Monogamy is imperative. A deceived husband is at liberty to wreak vengeance in any way he chooses upon the adulterer.

The system of blood-brotherhood-bond between the Bambuti and the Babira is permissible. Two pots of food are prepared, into each of which both participants shed drops of blood, which they take from the arms. Then they eat the food.

Both the Babira and the Bambuti have a superstitious dread of twin births.

Two skinny little old pigmies in Kapamba's village told me that formerly their people used to kill and eat their enemies, and that women used to take part in the cannibalistic feasts.

At Pumba, the last Babira village, a horde of pigmies led by their patron, the village blacksmith, came to greet me with song and dance. It was also the last festive reception of the kind I was to get amid the dim forests of the Ituri. Ten months previously they had heard of the arrival of " Baba wa Bambuti " on the other side of the Ituri, and had been daily expecting me, until they heard that I had travelled towards the north-east.

My investigations were now concluded among the Ituri pigmies. I had to forego, through lack of time and the difficulty in getting bearers, my scheme of journeying westward to the valleys of the Mombo and of visiting Makala. And as, moreover, my vitality was at a low ebb, I proceeded to the Ituri accompanied by a gang of pigmy bearers.

Pengi is a Wangwana settlement, a sort of suburb of

s

Avakubi. The visit of the sultan and the importance of the village made it easy for me to get a caravan of bearers together quickly, as there was no boat available to take me down-stream. Not until I reached Kaitschui's village did I secure a canoe, which brought me to Kero, whence, on the next day, I reached Avakubi, accompanied by my servant Moke, while another canoe followed with my baggage.

The results of my investigations along the Ituri were so satisfactory in every respect, that I was able to take a much-needed rest before undertaking my next task of studying the pigmies of French Equatorial Africa, who had been included in my original plan. I still had to find out, whether the pigmies there had any connection with those of the Ituri.

A later book will deal with the journey, as well as with my experiences among the various negro tribes. As the equatorial pigmies are a race of half-breeds or, as the scientific term goes a pigmy-form race, it would be out of place to deal with them here. I would have preferred to have been able to have stayed longer in the Ituri region, and to have investigated the outlying districts where there are pigmies. I should have liked to have tried to find if there were, anywhere, an organized community of the little people with more racial solidarity than I had so far encountered. Unfortunately a return to the Ituri was impossible, firstly, because the journey was too long, and secondly, my health would not permit a repetition of my rough-and-tumble method of living in pigmy camps in the Congo forests.

In Avakubi I had my hands full with packing specimens and souvenirs which had piled up enormously. Moreover, I had to complete my notes about my research work, especially with regard to the pigmy languages and dialects.

My hope that I would travel by the Avakubi–Bafwasende–Stanleyville motor service on its maiden trip was not fulfilled, as the road was unfinished when I had to leave. I decided upon the seven-day down-stream trip on the Ituri. A splendid boat with nine oarsmen was placed at my disposal. Leaning back in an arm-chair I saw the ever-changing forest vista, and dreamily listened to the songs of the rowers, who with mighty sweeps of their blades took the boat past rapids and crags with the speed of an arrow. Treacherous submerged rocks, whose presence was indicated by the rippling of the water and by whirlpools and cascades, were constantly providing us with plenty of excitement. In such emergencies the boat hugged the bank, while local oarsmen brought us through the danger zone. Our baggage was generally unshipped and carried overland for the time being. I spent the first night in the village of a friendly Mubali negro, who was worried on my account, because on the previous day lightning had struck and damaged the rest-hut. He could not comprehend why, despite this fact, I should insist on sleeping in the hut.

Our next halt was at Bombili, which commands a view of the estuary of the Nepoko, which pours its waters over crags into the Ituri with a mighty and eternal roar. The Bombili has grim associations for the Babali. A few years ago ten of their tribe were hanged, for being members of the Anyota Secret Society, as they had been implicated in the murder of many men. The site of the giant gallows is no longer visible, yet any Mubali can point out the exact spot where it stood.

In Bombili we got a change of boat and oarsmen. The Government maintains a fairly good service of boats on the Ituri. Our new oarsmen tried to dawdle over the trip as much as possible. They had sized me up as being rather soft, and they counted on my ignorance of the neighbourhood. On the latter point, at any rate, they were grievously mistaken, as I had before me an excellent chart of the river route. When I saw that they were contemplating spending an extra day on the job, and stopping at a riverside village for a bit of fun, I absolutely refused to give my consent as I could not afford to waste time. When, in spite of what I said, they started to row towards the bank, I lost my temper and acted in a way that I should never have conceived possible before. I hurled everything I could lay hands on at the skipper's head. With a frenzied leap he shot overboard, followed by all the other oarsmen. The leaderless craft drifted idly down-stream. To tell the truth I was feeling heartily ashamed of having lost my head, when I saw my crew swimming like rats in the wake of the boat. They clambered aboard, took the oars once more, and sent the little vessel flying along at a terrific rate. The tempo of their singing, which they resumed with zest, was attuned precisely to the lightning sweep of their blades. I was no longer the good Muzungu, who gave them lots to eat. The burden of their chant was that the Baba wa Bambuti was a bad man who hurled sticks and stools at people, and drove them into the river, and so on. It mattered little to me what they sang, so long as the inspiration of their lay gave zest to their rowing. Late in the evening we reached our halting-place. As the boat drew near the anchorage, the oarsmen shouted in a warning tone to the negroes, who had been attracted to the bank by the singing, not to fool around, but to do the Muzungu's bidding as quickly as possible, as he was " wa makali " (not in joking mood). The consequence was that not only did the oarsmen get plenty of food, but the chief offered me a goat, which I declined with thanks.

Opposite Panga the Ituri thunders down a mighty cascade. This marks the limit of the boat service from Bombili. Babeyru oarsmen steered our boat for over half a mile through waterfalls, that sweep downward among jutting crags with tremendous speed. Holding my camera, I stood up in the boat and tried in vain to film the majestic scene. The boat, wreathed in flakes of foam and flying spindrift, was tossed violently to and fro at such a rate that I sat down rather abruptly or rather flopped back with a jerk into my seat, and had to grip the gunwale with both hands to save myself from being catapulted into the seething water.

When we reached still water, we got once again a new relay of oarsmen. In the afternoon we sighted on the steep right bank a negro village, behind which black clouds welled up from the horizon, and we heard the rumble of an oncoming thunderstorm. The oarsmen pulled for all they were worth to get the craft to anchorage before we got the full force of the storm. Scarcely was the baggage safely stowed away, when the rain came down in buckets, accompanied by continuous lightning and thunder claps. It passed as suddenly as it came, and a gorgeous rainbow spanned the eastern sky.

BAMBUTI WOMEN FROM PUMBA'S VILLAGE CARRYING BABIES
IN SASHES

MY CARAVAN CROSSES A RIVER IN THE ITURI FOREST

(Page 267)

"I DECIDED FOR THE ROMANCE OF A SEVEN DAYS' TRIP
DOWNSTREAM ON THE ITURI"

(*Page 274*)

PIGMY CHILDREN PLAYING THE GUITAR

All the local pigmies had been prevented by the storm from coming to greet me, but they sent four young fellows to represent them. They were Baleu pigmies, and I chatted with them until a late hour with the aid of an interpreter.

A three days' journey brought me from Panga to Banalia, whence I motored to Stanleyville, and went down the River Congo in a huge paddle-steamer.

Just twice more on my way I heard about pigmies. Fellow-passengers on the steamer had seen some of them on the upper reaches of the Lomani near Chosa, where, in days gone by, Greenfeld and Wolf had met them. And a missionary from Elizabethville, below Basoko, stated that a bit inland off the Congo banks pigmies dwelt, who were called " Tikitiki," a name that recalls the Azande. The missionary thought that the word might be a corruption of " kikikiki " which means " little."

I got definite information months later about pigmies in the Kasai region in the forest near Lusambo from Luluaberg missionaries, who had a great deal to do with them.

Towards the end of March I reached Coquilhatville, the capital of French Equatorial Africa, whence my route lay inland, to the Bachwa, the half cousins of the Bambuti of the Ituri.

CHAPTER XIV

THE LIFE AND WAYS OF THE BAMBUTI

HAS the picture I have drawn of the Bambuti been a true one, at least in its salient outlines? Has my description of their daily round of toil, gossip and gaiety tallied with the actualities of their grim battles for existence in the virgin forest? I certainly strove earnestly to keep my original plan of giving in faithful detail the stark facts which I observed during the long months I lived among the pigmies. And yet, now that I have completed my sketch, I have an uneasy feeling that perhaps I have over-emphasized the bright tints and under-stressed the shadows—that with lapse of time and change of clime I have visualized the Bambuti as a more lovable and a better people, and their gipsy shiftless existence as more romantic than they really appeared, when I lived among them, and had to put up with all their callow crudeness. Still, despite this misgiving on my part, I know that I have done my best not to see them in the roseate hues which distance lends, as will be evident from my blunt portrayal of unamiable kinks in their character and of the unpleasantness of some of their personal habits.

I hope sincerely that, taking all in all, my book has done justice to the Bambuti, as I have aimed, not at sensationalism, but at truth—at bringing the world in touch with the weird and strange, yet intensely human existence and outlook of the hitherto almost unknown pigmies of the Ituri.

These were real men whom I saw in the Ituri forests, and my purpose was to depict them as real men, not as monsters, as beast-men, living, so to speak, on the verge of humanity—on the borderland between man and beast.

Those writers who have endeavoured to depict people living in remote undeveloped regions as freaks, and to give the reader as inaccurate and fantastic an account of them as possible, have always failed in their purpose, because even the seemingly strangest idiosyncrasies in morals and customs cease to be bizarre and meaningless when they are considered in connection with the mentality of a people and their environment. They seem as quite normal and logical sequences to both mentality and environment.

One must take a survey of their daily round as the foundation of their social and mental outlook. The reader will thus get a glimpse of this environment from which a people have sprung, and he will be in a position to understand their spiritual outlook and their temperament.

It is only by living among the pigmies that one can realize how difficult it is to comprehend the outlook and the attitude towards life of such a remote people. At first we see characteristics that repel us rather than show common contacts ; we see the primitive, rough and brutal man, but not the soul—not the spiritual life masked by his harsh exterior Even the negro peasant thinks he is justified in looking on the pigmy with a blend of condescension and contempt in virtue of his economic superiority over him. But, if it goes to that, is it not our own economic advantages over them that have engendered in us the illusion that all primitive peoples are far inferior to us, and that we have a right to treat them—or, rather, ill-treat them accordingly ?

And has not our self-sufficient, casual, patronizing attitude towards such nations and their culture been responsible for this erroneous view ?

Even at the present day considerable numbers of people are inclined to look down on the African negroes as wild animals, despite the fact that so many conscientious and painstaking explorers have long since dispelled the illusion about their savagery and their backwardness. The fact that they differ from us does not necessarily mean that they are backward. In many ways they are by far our superiors. People foreign to us are only savage until we have seen the error of our original stupid view of them, and until we are in the position to study their peculiar habits and outlook. In short, our ignorance is the cause of the gulf between us and them.

And, taking an exactly similar attitude towards the pigmy as we take towards himself, the negro looks down on him " as a wild animal—as a chimpanzee "—simply because the pigmy's way of life is as strange to the negro as the negro's is to us. The barriers between different civilizations stand in the way of an understanding and appreciation of their mutual merits.

I have already emphasized the fact that economic causes are mainly responsible for divergences between the peoples, and it is obvious that man's progress culturally has been *pari passu* with improvement in his economic environment. Considering the matter, then, from the economic point of view, we definitely place the negro on a far lower scale than ourselves, and the pigmy on a far lower scale than the negro. Our respective attitudes, based just on our standards of life, are merely relative, and have no real bearing on our respective evolutionary or cultural precedence. The economic development of a primitive people is mainly dependent on environment. But as the existing economic conditions react upon the outlook on life and the social system of a people, we must pay the greatest attention to these conditions, as only thus can we arrive at an appreciation of the standard of culture of the community. And so we get an opportunity of sharing, to a certain extent, at any rate, the ordinary life of the people under consideration ; we get a better insight into their peculiarities and their points of divergence from us. We begin to see that they are men just like us, but men living in a differently conditioned environment, and dependent on that environment. The sorting out of the thousands of threads that link the primitive man's processes of thought and action with his surroundings and enmesh him on all sides, will unravel for us the maze of his enigmatical existence.

The pigmy has evolved into what he is through his battle with the wilderness—with the limitless untrodden forest. Viewed amidst these wild surroundings, he seems to us to

A MIBIRA NEGRO AND A PIGMY WITH TRIBAL MARKS

A PIGMY KITCHEN

A HALF-BREED AND A PIGMY

A PIGMY BUYING BANANA BEER

In the foreground to the left is the trough in which the bananas are brought
to the brewing vats.

lead a complete, fully-rounded life. Sometimes we see him give proofs of great ingenuity, and we see that he is not only able to support himself by his own resourcefulness, but that he enjoys doing so. Born in his harsh environment, he lives contentedly in it. Left to his own resources in such surroundings, a white man would go under just as quickly as would the pigmy if he found himself thrown friendless and alone into the heart of one of our great industrial cities.

Any man who has endeavoured to adapt himself to the habits of life of a primitive people, knows what a difficult task it is to make himself quite at home with them, especially as he finds himself obliged to jettison almost the entire ballast of our modern civilization. But the more he succeeds in shedding his own civilization for the time being, the more likely will he be able to understand that of his aboriginal hosts, and to grasp the gist of his strange environment. And the man who has nothing but contempt for what he has seen among a primitive people, and who feels that he has no common bond with them, has never probed into the soul of that people, and their culture will ever remain a mystery to him.

The Ituri pigmies number some twenty thousand, all told—a small population for such a vast region. From my personal observation of those little wanderers, I can say confidently that I think they are the happiest people on the earth. If they have sufficient food for the day, they do not worry about the morrow, and they live in perfect contentment and security, isolated from the big world in the small cosmos of their clan or the still smaller cosmos of their family group.

The pigmies are a very vital and hardy race, and it is absurd to talk of them, as so many do, as a moribund stock. But though there is no menace of internal decay, there is the imminent external menace of their extinction owing to the encroachment of the negro and the white man. The white man's civilization is forcing the negro deeper and deeper into the forest with the result that the scope for the untrammelled, nomadic existence of the Bambuti is considerably curtailed. This encroachment on his forest domain is numbing the little

man's inmost soul. Moreover, civilization is bringing in
its train a host of diseases and ailments among these
children of nature, which inevitably must entail their
extinction.

Who will save the Bambuti from their doom ?

INDEX

A

Abemon, a negro chief, 212
Abiti, famous pigmy drummer, 71, 72
Abitiri, officials who conducted secret ceremony of initiation, 256
Ade, term applied to boys who are being initiated into tribal customs, 257
Adengu, a pigmy, 52
Adzapori, a half-breed, 37, 76, 77, 91, 126, 127
Afé. *See* Efé
Agali, first pigmy the author saw, 24, 25, 26, 51, 55, 56
Agbendu, a medicine-man, 77, 87, 99, 100
" Africa Speaks," 97, 98
Agomu, a very tiny pigmy, 142–144
Ai, legendary pigmy character, 186
Akandu, 97
Aká (or Akka), one of main subdivisions of pigmies, 40, 181–183, 272
Akapura, a pigmy elder, 126
Akoa, a Gabun tribe, 20
Albert, Lake, 251
Aleku, negro village, 192, 193
Alianga, a pigmy chief, 28, 32, 33, 47, 48, 49, 78, 83–87, 96, 101, 104–106, 123
Ambutsi, a negro village, 246, 247
Andaman Islands, 14
Andeporu pigmy clan, 195, 208
Andudu town, 190–194, 208, 209, 216
Angode, negro village, 217
Ants, 202–204
Anyota secret society (leopard men), 111, 173, 275
Apare River, 22, 38, 47, 117, 149
Ape, anthropoid (" Sheko "), 31, 32, 63
Apollo, a negro missionary, 258
Arao, a vivacious pigmy girl, 50, 51
Arumimi River, 140
Asangwa, an aged pigmy, 52, 60, 77, 83–86, 88, 98, 106, 108, 125
Asaragba, a trumpet, 250
Asobe (God), 150
Asua. *See* Aká
Asunguda camp, 38, 45, 103, 178, 206
Asunguda River, 34, 39, 49, 66
Atikitiki. *See* Baka

Aué. *See* Efé
Augustine, Saint, 20
Avakubi, a station, 103, 111, 133–140, 146, 147, 191, 193, 251, 274
Awasa, a negro village, 218
Awasomba, pigmy clan, 259
Azande, negro tribe, 147, 277

B

Babali negroes, 21, 22, 38, 39, 111, 119, 132, 173
" Baba wa Bambuti " (Father of the Pigmies), 21, 23, 30, 31, 136, 194, 276
Babeyru negroes, 133, 276
Babira-Bakumu negroes, 40
Babira-Bambuti pigmies, 149
Babira negroes, 39, 263
Babonge, a negro village, 178–180
Baboti, pigmy clan, 47
Bachwa pigmies, 277
Badike pigmies. *See* Aká
Bafwabaka mission, seat of, 176, 193
Bafwabane, pigmy clan, 47
Bafwaguda camp, 47, 63, 103
Bafwaguda pigmies, 47, 51, 63, 92, 98, 99, 119
Bafwasende, pigmy clan, 21, 34, 90
Bafwasengwe, pigmy clan, 92, 119, 123, 127, 132, 137
Bafwasili village, 111
Baka, pigmy clan, 183
Bakango-Bafwasengwe, a pigmy clan, 118
Bakango pigmies, 38, 39, 40, 78, 80–82, 92, 100, 101, 103, 119, 123, 148
Bakbara, a pigmy girl, 52
Baketi, spirits, 164
Bakkebakke, pigmy clan, 20
Balendu, negro tribe, 252
Balenga, negro tribe, 147
Balese, negro tribe, 41, 205, 217, 220, 233, 247
Baleu, pigmy clan, 182, 277
Balika, negro tribe, 40, 176
Bambina, Alianga's wife, 64, 65
Bambuba, negro tribe, 41, 233
Bamunzi pigmies, 185, 188
Banalia, a negro village, 277
Banande, negro tribe, 251, 252